CAMBRIDGE LIBRARY COLLECTION

Books of enduring scholarly value

Travel and Exploration

The history of travel writing dates back to the Bible, Caesar, the Vikings and the Crusaders, and its many themes include war, trade, science and recreation. Explorers from Columbus to Cook charted lands not previously visited by Western travellers, and were followed by merchants, missionaries, and colonists, who wrote accounts of their experiences. The development of steam power in the nineteenth century provided opportunities for increasing numbers of 'ordinary' people to travel further, more economically, and more safely, and resulted in great enthusiasm for travel writing among the reading public. Works included in this series range from first-hand descriptions of previously unrecorded places, to literary accounts of the strange habits of foreigners, to examples of the burgeoning numbers of guidebooks produced to satisfy the needs of a new kind of traveller - the tourist.

The Captivity of Hans Stade of Hesse in A.D. 1547-1555, Among the Wild Tribes of Eastern Brazil

The publications of the Hakluyt Society (founded in 1846) made available edited (and sometimes translated) early accounts of exploration. The first series, which ran from 1847 to 1899, consists of 100 books containing published or previously unpublished works by authors from Christopher Columbus to Sir Francis Drake, and covering voyages to the New World, to China and Japan, to Russia and to Africa and India. First published in English in 1874, this book contains Hans Stade's autobiographical account of his capture by the indigenous Brazilian Tupinamba people in 1554, and his description of their customs. Stade was held prisoner for a year, and according to his sensational report he witnessed many acts of cannibalism and was offered roasted human flesh by the chief of a Tupinamba village. The nineteenth-century editor Richard Burton added a substantial preface describing the geography of the area of Brazil in question, where he himself had spent three years of 'exile'.

T0381758

Cambridge University Press has long been a pioneer in the reissuing of out-of-print titles from its own backlist, producing digital reprints of books that are still sought after by scholars and students but could not be reprinted economically using traditional technology. The Cambridge Library Collection extends this activity to a wider range of books which are still of importance to researchers and professionals, either for the source material they contain, or as landmarks in the history of their academic discipline.

Drawing from the world-renowned collections in the Cambridge University Library, and guided by the advice of experts in each subject area, Cambridge University Press is using state-of-the-art scanning machines in its own Printing House to capture the content of each book selected for inclusion. The files are processed to give a consistently clear, crisp image, and the books finished to the high quality standard for which the Press is recognised around the world. The latest print-on-demand technology ensures that the books will remain available indefinitely, and that orders for single or multiple copies can quickly be supplied.

The Cambridge Library Collection will bring back to life books of enduring scholarly value (including out-of-copyright works originally issued by other publishers) across a wide range of disciplines in the humanities and social sciences and in science and technology.

The Captivity of Hans Stade of Hesse in A.D. 1547-1555

Among the Wild Tribes of Eastern Brazil

HANS STADE
EDITED BY RICHARD F. BURTON

CAMBRIDGE
UNIVERSITY PRESS

CAMBRIDGE UNIVERSITY PRESS

Cambridge, New York, Melbourne, Madrid, Cape Town, Singapore,
São Paolo, Delhi, Dubai, Tokyo

Published in the United States of America by Cambridge University Press, New York

www.cambridge.org
Information on this title: www.cambridge.org/9781108012379

© in this compilation Cambridge University Press 2010

This edition first published 1874
This digitally printed version 2010

ISBN 978-1-108-01237-9 Paperback

WORKS ISSUED BY

The Hakluyt Society.

——•——

THE CAPTIVITY OF HANS STADE
OF HESSE.

No. LI.

THE

CAPTIVITY OF HANS STADE

OF HESSE,

IN A.D. 1547 1555,

AMONG THE WILD TRIBES OF EASTERN BRAZIL.

TRANSLATED BY

ALBERT TOOTAL, ESQ., OF RIO DE JANEIRO,

AND

ANNOTATED BY

RICHARD F. BURTON.

" Floriferis ut apes in saltibus omnia libant
Omnia nos."
LUCRETIUS.

" Da veniam scriptis, quorum non gloria nobis
Causa, sed utilitas officiumque fuit."
OVID, *Epist.*

LONDON:

PRINTED FOR THE HAKLUYT SOCIETY.

M.DCCC.LXXIV.

COUNCIL

OF

THE HAKLUYT SOCIETY.

PREFACE.

Section I.

It was my fate during nearly three years, between November 10th, 1865, and July 28th, 1868, to endure exile as H.B.M.'s Consul for the port of Santos, in the province of São Paulo, the Brazil. There was little occupation on high days and holidays, except to visit the sea-board and "kitchen middens"; and, as there are no roads along the shore, many of my excursions were made in open boats—trips which gained dignity by the perpetual presence of danger. During these excursions, I passed again and again through the Rio Bertioga, a channel which separates the once populous and still luxuriant island of Santo Amaro from the mainland; and I landed, not unfrequently, at the ruin opposite the Forte da Bertioga. The stone-heap occupies the site where Hans Stade, the author of the following pages, served as gunner, and whence he was carried off captive by the cannibal savages, who, in those days lived alternately upon the sea-coast and the interior plateau. Of the wild tribes, not a living specimen remains; but, like the Guanches of Tenerife, they have left manifest traces of " red" blood in the veins of their modern

b

successors. And, whilst their wigwams have long
vanished from the earth's face, their enormous "kitchen
middens", called by the natives Sambaqué, and by the
Portuguese Ostreiras, containing thousands of cubic
feet, and composed chiefly of Venus (berbigões), oyster
and mussel shells, still stud the coast line and supply
the granitic and primary regions with lime, which
will presently be exhausted.

Before my transfer from Santos to Damascus (1869),
I had strongly recommended a friend, Albert Tootal,
to expend the moments which he could spare from
more important matters in translating Hans Stade.
He followed my advice, and all those who take an interest in wild tribes, and especially in the Brazilian
savages, owe him a debt of gratitude. Also at my
suggestion, he preserved the chaste and simple style
which best suits the subject ; which accords with the
character of the unlettered gunner, and which seems
to vouch for the truth and the straightforwardness of
the traveller. And the matter is not less interesting
than the manner : it has the intrinsic value of ranking
amongst the very few works written by eye-witnesses
during the early sixteenth century, and it throws important light upon a point which unreasonable doubts
have lately darkened. Not long ago we were assured
that man does not outlive a hundred years, and the supposed error of Flourens led his correctors into an error
still greater. After that freak, that "crotchet of criti-
cism", the existence of cannibalism, which seems at
different ages of the world to have been the universal
custom of mankind, was called in question. Hans

Stade now steps forth and delivers his testimony about a people who were literally "fleshed with human meat".

I must apologise to Mr. Tootal for long delay in my share of the work. The translation was finished in 1869, and it was taken to Syria for the purpose of adding an Introduction and a few explanatory Notes. But I unexpectedly found at Damascus duties and studies that occupied the whole of my time, and the various troubles to which allusion has been made in "Unexplored Syria", left me as little will as leisure for the work. When suddenly recalled from my post, friends advised me to try the tonic effects of a summer in Iceland ; in fact, until the present moment, when settled *pro tempore* at Trieste, I have lacked opportunity to fulfil my humble part of the contract.

Mr. Tootal is alone answerable for the accuracy of his translation. To my responsibility fall the Introduction and the Notes. Its bibliographical portion was kindly undertaken by Clements R. Markham, C.B., etc., whose various literary avocations, to say nothing of official labours, enable him to be, like most hard workers perforce thrifty of their time, a man of comparative leisure. He has also the advantage of consulting libraries and of collecting *vivâ voce* information —conditions hardly to be expected in a highly commercial sea-port.

SECTION II.

Before proceeding to the old inhabitants of the country, I will describe the passage of the Bertioga, and a cruise along the coast of São Paulo as far as Ubatúba, which forms the scene of Hans Stade's captivity. Of the various excursions made by me, those will be most useful which took place in mid-November, 1865, and August, 1866. At the former season it is necessary to choose fine weather, when the fish do not spring, and when the distant hills do not look as if you can touch their feathered flanks : without this precaution the surf will not allow men to land. During the last-mentioned month, the traveller still finds the hot, fever-giving winds, the dry tornadoes and the dense fogs (Cerração), mentioned by Pero Lopes in 1531.[1]

The beautiful Rio Bertioga, popularly known as the Rio Grande, is a sea arm winding nearly east and west, about fifteen statute (=10 direct geographical) miles long, and from three miles to a few hundred yards in breadth ; it has a double flow, as the centre forms a water-parting ; the western half runs westward into Santos Bay, and the other into the Southern Atlantic. At times this Euripus shows the vivacity of a sluice. The depth is rarely under two fathoms, and the bottom is soft mud.

The only vehicle which chanced to be procurable in November 1865, was a " Batelão", a short thick " Ein-

---

[1] Diario da Navegação, etc. Alluded to further on.

baum", with additions fore, aft, and at the quarters. These nut-shells will ply north, hoping for a calm sea, but nothing can persuade them to tempt the "Costa *braba*" (wild coast) to the south of Santos. Paddling away from my pleasant station, the "Wapping of the far West"; early in the morning we left at the nearer extremity of Santo Amaro, the old fort Itapema ("flat stone"), now a heap of dull yellow masonry, backed by two large kitchen middens, which by this time have probably disappeared. Some care is requisite when entering the sea-arm's narrow mouth, as the northern jaw is foul with hidden rocks. The distant view on both sides is high and grandiose; the immediate banks are low and swampy, with lumps of detached hill, amongst which the sphynx-form, as about the granite regions of Rio de Janeiro, is not uncommon. The ragged mangrove bush, with its undergrowth of tufted sprouts, is a glorious breeding-place when the ebb-tide discovers huge mud flats, the homes of various pests known to the natives as Mutuca, Perna-lunga, Pium Carapana, and Maruim.[1] A few cottages of dirty bilious clay, covered with rusty tattered thatch and

---

[1] The Mutúca or Motúca, generally called Butúca, is the local gadfly (Hadæus lepidotus. Perty). The Perna-lunga (Daddy-long-legs) is the true "Mosquito", a Spanish term which well describes the Sand-, or "Little fly", but which becomes ridiculous when applied to M. Maringouin. The Piúm (a Simulium) is the angry biter, better known as Borrachuda, the drunkard : it attacks you by day, and it is a little larger than the Carapaná. The Mucuîm or Mocoim is a small scarlet Acarus : the term, however, is now generally applied to the sand-fly, by the "Indians" termed Maruim, and by the Portuguese "Polvora" (gunpowder). This is a prime

fronting, perhaps, some square yards of cane, occupy
holes cut in the luxuriant green bush, and roughly-
made canoes are drawn up the black mire—we might
be prospecting one of the " Oil Rivers" in the Bight
of Biafra.   But though the mud is fetid, the people
are said not to be unhealthy.

On the right hand we pass a Morne (earth cliff), denoted by a Ranch or hovel for the use of lime burners.
To the left is the Morro de Cabrão, which rises darkly
from the light green mangrove,

> " A glorious scene, and as the ranks ascend
>   Shade above shade, a woody theatre
>   Of stateliest view,"

we especially note amongst the tangled and cordaged
trees a beautiful Veronica, locally called Nyaganháca-
tiró.   Each is a garden of flowers, purple-mauve
in youth, pink in middle life, and virgin white, like
the dog-roses of Dalmatia, with the hoar of age : all
these colours blooming at the same time.   There is the
normal peculiarity of the grand Brazilian forest, the
gigantic white trunks thrown out in strong relief by
the black-green shade, and the light yellow-green verdure of the Capoeira or second growth, contrasting with
the mottled glooms of the Mato Virgem.   The Rhine, in
summer, can show nothing like the might and majesty
of this "Flowery Forest"; and the vegetation dwarfs the

pest in all unexposed places where the sea-breeze cannot blow
them away : the infinitesimal fiends are most troublesome in the
mornings and evenings, and they are said to rage most furiously
at the change and full of the moon.   Dira lues ! rightly exclaims
P. Anchieta.

tallest of English oaks and the noblest of European elms, as though they had passed through Chinese hands. Art is wholly absent. Smoke winding from the bush alone shows that the woodland contains homesteads and farms ; whilst palms, as in Africa, denote the presence of man—this contrast between the works of nature, first-hand and second-hand, is here ever present to the mind.

The several features of the Bertioga are the Volta Grande, where a sweet-water stream from the Cabrão forms a riverine island ; various " Furados" (creeks) in the mangrove bush ; the Rio do Quilombo (of the Maroon village) draining the mountains and telling its date of olden days ; and, on the right bank two unclean ditches known as the Rio dos Portos and the Rio da Boa Vista. Every site is named,—names are retained for places even when houses have long returned to earth. Some ugly bends deform the stream, where lies a small archipelago, and for about a league and a half the mangrove country lasts : beyond it, the rhizophor still fringes the brown water, but the shore grows higher, and bald patches of yellow rock appear. The wondrously shaggy Serra looks as if man had never placed his foot there. In wet weather cloud-flecks cling like handfuls of wool to thorny shrubs. Now it shows with sharp distinctness a sky-line jagged like a saw, while, misty in the far distance, loom the blue cliffs behind Enseada. And over all are the glow and play of a tropical sun, a dancing of the bright clear air, and the diamond sparkle and iridescence of the sea as it catches the direct or the slanting light. The storm-tossed Portuguese must have found a peculiar charm in this Rio Formoso of the western hemisphere.

Presently we arrive at the half-way house, the Lagõa de Caeté (of good wood), a small Mediterranean, long and shallow, which mirrors the tall Serra and its hilly and knobby outlines. The current begins to run eastward and to mingle with the South Atlantic : the view waxes still finer, and we taste the sweets of the un-adulterated sea-breeze. On the mainland bank and raised above the marsh is the Quinta (villa) of Colonel Candinho Albuquerque, whose lime manufactory is close to the water's edge, not far from the Cabussú river, a mere surface drain of the Serra. The small white house, with double roof, two windows, and a door, is approached by steps, some of stone, others cut in the stiff yellow clay. The extensive sheds and out-houses show dogs and poultry ; but no negroes are working in the now neglected coffee grounds which surround it ; and the large guavas and cedars, palms and palmitos, flower and fruit all in vain. Many pro-prietors from Santos have boxes up the Bertioga, where they come to eat fish and to shoot the deer and the Anta (tapir), now so rare in the neighbourhood of civi-lisation. Here, however, the mosquitoes muster too strong for enjoyment.

On the right hand the bearded hills and knolls of Santo Amaro slope gradually to the water-brink. The island,[1] once populous and cultivated, and still pre-

---

[1] It was called by the natives Guaimbé (Simam de Vasconcellos prefers Gaibé), from a pestilent weed which overran it. "Sanctus

serving ruins of Engenhos or sugar-houses, has become a mass of luxuriant second-growth. With the exception of rice, which much resembles that of Carolina, agriculture is a poor trade : as in Santos Island, the climate forbids it; the burning sun ever alternating with flooding rains, and the plague of Sauba,[1] more than compensate for all the fertility of the soil. Yet Fray Gaspar da Madre de Deos, the monographer of his native province,[2] attributed in the last century the poverty of his compatriots to their contempt for Triptolemus, and declared that their indolence has covered large Fazendas (plantations) with bush.

Santo Amaro island still shows beyond the Caeté river the small white Ermida (chapel) of Curumahú, which rejoices in an image known as Nossa Senhora da Representação, and the stream of the same name leads to the Casa do Perequé, an estate on the north-eastern side fronting the sea. Further again is a gap in the brake-covert called the Burraccão (big hole), which has a short cut over the hills to the Praia de Yporanga near Perequé.

A little beyond Colonel Albuquerque's house lie the Sitio (farm) and Ostreira of Manoel Luiz Fer-

Maurus" was a disciple of St. Benedict and the patron of broken bones.

[1] The correct Tupi term was Yçaýba, which we should write Isaýba.

[2] Memorias para a Historia da Capitania de S. Vicente, etc., por Fr. G. da M. de Deos, publicadas em 1797. The author was a Benedictine monk, and a correspondent of the R. Academy of Sciences, Lisbon. He left a second volume in manuscript, which is said to have been stolen by some " curioso"—not an unfrequent occurrence in the Brazil.

reira, popularly known as Manecco Manguáta. The
little yellow box, built upon a hillock, with a landing-place like those of the Tanganyika Lake, is the
best in the whole line ; it is faced on the mainland
by the Prainha, a cleared, grassy space, dotted with
palms, and boasting of a boat-house ; whilst beyond it
the Rio de Uriri denotes the site of a huge shell-heap.

The Corral de Peixe (fish kraal), here a common
feature, attracts our attention. It is a winding fence
thrown across, or half across, the sea-arm ; the material
being bamboo poles connected by the black Imbé (Philo-
dendron imbe), which my friends on the Bonny river
would recognise as "tie-tie". The victims are driven by
the tide through a Giqui, funnel or narrow passage, into
a Camara or bulge ; thence a struggle for escape leads
them into a second ; and, finally, they enter the last
pocket known by the tunny-fishers' name—"Camara da
Morte". Here two men, standing upon the fence, ply a
large hand-net fastened to a pole. The produce consists
of some eighty or ninety species, of which the most common are known as Savelha or Sardinha and Cavalla ;
Gallo and Corvina ; Bagre and Robalo ; Paraty, Paru
and Parambeta ; Pescado jacú, Pescado branco, and
Pescado amarello, the latter often weighing twenty
pounds and worth 6$000. The less common are the
Sherma and Caratinga ; the Badeja and Caranha ; the
Goette, the Pescado Selvagem, the Pescado Cangoá, and
the excellent Garupa and Garupeta.

As at Fernando Po, the fisherman can easily clear
£5 by a single day's haul ; yet, with all this wealth
at hand, the people, from the Amazons to the Plata,

actually import Bacalháo (salt cod) from Newfoundland,
and, with the sea at their feet, they will not take the
trouble, or rather it is not worth their while, to lay out
Salinas. One of the divers boasted that he could remain ten minutes under water, and I put him on the
path of making a fabulous fortune in England or in
the United States. The "patroon", who, like many of
his class hereabouts, had been three times captured by
English cruizers when slaving on the West Coast of
Africa, and who consequently "knew a thing or two",
scoffingly compared the boaster with the renowned
Padre Anchieta, who could pray and read his breviary
for three-quarters of an hour at a time under water.

The river presently narrows and makes a distinct
bend to the north of east. The last projection, on
the right, is the Ponta Grossa, a commanding ridge
with a large clearing, green as a parrot's plume, which
has not had time for second growth, although the old
sugar plantation is utterly deserted. Opposite is the
Rio do Pilar, *alias* the Barra do Bucuhy, a stream
which extends, they say, some twelve leagues inland
and supports various Fazendas, whilst the banks supply
tanneries, especially that of M. Porchat, with mangrove
bark. Up its valley runs a Picada (bush-path, as
opposed to a Caminho franco) connecting with the
settlement of Mogy das Cruzes on the plateau of
São Paulo. Gold-dust is said still to be found in the
upper waters, the Rio Itutinga, and the head of the
Tapanhahú (Tapañahú). The mouth is blocked by
electric wires which ought to be submerged.

After some four hours paddling we sight the open

sea from the embouchure of the Bertioga, where the hills draw off. On the left is still the tall Serra do Mar, the eastern ghauts of the Brazil, which rival the Camarones mountains in portentous luxuriance of vegetation. The Itaguáre height, with its crystal vein of water, is conspicuous, and we count upon the face of the rock-wall seven cascades, diminished by distance to the size of thin twisted glass cylinders in the old style of Swiss clock. The nearest point ahead is the bluff headland known as the Morro, or Ponta da Enseada (da Bertioga); beyond it rises the islet of Monte Pascoal, bluer than the air; further still is the heap called Montão do Trigo, and lastly the Alcatrazes lie low in the water, shaped like an elephant's back, and thrown out by the azure curtain of charming São Sebastião. This fringe of scattered islets affords excellent shelter, and forms in fact a natural διῶρυξ, through which even canoes, during the calm season, ply between Santos and Rio de Janeiro. They are Continental, not Pelagic, to adopt Von Buch's distinction; almost all are inhabited except where water is absolutely wanting, and it is probable that they were occupied by "Indians" in the days of yore.

The eastern mouth of the Bertioga is some 600 or 700 yards wide, and from two to three fathoms deep; it is said to have no bar, the curse of Brazilian as of tropical African rivers, and I certainly never saw the sea break across it. Inside is a safe anchorage of eight fathoms, forming a first-rate harbour of refuge for small craft making Santos from the north: thus they save the twenty rough miles round Santo Amaro. In

the days when Fr. Gaspar wrote, it was generally believed that the Discoverer and First Donatory of the
Captaincy, Martim Affonso de Souza, entered the Bertioga channel when outward bound. But the log-book
of his brother, Pero Lopes de Souza,[1] clearly shows
that, after leaving Rio de Janeiro, the squadron in
twelve days made Cananéa, and did not touch at the
parts about Santos, till homeward bound, on January
22nd, 1532, when S. Vicente and the Bertioga fort
were built. He had sailed from Portugal on December
23rd, 1530, and reached Rio de Janeiro, not in
January, but on April 30th, 1531 : thus he was too
late to name, as some have supposed (Southey, I, 42),
the several ports upon the Brazilian coast. The old
Portuguese navigators, it has been well remarked,
travelled almanac in hand, baptising every place after
the patron saint who presided on the day of discovery.
For instance—

Cape S. Roque is so called from Aug. 16.[2]
Cape S. Agostinho   „   „   „   28.
Rio de S. Miguel   „   „   Sept. 29.
Rio de S. Jeronymo   „   „   „   30.
Rio de S. Francisco   „   „   Oct. 4.

---

[1] Diario de Navegação da Armada que foi à terra do Brasil em
1530. Escripto por Pedro Lopes de Souza e publicado em 1839,
em Lisboa por Francisco Adolfo de Varnhagen, etc. Rio de
Janeiro. Freitas, Guimaraens e Ca. Rua do Sabão, 1847. It is a
highly interesting specimen of an old log-book, settling not a few
disputed questions.
[2] The change from old to new style was ordered by Pope Gregory
XIII in A.D. 1582.

Rio das Virgens is so called from Oct. 21.

Rio de Santa Luzia (Rio Doce?) Dec. 15.

Cabo de S. Thomé   „   „   „   21 (? 22)

S. Salvador da Bahia de todos os Santos
(discovered November 1st, 1501,
popularly placed on December 25).

Rio de Janeiro   „   „   Jan. 1.

Angra dos Reis Magos (Epiphany,
or Twelfth-day)   „   „   „   6.

Ilha de S. Sebastião   „   „   „   20.

Porto (or Rio) de S. Vicente „   „   21.
(22nd (?) festival of SS. Vincent and
Anastasius).

M. F. Adolfo de Varnhagen (note to *History*, vol. i,
p. 425), finds S. Augustine mentioned in A.D. 1504 ;
St. Vincent is on the map of J. Ruysch, dated 1508,
and Cape S. Thomé and Angra dos Reis appear before
1519 (*Navarrete*, iv, 210). He is therefore justified in
attributing the nomenclature to the first exploration of
the coast by Gonçalo Coelho in 1501, who, by order of
D. Manuel, carried on board, as pilot and cosmographer,
the much-maligned Italian *savant*, Amerigo Vespucci.[1]

---

[1] See "Amerigo Vespucci, son caractère, ses écrits, sa vie et ses
Navigations", Lima, 1865." " Le Premier Voyage de Vespucci
définitivement expliqué dans ses détails", Vienne, 1869, and "Nou-
velles Recherches sur les dernières Recherches du Navigateur
Florentin, et les restes des documents et éclaircissements sur lui,
avec les textes et une postface", Vienne, 1870.

M. Varnhagen has not only established Vespucci's character for
rectitude and integrity ; he has also had the courage to prove the
priority of the much maligned navigator in American waters ; and

We anchored, in deep water, under the Fortaleza da Bertioga on the northern or mainland shore. The word, according to Fray Gaspar (p. 21), is a corruption of Buriqui oca, "the house of Buriqui," a kind of reddish monkey formerly abundant : at first it was applied to the hill behind the settlement, on the northern point of the Serra de Santo Amaro, but generally it extended to the neighbourhood and to the whole sea arm. Vasconcellos (iii, 63) calls it "Biritioga", and the author of the *Noticia do Brazil*, "Britioga" (Part I, chap. lxi). They erroneously suppose that the Indians, when they saw the work, named it "house of Buriquis," because its garrison had ruddy hair like those simiads. As will be seen, there were two forts at the mouth of the Bertioga : they were called after SS. Felippe and Santiago, and the former was founded on the island by Martim Affonso. Hans Stade names it only the "Fort of Santo Amaro."

The C. O., Manuel dos Santos, who commands a garrison of four men, did the honours of the modern establishment. The building has evidently been renewed upon the olden plan, and hodiernal plaster takes the place of ancient stone. It is in the usual style of its date, built of boulders and lime, with a straight curtain commanding the water, whilst two side faces afford flanking fire. Each angle is provided with its pepper-castor sentry-box : the *terre pleine*, revetted with uncut slabs,

he makes it certain that Vespucci saw the American continent in A.D. 1497-1498, while Columbus, who did not sight it till August 1498, died in the belief that he had discovered the easternmost part of Asia.

is thirty paces in length by seven deep. Six old carronades, for which there is no powder, lie about anywhere except near the embrasures, and only one rusty
gun overlooks the wall. In rear of the battery is the
normal roof of red tiles, denoting the Quartel or barracks. The door is off its hinges, and a canoe occupies
the guard-room. To the right are the commandant's
quarters, carefully shut, and, as the holy-water basin
and a wooden cross nailed to the wall suggest, the left
wing is the chapel of São João Baptista.

We may see this kind of thing in any part of old
Iberia; for instance, at Algeçiras, in the Bay of Gibral-
tar. Europe, however, usually whitewashes the smaller
buildings ; this is spotted like a carriage dog, the
result of abnormal moisture. The little village of
eight houses, with a population of seventy-two souls,
lies behind the sand-spit which supports the fort :
some of the tenements are neat and clean, showing
all the implements for fishing, and the usual multitude of children born of and bred by ichthyopha-
gous populations. They are built on no regular
plan, and the streets are reduced to narrow footpaths,
winding amongst shrubs and palms. A certain Pinto
will supply breakfast, and the commandant, who
passes most of his time in making nets of Tucum
fibre (Astrocaryum tucum), has a little store of
rum, beer, sugar, and other necessaries ; but he com-
plains that business is not brisk. Opposite this Fortaleza is one of the *incunabula* of the Luso-Brazilian
Empire, the site of the old tower of earth and mud
built in A.D. 1532 by Martim Affonso, the great Dona-

tory, and rebuilt in 1552 by Thomé de Souza.[1] After
the fashion of the ancient world the first captain
wisely preferred, to the. continent, the island-site,
where defence was easy, where troubles with the
natives, who infested the place with hostile canoes,
would be least dangerous, and where exports, then the
object of colonisation, would most readily be embarked. Indeed, he forbade his people to visit the
interior without special leave, trusting that in time,
after the shores had been occupied, an increasing population would spread inland : these sensible precautions
were abolished by his widow, Dona Anna Pimentel.

When the Indians saw the Portuguese disembark
they fled, headed by their Cacique, to the uplands, and
reported the matter to the great warrior chief of the
Goyanazes, Tebyreça, Anchieta's Teveriçá, Lord of the
Prairies of Piratininga—now São Paulo, or, more
classically, Paulopolis—who had married his daughter
to one João Ramalho, a Portuguese refugee. The
latter, suspecting that a handful of his fellow-country-
men had been driven ashore like himself, accompanied
the Regulus who, with three hundred braves, marched
upon the Bertioga, and arrived there on the third day
to find the tower built and the guns mounted. Martim
Affonso made preparations for a regular defence, when
a white man walked up within hearsay and welcomed
the astonished Portuguese in their own tongue, bidding

---

[1] There was no "Governor and Captain-General" till A.D. 1549,
when that title was given by D. João III to the Captain of São
Salvador da Bahia, that he might have authority over the other
captaincies.

them not to fear. Ramalho was then presented to the captain, related his adventures, and promised assistance. Tebyreça, who afterwards prefixed to his name Martim Affonso,[1] in sign of baptism and of love for his white friend, was received with due respect, and hastened to make a perpetual alliance with the strangers. Then all was joy. The guns fired, to the terror of the "Red men", and the latter in kilts and coronals and beautiful plumage, sang, danced, and shot their arrows in the air. The other wild tribes that came hastening to the fray, found the Piratininganos and Portuguese on the best of terms ; and the Goyanazes, who mostly lived in the interior, easily permitted the foreigners to occupy the coast upon the sole condition of the fisheries remaining free.

The site has seen many a change since Hans Stade was captured,[2] in 1553-1554, and the last building was an Armação (whaling station), also in ruins and overgrown with bush : a stranger would pass it without a glance. The landing-place is within the river immediately behind the Morro da Paciencia, so called because peculiarly trying to craft going south : here are grand table-rocks of pink granite, but the least sea prevents disembarkation. There is a stone wharf like that at the present approach to Santos,[3] but the seats

[1] He must not be confounded with another "celebrated Indian", Martim Affonso de Souza, alias Ararigboia, who beat the French invaders in 1568.

[2] See chapter xlii.

[3] The "Brazil and River Plate Mail" (April 23rd, 1873) informs me that at length the Santos Docks, whose concession was modified by the decree of April 1st, 1873, are to be begun at once, and to

and blocks are now almost buried in mud. A slippery path leads up the slope, and the dense bush suggests caution : at this season (November) snakes are supposed to be abnormally active. Reaching a field of sugar-cane, we turned to the right, descended some ruinous steps, and found the remains. The chapel of São João da Bertioga preserves an arch of cut stone between the body of the building and the high altar ; a pediment, and a dwarf tower; the sanctuary is broken and the roof has fallen in. A bartizan and a curtain, with a bluff shoulder facing the sea, show excellent masonry, and the wall that crowns the corner looks as if freshly made ; probably the stones were brought from Europe by Thomé de Souza. Truly a wonderful race were these old Portuguese, who seem, like their sires, the Romans, to have built for eternity. According to the people, this later fort was never finished : the bush was cleared out about two years before my visit. Up hill, where stretches a fine sheet of verdurous second-growth, tier upon tier of tenderest green domes and domelets, like giant parasols, are the ruins of another bartizan.

At the Fortaleza we must dismiss the wet and cranky Batelão, which objects to venture into the smoking Enseada, or Bay to the east, swept by the full force of the Atlantic, and very dangerous after a

be finished in five years. They are to consist of a floating apparatus 800 feet long by 210 wide. The other works will be an embankment 3000 feet long, from the Government wharf to near the Custom House; with wharves, warehouses, and landing-stages in the river-front; an enlarged Custom House and Marine Arsenal, in appropriate places, and a new street pierced through the city.

south-wester. I was lucky enough to find a Canôa de
Voga, the Santa Maria. Its hull was a giant Jequitibá
(Couratari legalis, Mart), some 50 palms long by 4
deep, and 6½ in breadth, and it carried 400 arrobas
(× 32 lbs. = 12,800 lbs.), nearly six tons, whilst the value
was about £150. The sides spooned outwards; it was
supplied with additional boards at the gunwales, prow
and stern, and it was copper-sheathed above as well as
copper bottomed. The admirably graceful lines showed
its descent from the naval architecture of the savages,
and this may be observed throughout the Brazil: Venice
herself can boast nothing more picturesque. The
Santa Maria had only one mast, with ham-shaped sails,
and she was utterly ignorant of the jib which would
be useful : a Patrão (master) and six oarsmen composed the normal crew. The larger specimens are
decked fore and aft, and carry a foremast (trinqueta)
and square sail, with a mizen (mizena) and leg of
mutton ; they are not, however, so manageable.

The Santa Maria stands boldly out along the

Virgens plagas do Cabral famoso,

straight as a bee-line for the little fishing-village of
Enseada. It is distant eight long miles by sea,
but those who prefer a land journey can ride nearly
the same number of leagues. Looking back upon
the island of Santo Amaro we see the houses and
estate called the Fazenda do Perequé : now it is
the property of Sr. Valencio Augusto Teixeira Leo-
mil, and he would willingly part with his haunt
of ants, although coal, they say, has been found there.

The place has a bad name in history : before 1850 it was a landing-place for slaves, who were smuggled, as our seaboard once smuggled silks and brandies. On the 16th of May H.M.S. "Rifleman," Commander Crofton, whose cutter had been fired upon, and one of the crew killed, landed and burnt the Casa de Perequé. I spare further details, especially in these days, when

"All Afric's sons exclaim from shore to shore,
'Quashee ma boo! the slave trade is no more.'"

The bay (Enseada) is a long shallow arc protected on the north-eastern side by the Morro da Enseada, a stony point bending south : the land is the same tall rocky curtain which forms the Engua-guassú, alias Monjolo, alias Pilão Grande (Great Mortar) of Santos, and a break in it denotes, by a thin white thread, the Itutinga cataract. The settlement boasts a fine beach, but sadly exposed to the west wind. Gaps in the bush lead from the sand to the houses, which are those of the Bertioga : there are about forty tenements under the charge of an Inspector de Quarteirão (police magistrate); and one has lately been built at an expense of 300$000, say £30. There is a chaplain, and a little chapel dedicated to the Bom Jesus de Canna-verde; it accommodates some thirty-five women, who sit at squat, whilst the men stand outside, or kneel upon the bare stones. When Ladainhas (litanies) are recited there is a full gathering : the altar candles are lighted ; the calico awning and curtains contrast with the bare walls, and all is gay with roses—Catholicism and flowers seem in these regions to be inseparably united. A gun-shot denotes the end of the psalmody, which contrasts well with

that of the village church in England, and a second discharge shows the end of the "function", after which all
troop out chatting and laughing as they wend their
way homewards.

The people were formerly fishermen, but the "tainha,"
a white mullet (Mugil albula) the herring of this region,
whose shoals, according to the "peritos" (experts),
once numbered fifty to sixty thousand, have deserted
the coast : the same complaint is made everywhere between Rio de Janeiro and Conceiçao, whereas south of
the latter port "tainha" is still the staff of life. Agriculture has not proceeded beyond manioc, which thrives
tolerably : fruits abound, and a little cane is grown
for Melado (molasses) ; but sugar, coffee, and caxaça
(rum) are unknown. Formerly Enseada had a high re-
pute for " Batuqueiras," who performed much in the
style of the Egyptian Alimeh (dancing girls), and the
youth of Santos used to visit it on Saturdays accompanied by a large demi-john of spirits. Now it is vain
for a stranger to propose a " nautch "—modesty forbids.

Beyond Enseada the coast runs nearly west-east,
forming a system of headlands and bays, the latter
generally giving names to the former : as we advance
sun-wards the bights have less sag, and become mere
denticulations in the coast line. Three bluffs attracted my attention, the Tres Morros de Imburacé :
here the rocky, shallow bottom causes the sea to break
half a mile off, and this " Carréra " is much feared.

On August 1st, 1866, I entered the Rio de Una,
which now divides the municipalities of Santos and
São Sebastião. My visit was for the purpose of in-

specting a "gigantic marine monster," which had found
its way into the papers. The settlers, said the local
prints, called it "Peixe Cobra," because it swam like a
snake and "Igbahe Apena", or "Diabo Pelado" (bald
devil) : they represented it to be two hundred and sixteen feet long ; three years ago (1863) it had been
thrown up by the sea, and it remained alive three days.
The body was scaleless and gave no oil. The vertebræ
could not be seen, having been buried in the sand, but
the gigantic ribs lay on the shore, measuring almost
twenty-four feet long, three feet wide, and fourteen
inches in thickness : there was also a bone, sword-
shaped and triangular, measuring nearly fifteen feet ;
whilst another, which lay near the ribs and was nine
and a half feet in length, was judged to be part of the
head. It became, in fact, a regular Dragon of Want-
ley, which, with a tail unreasonably long, devoured
the shepherd as well as the sheep.

The bar of the Una was not pleasant to cross, there
are rocks in the channel, and it bends parallel with the
seaboard, forming a sand-pit : formerly the Abra de
Una was better, but nature has driven it to the eastward. On the right bank is a low, tiled, and yellow-
painted house, one of the twenty-four establishments
belonging to the Carmelite order ; the chapel is dedicated to the Senhor Bom Jesus. The brotherhood lets
it for 50$000 *per mensem* to a certain Antonio de
Goes Moreira, but will not allow the ground to be cultivated. The lessee led me to the *disjecta ossa* of
what was evidently a Balêa or whale ; the vertebræ
had been turned into stools by the cottagers, the people

had drawn oil from the tongue ; the tail-piece, which
served the newspapers as a sword, had been carried off,
and the ribs measured a maximum of twenty-four and
a half spans. The total length had been ninety-nine
feet, and similar godsends had lately been found at the
northern whaling establishment (Armação)[1] of São
Sebastião, and on the Ilha das Côuves (of cabbages).
The mammal was hunted off the Ponta de Arpoar,
(Harpoon point) to the north in August and September,
and in June and July to the south.

The people of Una have not the best of names.
Here three municipalities meet, the third being that of
São José de Parahytinga, and its position makes it
an asylum for thieves and murderers : shortly after I
left it, one João Marianna was assassinated at the in-
stigation of his wife. Off the mouth of the Rio de
Una is the round mound, called Montão de Trigo
(wheat heap) ; the islet is inhabited by some seven

---

[1] In the island of São Sebastião alone there are four Armações
dating from the days of its prosperity. The northernmost is called
Das Balêas ; once it belonged to Government, and now the white
house and chapel in the straggling fisher-village are the property of
Antonio da Costa Braga, who still works it. The second is of Antonio Lourenço de Freitas, closed. The third was called after Manoel
Serafim dos Anjos Ferreira ; it had been turned into sugar-works
by Lieut.-Colonel (National Guard) Alexandre Martinez d'Oliveira.
The fourth belonged to the late Manoel Pedro, and the house is
in ruins. Formerly some ninety to a hundred fish were harpooned
in the course of the year—1781 was exceptional, and gave 850
head — and whaling was the earliest source of wealth to the
colonists, together with the sugar-cane, brought from Madeira by
Martim Affonso (Fr. Gaspar, p. 49). During the last two years
there have been only six captures. The Gibárte whale (Rorqual ?)
gives only six pipes ; the Balêa, or right whale, twenty.

families, who cultivate coffee and catch as much fish as they please. The Alcatrazes, or Pelican Islands, a system of rock-lumps, are further out to sea, some seven leagues from land : there is water upon them, but no population : the solitude would be that of Saint Ronans. The aspect of the rock masses is barren and picturesque, and Capitaine E. Mouchez, who surveyed the coast in the frigate *La Motte Piquet* made the height only 180 feet above the " wasser-spiegel." The fringe of little outliers still continues along the shore ; the principal are the Tres Ilhas, with good soil, and the uninhabited Ilha do Gato (of the cat) : beyond it lies the Ilha das Côuves, which supports four families, and the scatter of Toque Toque, also deserted, at the mouth of the S. Sebastião channel. Toque Toque means a " tide-rip," here caused by the currents, thrown off by the island, meeting the stony Main-land-point Buraco or Ponta da Velha ; there is an-other, Toque Emboque, between the Tamanduá islet and Tobatinga point, further north. The most remark-able headlands and bays are the Buracéa, Juréa, Ju-quihy, Asahy, Praia da Balêa, and Boisucanga :[1] at the latter there is a little chapel, N.S. da Conceicão. Afterwards come Marezias, Toque Toque Pequeno, Calhetas, and Toque Toque Grande.

I passed, very unwillingly, a night at the Praia de Toque Toque Grande, a village now containing some

---

[1] Usually supposed to be a corruption of Boy-assú-cánga, the big Boa's head. The Boa, properly speaking, does not exist in the New World ; yet we have borrowed the word from its indigens. For further details, see chapter li.

forty-four huts and hovels of fishermen, who have perforce become cultivators. My object was to examine
some reported lead diggings, which, if they existed,
would prove that the highly-important Yporanga for-
mation, the Derbyshire of the Brazil, extends thus far
north. Old men spoke of the metal being found in
dry torrent-beds after rain ; there was a report that
some had lately appeared where the foundation for a
house was dug, and the elder fishermen remembered
weighting their nets with it. I made two excursions
in vain to the Cachoeira or water-fall, a mere thread
about one hundred feet long, falling down a gap between the tall bluffs to the north-east into a kieve,
containing the coldest water even in the hot season. From this place there is a land road to the town
of S. Sebastião, which leads for three hours over an al-
ternation of rocky projections and sandy inlets. We
preferred, however, the boat. The weather was peculiarly threatening: a brassy-yellow gleam in the eastern
sky followed the sunset ; puffs of wind like the breath
of a furnace ruffled the sea at intervals, and there was
a peculiar moan which seemed to announce disaster.
The rains were approaching, and men quoted the
saying—

" Nova lua trovoajada
Trinte dias de molhada."

We put off for the coast of S. Sebastião, which appeared a dark *cul de sac*, hardly inviting even to a returning fisherman—it sadly wants a lighthouse. Hardly
had the oars dipped a dozen times when a simoom-blast
came ploughing the sea like a tornado, and a succes-

sion of three huge waves raised us from the water and tossed us ashore, as if the large boat had been a walnut-shell. A few contusions were the only result. The people rushed down to our assistance, and we met with the usual kindly· reception of "shipwrecked mariners" at the hospitable house of Mattheus de Moura.

On the next day, by no means the worse for our adventure, we passed the high and rocky mainland point Toque Toque, which fronts the lone long Ponta da Silla, the south-western corner of the island São Sebastião, a little south of the Forte da Feiticeira, now a plantation. Followed the Praia Brava, with the Buraca da Velha (old woman's hole), so called from a dark rugged cave at its point : this section is steep and rocky, wild and narrow ; all give it a wide berth, as many canoes have been broken and lives lost, especially during the dangerous south-west wind. About one and a-half leagues from the town of São Sebastião are the small sandy Praia and the Ponta de Guiacá, an "Indian" word supposed to signify a den. Here is the Buraco do Bicho (beast-hole), one of the many tunnels in the honeycombed rock : it gets its name from some unknown animal that issued from it and sprang into the sea. The unlearned tell many "Worm"-tales about it, and the learned quote the Beast of Rhodes. The Guiacá is a large and well-timbered estate, with a chapel under the invocation of Na. Sa. da Luz, belonging to the Carmo (Carmelite Order). The last friar carried off all the movables in prospect of secularisation, and the place was offered for 800$000. On December 3rd, 1864, the slaves murdered their administrator, Antonio Augusto Teixeira, because he hired out some of their number beyond the limits of the municipality. It is followed by the Praia de Varequesaba, separated from the Praia do Cavallo Gordo by a point of grassy rock-faced soil; then come the Praia de Pitanguy, very romantic and solitary; two stony projections; the Praia Grande, fronted by a dangerous "deviling;" the Lage da Araça, or da Praia Grande; and lastly, the Ponta da Araça, where lies an old and decayed battery, with guns along the wall, a red-tiled house behind, and a small whitewashed chapel dedicated to São Sebastião.

We are now within the canal de São Sebastião, sometimes called Toque Toque, one hundred and forty indirect miles from Rio de Janeiro. Here the coast bends suddenly from west-east to north-east, and is fronted by the continental island of São Sebastião which, viewed from a distance, seems part of the shore. Between the two is a land-locked channel, a vast harbour nine to ten miles long by two to three broad: it is easy of access for the island, with a coast line of fourteen miles, which has few important projections. The depth averages twelve fathoms: the middle is a sandy and stony bottom, and on both sides there is a slate-coloured clayey mud. When the tide is out landing is difficult: at high water you step upon hard sand, and the veriest sketch of a pier would suffice for public comfort. This channel, which casts the harbour of Lerwick far into the shade, mimics a lake; it is generally smooth as ice, and the scenery is fair as

that of the fairest river. An English naval officer declares the Brazilian coast to be deficient in ports : in
these parts at least it has some of the best that can be
imagined.

I visited more than once the town of S. Sebastião da
Terra Firma, so called to distinguish it from the island
and its capital, and I always lodged at the house of a
bachelor friend, Benedito Fernando Coelho, President
of the Municipal Chamber (Mayor). Originally it was
a small village, subject, like all the coast places north
of Bertioga, to its head-quarters, the Porto de Santos
—Sanctorum oppidum. It was created Villa de Sam
Sebastiam, on March 16, A.D. 1636, by Pedro de
Motta Leite, sixth Capitão Mór of São Vicente, in the
name of the perpetual Donatory, D. Alvaro Perez de
Castro Souza, Count of Monsanto : a copy of the
old document made in 1741, and very much worm-
eaten, may still be seen in the municipal building.
The population then consisted of some sixty " mora-
dores" (colonists), and its jurisdiction extended nine
miles south to the Una River. It was presently prolonged to the Rio Sahy, but Law No. 44 (of April 5,
1865) revived the older state of things. Northwards
the frontier once ran to Tabatinga, a distance of
thirteen leagues ; but when Caraguatatuba was raised
to the rank of a Villa (town), the line was drawn at
the Juquirequiré River, distant three leagues. Its early
reputation arose from the neighbouring gold mines of
Araguára ; the site, however, as often happens in the
Brazil, is now forgotten.

The town of S. Sebastião consists, like its neighbours,

of a Rua Direita (straight or high street) and a
Largo (square), both well grown with grass. It is very
badly placed in a low plain of thick mata (bush)
under a buttress perpendicular to the main chain of
the Serra, which here edges away from the sea :
it is backed by a dangerous swamp, and bounded to
the north by an unclean drain. Yet the people boast
of their climate, and declare that the land is fertile and
the water is abundant. From afar it is denoted by two
large double-storied houses, apparently uninhabited ;
they are the common many-windowed and balconied
claret-cases with foundations and corners of good stone.
The landing is not pleasant : formerly there was a fort,
now turned into a drying-ground for coffee, and its four
old English carronades lie dismantled upon the sand.
The shipping is represented by a few small craft, chiefly
Lanchas and Sumacas for the Cabotagem or coasting
trade, by half a dozen drawn-up canoes, and by the same
number of " Canôas de Voga" discharging Carne seca—
jerked beef. The population of São Sebastião and its
jurisdiction, although much of it, including Caraguatatuba, has been curtailed, still represents six thousand
souls, which the enthusiastic exaggerate to double. I
have every reason to remember with pleasure and
gratitude the hospitality of my excellent host and the
kindness of the São Sebastianenses.

In 1590, São Sebastião, being then a village, had a
filial chapel of São Gonçalo under the Villa de Santos ;
when visited by the Administrator of Rio de Janeiro,
Doctor Lourenço de Mendonça Prelado, he ordered
the building to be removed a gunshot from the shore,

where the Matriz of São Sebastião now stands. The latter is a long low building, which lacking stone foundations cannot be raised higher; the tower is to the north, not a common arrangement here as in Styria. As usual, it is unfinished; three side chapels have been furnished by private piety, but three still want columns and other necessaries. Below it lies a mass of human remains; the dead were buried there till 1862, when a small cemetery was erected by public contributions, the government giving its share of 400$000. Again, the mortuary chapel is unfinished. The main square shows vestiges of antiquity in the Portuguese pillory with hanging bars to accommodate four: *levantar pelourinho e fazer Villa* was the good old feudal phrase for founding a settlement.[1] Behind it is the prison, in which I found a negro confined for the Guiacá murder. The main square (Largo da Matriz) contains a small dwelling once inhabited by the "Palmerston of the Brazil," the late Marquez de Paraná, who here began his career as Juiz de Fora. The Casa da Camara (Town Hall) was opened, like the prison, in 1865.

In the long Rua Direita stand the empty barracks and magazine (Trem or Armazem de Artigos bellicos); the latter was built in 1825 by the military commandant and last governor of the Villa, Lieut.-Colonel Lopo da Cunha d'Eça e Costa. In these piping times of peace the guns have been transferred to Santos. Forts were once numerous. North of the town lay

---

[1] For the "ceremony of creating a town in the New World", see Southey (iii, 885), who borrows from the "Milicia Indiana of Captain Bernardo de Vargas Machuca. Madrid, 1599."

the Fortes da Sapituba, da Ponta da Cruz, whose guns cumber the ground, and da Ponta das Cannas, the most salient point : the latter has an old wall of cut stone, probably dating from 1800, and pierced for eighteen pieces ; it is in ruins, and has served to build the houses. South is the Forte da Araçá (·Araxá), opposite the island-work " da Feiticeira." In this direction also is the temporary Matriz of S. Gonçalo, and a brook called " O Ribeiro," coming from the south-west ; the upper part supplies drinking water, and the lower is handy for washerwomen.

Of course there is a Rua da Quitanda (market street), but the supplies are very limited. The people content themselves with cultivating half an acre of manioc, and fish when they please ; fresh meat is rare, and the many cannot even afford Carne seca. There are a few shops of the *omnium gatherum* style in the grassy streets ; two bakeries supply bread half-raw, and the square boasts the normal poor apothecary. The people mentioned an Irish doctor, Alexander Newcator, who married a Brazilian wife, and eventually came to grief.

São Sebastião contains two well-frequented schools of first letters for each sex : according to the law of the Empire (October 15th, 1827) they teach Portuguese grammar, arithmetic, the elements of geography, morality, and the religion of the State. The earliest creation was in 1800, under the Professor Alexandre Bento de Barros. At the same time a Latin *cum* French school was established : it was shut in 1861, as it wanted the legal number of pupils. There are also elementary schools at the neighbouring places, the Toque-Toques (Grande and Pequeno), S. Francisco, Enseada, Caraguatatuba, Massa-guasú, and Cambory.

I made a short excursion north of S. Sebastião to the Bairro de São Francisco, in order to inquire about some antimony reported to have been found there. A grassy hill beyond the town gives a fine view ; further lies the large Fazenda de Santa Anna, belonging to Antonio Francisco da Rego. The stone aqueduct shows that it was once important, and supported a number of slaves ; now the house is neglected, and the orchard is a fine breeding-place for weeds. The next baylet contains a tilery, and a pottery manufactory higher up. The walk is pleasant, the sands are overrun with the delicate blue Ipomæa Maritima (here called Salsa da praia), like our convolvulus ; and I recognised with pleasure the fleshy leaves which welcome the traveller to inter-tropical Africa. Inland are heaps of a Cardomum-like plant, the tall Sapé grass, and the arrowy Ubá (properly Vubá, Arundo Sagittaria), resembling sugar-cane. The Páo d'Alho (Garlic tree, Seguiera alliacea) flourishes everywhere, even on the beach ; the people have an idea that its wood deflects the needle, and will hardly trust their eyes when they see that it does not.

After walking a league I reached the Bairro de S. Francisco, one of those small outlying places which astonish the traveller in the Brazil.[1] In a village with a

[1] I have noticed a similar surprise at that " templum miræ magnitudinis", Na. Sa. da Conceição dos Morrinhos on the Rio de S. Francisco (Highlands of the Brazil, ii, p. 271).

d

single street of scattered houses, backed by cocoa-nuts
and large clearings, and fronted by a Praia (beach) bearing a few canoes, rises a vast and lofty building of the
best masonry, approached by a fine ramp of masonry,
and faced by a substantial stone cross. To the north
is a chapel of the Third Order of Franciscans, now a
Matriz: in the centre and fronting east is the convent
church, with a portico supported by two piers and
flanked by a tower. The southern building is a huge
convent, which once accommodated a score of monks,
and might have lodged a hundred. Azulejos (Lisbon
glazed tiles) upon the tower, the dome and the façade,
prove that no expense was spared : both places of
worship show St. Francis and his stigmata, whilst both
have black St. Benedicts in gorgeous array, each holding a white baby.[1] But everything is in the last stage
of neglect ; the kitchen, with the vast chimney, looks
utterly deserted ; the cloisters are falling to pieces ;
the floors are dangerous, and the torn music-scores are
scattered on the ground—I saw something of the kind
on the Congo River. Tradition says that the land was
given by an old "Morador" (colonist), Antonio de
Abreu, and doubtless a whole regiment of slaves, and
probably of Indians, was employed upon the construction. It belongs to careless owners in Rio de Janeiro ;
the difficulty is to know what to do with it, were it
even secularised. The Freguezia (parish) is one of the
most populous in the Province, but men have changed

---

[1] One morning I awoke and actually found a black Benedict
in a most peculiar costume, placed right above my head. The
white Saint Benedict in these regions is called São Bento.

their habitations, and there are no monks to be lodged. At the Bairro, antimony was ignored by all the in- habitants.

The continental island of São Sebastião (A Ilha Fron- teira) invites a visit. In fine weather, when the sea is blue and the landscape is clearly outlined, the aspect is charming. The length of the long narrow feature, which is hatchet-shaped, the edge being to the south, is eight or nine miles, and the breadth two to four : consequently it shares with St. Catherine the honour of being the largest island off the Brazilian coast be- tween the Amazonas and the Plata river. We find it mentioned by old travellers, especially Hans Stade and Andrew Battel of Leigh ; from the former we learn the Tupi name, Meyen or Meyenbipe, which is now clean forgotten. Near the southern shore the water is deep ; ships, however, must be cautious when approaching Villa Bella about the north-western third. The surface is high, broken, and picturesque ; a single Serra runs down the length, bifurcating about the centre to south-east and south-west : it is generally covered with wool-pack in the morning, whilst opaline mists lie in the hollows. The outline is somewhat volcanic in shape, especially the Central Peak, in whose flanks the rains have ploughed deep hollows. Thick trees run up to the summit, clothing every inch of ground. The people have had the sense not to dis- forest the upper island for plantations where the soil would be cold and useless : consequently the humus and vegetable matter have not been swept into the sea. In the middle altitudes are clearings and grassy

d 2

fallows ; the cultivation is better than on the main
land, and coffee extends 1100 feet high. The aspect
reminded me of Brava Island in the Cape Verdes, but
Africa must here yield to the Brazil.

All the hill points[1] are not named. The pyramidal
north-eastern peak is called the Pico do Poço after a
Cachoeira or waterfall. Viewed from the north, it is
bell-shaped, with a Mamelon on the summit, like the
Old Man of Hoy. The north-western summit is the
Monte da Pacuiba, green, and rising to a point from
its spreading roots the Ponta da Pedra and the rushy
Ponta das Cannas. The central height, steep and
regularly pyramidal, with a bare stony buttress to the
north, is known as the Morro or Pedra de Baipi, or
Baijipi, possibly from the name of the cannibals who
used to attack the people of Caraguatatuba, and who
were driven away by the colonists of Santos. To the
south is a well-wooded and rounded hill, "O Frade", a
humbug compared with " O Frade" of Paraty, further
north, which much resembles a hooded Franciscan.

On August 5th, 1866, I ascended the Baipi. The
path was decent as long as it passed over the plantations and the grassy hills, but it became very troublesome when it plunged into the steep virgin forest along
a succession of Cachoeiras. The Criciúma bamboo,
which at a certain angle cuts like glass, molested the

[1] The Royal Geographical Society calls everything above 1000
feet a mountain. In this matter I prefer Ritter, who extends the
hill to 2000 feet, the low mountain to 4000, the middling to 6000,
and the Alpine to 10,000. Beyond this height the altitude becomes gigantic (*riesen gebirge*).

hands unprotected by gloves, the Sipós (llianas) tangled the feet, and the Caraguatá thorns were more injurious than the "wait-a-bit". The people spoke largely of coral serpents, rattlesnakes, Jararácas, Jararacussús, and other trigonokephali ; but in places so damp I made sure of not finding them. The bats (Noctilio and Molossus) are very common, whilst the Morcego or vampire, known by its musky smell, does not confine itself to insects—I have described its habits of phlebotomy in the *Highlands of the Brazil.* Here the people hang up an owl's skin to keep it away from themselves and from their cattle, which it afflicts with poisonous sores. We passed several Tócos (caves), in which runaway negroes had taken refuge. Presently we emerged from the virgin forest upon a stony sugarloaf, whose summit is about 2000 feet above sea level ; here ropes were wanted, and the guide refused to advance. It afforded a grand prospect of the northern coast about Caraguatatuba and the mountain walls of the Serra do Mar working round to the east.

We could see on the verge of the open Atlantic to the north-east the Ilha dos Búzios (Cowrie Island), a lumpy feature like the Cypræa, which gave it a name, but somewhat saddle-backed ; it contains water in abundance, and supports about a score of families, whose mainland is São Sebastião. Still nearer the shore and east is the uninhabited island of Vittoria, a local name adopted by Captain Mouchez ; it is generally included with its little outliers in the Búzios group. Want of water forbids population, but coffee grows luxuriantly. South-west of Vittoria is a snug

bight, the Bahia dos Castelhanos, so called from a
Spanish ship wrecked there.

The landing-place, whence Baipi can best be ascended, is the settlement of Perequé opposite the town
of S. Sebastião. A flat ledge under the heights carries
about two hundred houses, large and small, scattered
about and buried in the bush, or abutting upon
plantations—everywhere here, as in Africa, the waving
cocoa-nut trees show the presence of man. About a
dozen whitewashed bungalows form a straight line
along the shore, and the same number of shops supply
the necessaries of life—the baker complained to me,
however, that his trade would not keep him alive ; he
had sold only two vintems worth of bread that morning. A little south of Perequé and hugging the
western shore, is the green Ilha das Cabras.

A walk of two miles from the north leads from
Perequé to Villa Bella, the chief town in the island of
São Sebastião. On the way we pass a local lion, the
Cachoeira—cataract or rapid—beyond which the road
is very good. The water is scanty between June and
August, dividing it into two sections, which course
down a steep incline of granite : about Christmas
time it becomes a single sheet. There is a similar
feature north of Villa Bella, and a third upon the
mainland. All are charming streams, with Mesas or
large sheets of granite, and either falling into Poços
(kieves) or into swamps and *débris* of rock, the ruins of
the mountain, which they themselves have made. The
Tócas or caverns, which produce luxuriant orchids, are
favourite places for Troglodytic picnics : one of them

is called the Tóca do Mendez, from a "pardo" (Mulatto),
who here took refuge from conscription. Brazilians
especially affect the "agua batida", broken water,
which, dashing from high rocks, is thoroughly aërated.
On September 7th, 1865—Independence Day—
Commander Napier, R.N., of H.M.S. *Triton*, a sister
ship to the *Antelope*, and I, landed at Villa Bella and
inspected the old-new settlement. From 1600 to 1806
the island formed part of the municipality of São
Sebastião, till the "beautiful town" was founded by
the Capitão Mór Julião de Moura Negrão, and was in-
augurated in 1808-9 by Dr. Joaquim Procopio Picão
Salgado, the Ouvidor (Chief Justice) of the Comarca
de São Paulo. Hence it is also known as Villa Nova
da Princeza. The site is a sandy, boulder-studded
flat at the foot of the hills outlying the mountains, and
it commands a glorious view of the winding channel,
with its salient and re-entering angles. Villa Bella is
bounded north by a gorge, whose vast blocks, angular
as well as rounded, are small conservatories of orchids
copiously irrigated by the rain, and the mouth is a
tract of "bents" and reeds. At times a dangerous
torrent rolls down the bed, and the broken wooden
bridge should be removed higher up. The church, Na.
Sa. de Ajuda, stands on a dwarf rise fronting a square
which contains the now empty prison and the municipal chamber above—the broken-down feudal pillory
will be turned into a cross when funds are forth-
coming. The place of worship is a towerless, barn-
like structure, with three holes in the long sides and
an aperture by way of wheel window in front. A

ramp was proposed for the entrance: it was unfinished in 1865, but in August 1866 considerable progress appeared. The belfry is a kind of gallows, to which the bells hang, as in the Congo regions. Inside, the high altar shows the mother and child, with Sta. Barbara in blue on the proper right, and a black Benedict in Papal robes and bosomed baby to the left. The confessional is a mere grating—I should think' it a great advantage if confessor and penitent did not know each other, but certainly neither would agree with me. The font is painted light ultramarine, a favourite colour in the Brazil. The sacristy is poor and unfinished, and the cemetery behind the church is still a kind of "Campo" (open bush) unwalled, and denoted only by a cross. The Fête of the Padroeira (patroness) is on February 2nd.

The houses form a street, Rua da Cunha, along the sea, which seems to be empty except on Sundays and holidays. The only Sobrado (two-storied tenement) is the jail, and there is a single Meio-sobrado raised upon masonry foundations. The walls are decorated with crosses of lath painted black, upon whitewashed grounds; the roofs are tiled, and, besides the eleven of somewhat superior construction, there are a number of ragged and grey-thatched hovels forming three rudimental cross-streets. About the middle of the settlement and denoted by a tall palm, stands an old and crumbling battery of earth and stone. The good brass guns have been sent, we were told, to the seat of war in Paraguay: those that remain are chiefly the ancient twenty-four pounders, and all except one bear the

broad arrow of England. To the south of the settlement, and opposite the Rua dos Benedictinos, lies the
little chapel of St. Benedict, still unfinished ; yet
corpses are buried in it. It owes its existence to the
Mulattos, who, being a proud race, will have their own
place of worship, but will not, or rather cannot, afford
the luxury. The "movement of commerce" is represented by one shop of dry goods, and four of Molhados,
wet goods,—in plain English, liquor.

As we landed for the usual official visits we were
met by the notables of the place. Foremost was the
municipal judge, Dr. João dos Santos Sarahyba, in
black velvet cap, silk robes, and laced cuffs ; the Sub-
Delegate of Police, Sr. José Martinez da Silva, both of
them depending upon the town of São Sebastião, accompanied him ; also the intelligent young Vigario, Rev.
José Vicente Cabral of Ubatúba, who has lived here
but a short time, and is not "Collado" or permanent.
He had studied at Rio de Janeiro and São Paulo, and
it was easy to understand that he would willingly have
exchanged this pomp of skies, this calm of seas, this
grandeur of rocks, this luxury of vegetation, this
gigantic and monotonous magnificence of scenery, for
the dirty picturesqueness, and the human interest of a
back alley in a civilised city. Hardly a man in a
million can enjoy nature unadorned ; the *belle sauvage*
soon palls upon the senses, and love declines from in-
difference to absolute aversion. The people are in a
primitive state, as may be seen by their pulling off
their hats and wishing one another good night when
they hear the "Ave Maria". They live mostly in their

Roças, little clearings, and their only amusement is on summer evenings when the drum summons them to a dance. They are all poor, and, as is usually the case in these small places, they are reserved, not to say surly, to foreigners. But there is a reason for this. Some three years before our visit a drunken Frenchman, M. Perlet of Nantes, made himself peculiarly disagreeable, and one fine day he disappeared—his compatriots declare that he was murdered: the people represent him to have been drowned. The officials, who were very kind and communicative, informed us that Villa Bella contains some two hundred fires; the island supplies Santos, where nothing will grow, with Farinha (Manioc-flour), Feijão (beans), Batatas (sweet potatoes), various vegetables, as the Guandú (Cajanus flavus), and a little saffron; with fruits, such as oranges, plantains, Abacatis (Persea gratissima, the Avocado pear), and Jaboticábas (Eugenia cauliflora), the latter remarkably good. The Purgeira (Jatropha curcas), whose "physic-oil", used by Lisbon lamps, has often kept sundry of the Cape Verde Islands from starving, is here a weed, and neglected accordingly. The sugar-cane, of three kinds: the Creoula, Cayenna, and Preta; the latter, a purple variety, little prized, has of late years made way for coffee, and this "fruit", despite want of hands, became the principal export till 1856, when it was attacked by a disease, which had not disappeared in 1866. The "bush-", or wild coffee, had not suffered; the cause, therefore, must be sought in keeping the tree upon the same ground—a general failing in the Brazil. The rice of the Ribeira de Iguape, further south, has degenerated, because the seed was never changed. About Villa Bella there are no ploughs and few carts : the animals are horses, cows, and goats.

I will now continue my cruize on August 6, 1866. The "Canôa de Voga" carried me slowly up the noble channel of St. Sebastian, the breeze being from the west and the tide against us : the current depends chiefly upon the wind, flowing up coast with the souther, and *vice versâ*. The correspondence of the uplifted strata in shape and angle (about 45°), suggests that an earthquake once parted island from continent, and that there was a dome of rock where the sea now rolls up to the cliffs. The same was said of Sicily,

> " Hæc loca si quondam et vastâ convulsa ruinâ
> (Tantum ævi longinqua valet mutare vetustas)
> Disiluisse ferunt,"

and "Rheggio" embalms the belief which is not held by modern geologists. About one league north of the Villa Bella is the Forte do Rabo Azedo, whose small and almost unarmed garrison, on November 8, 1826, drove off the Argentine Admiral, William Brown, and forced his war schooner the "Sarandy" and a transport brig to retire. Near it lies Vianna, a little village of a dozen whitewashed houses, built in a cove which receives a small mountain stream : the site is a mound of earth and large boulders, fronting the bright sands and backed by woods of the darkest verdure, speckled with the verdigris green of the sugar cane. Beyond it is the Armação das Balêas, whence a line of road dotted with huts, and plantations of brown soil, leads to the chief town of the highly picturesque island.

The north-western extremity is the Ponta das Cannas, a projection from the Monte da Pedra ; it fronts the Ponta de Arpoar (Harpooning point) of the main land beyond the Bairro de S. Francisco, the convent whose straight lines stand well out from the curves of the tangled dark-green bush. Harpooning Point has a cross upon the rocks, showing that a man was drowned there : now the Devil, as the people say, has no power to enter the place. Our last look at the Pedra showed a remarkably sharp cone.

Beyond the channel we debouched upon a broad, shallow open bay of sand and mangrove,[1] con-

---

[1] The mangrove of these regions, as on the coast of Africa, is of two kinds :

1. The white (a Myoporinea, called by the " Indians" Sereiba-tinga, Serei-tinga or Sereibuna (?), and by the Portuguese Mangue Manso, M. Branco and M. Amarello, or more generally Mangue Bravo) which grows a tall tree on sand-banks where salt water does not extend, and even on raised cliffs. Its bark, a strong astringent, is used in medicine and for tanning, and its straight trunk makes good telegraph posts, whilst the wood is one of the best for fuel.

2. The red (Rhizophora Mangle, Guapariba, Mangue Verdadeiro, Amarello or Vermelho) flourishes only where fresh and salt water meet, and it grows again at once if the roots be not cut. The bark is a more powerful astringent than that of the white; the wood supplies house rafters, and the ashes are used in sugar refineries. The people will not stake it in fish weirs, believing that the bark drives away the game. The red, but not the white, mangrove strikes down shoots like Banyan trees (Ficus Indica). To the vegeto-animal matter, which it collects round its roots the people attribute miasmatic and febrile effects.

The old monk, Yves d'Evreux, calls the mangroves "Aparturiers" and "Aparturies" (probably a parturiendo), and, by means of them, explained to his savages the " Mystery of the Incarnation": the

sidered very dangerous for small shipping, but with good riding ground in calm weather. On our left, under the tall mountain walls, lay the Barra das Cana-veiras, a low and mangrove-grown tract with green water, which to the practised eye at once suggests a river. This is the Jujuiriqueré, anciently known as the Curupaçé, and here began the old Captaincy of Santo Amaro, which extended three leagues down coast, and which is now merged into the province of S. Paulo. Two miles beyond the Arpoar, and deep in the bay, is Caraguatatúba, *alias* the Villa de Santo Antonio do Morro de Caraguatatúba e Capella de Na. Sa. da Conceicão.

The town is not easily approached in rough weather, and the canoe is severely tried by a long, low line of breakers. The beach is garnished with a large shed, acting as boat-house ; and the abodes, some fifty fires, scattered about the bush, give the settlement a deso-late, dreary look. All are ground floors, even the Municipal Chamber : the church on the west is the mere skeleton of a place of worship, under repair, and not even plastered. Almost all the houses are shut, except the three Vendas (liquor-shops). A single old gun upon the ground shows that it was once defended. The place seems permanently ruined since the col-lectorate was transferred to São Sebastião, and it now keeps itself alive by supplying the chief town with bacon and cheese, coffee, beans, and maize. Caraguata-

upper growth was the heavenly nature with the hypostatic union, the lower was the Incarnation. I need hardly cite St. Patrick and the Shamrock.

túba is still very unhealthy, and the cause is manifest in the Pantanaes (morasses) which hem it in. During its most prosperous days it was well drained, but the neglect brought on a pestilence which destroyed almost all its inhabitants. After the rains, which are heavier even than at Santos, the neighbourhood is under water. There is a chalybeate spring which might be, but which is not, utilised by the people.

Caraguatatúba was founded in A.D. 1600, by Manoel de Faria Doria of Santos, said to be a son or nephew of Andrea Doria of Villa Oneglia in the western Riviera of Genoa, who attacked the Turks under Dragut Rais on the Neapolitan coast in 1552 : the family still flourishes at Santos.[1] It soon became a Villa, whose limits were Ubatúba on the north, and the Curupaçé river to the south. When desolated by pestilence its villa-ship was transferred to Ubatúba. The Provincial Law (No. 18, of March 16, 1847) created it a Freguezia (parish) under the municipality of São Sebastião. In 1828 it again suffered from "Maletas" (typhus), causing the patients to vomit blood, and to die at the shortest notice. By another Provincial Law (No. 30, of April 20, 1857), it became a Villa for the second time, forming part of the "Termo" (district) of São Sebastião. The Tropic of Capricorn is said to pass over it: a road four leagues long connects it with the chief town, and telegraph posts mark out the line.

The position of São Sebastião and the steepness of the hill curtain behind it, rendered a road to the Serra

[1] Others say that Manoel was a son of Doge A. Doria's son, the Admiral who defeated the Ottomans at Lepanto in 1571.

Acima (uplands) difficult and expensive. About 1832, a Picada or bridle-path was run up a branch ridge (Espigão) of the main wall to São José de Piratininga, distant about thirteen leagues, by two ecclesiastics, Padre Pinto and the Vicar Padre Manoel de Faria Doria. But the last died in 1843, and the Doria road was left for natives to destroy. In 1785, the Capitão Mór of São Sebastião, Manoel Lopes de Resurreicão, and others, dissatisfied with the dangerous ascents from Ubatúba and Paraty, which still remain, and unwilling to make the long detour viâ Pirassinunga, laid out a hill road. At present we see a red line winding over the dark green Serra : it leads in one day to Parahybuna, and the stiffness of the ascent is limited to five miles. But with such a port, what is the use of a highway ?

From Caraguatatúba to Ubatúba is a canoe run of seven leagues. You first cross the eastern half of the bay, so terrible in the east-south-eastern gales, foul with rocks and shallows, and showing a break half a mile long. Before arriving at the sandy Bahia, and the grassy bluff, " Ponta de Martim de Sá", we see a Prainha (little beach), a nook to the north-east, with a clump of white houses. At its natural pier sailors, coming from the north, land during bad weather, and find a path to Caraguatatúba ; another line also leads to Gitúba, the large Fazenda of Commendador José Vieira de Macedo. Beyond this point the coast-line is deeply indented with jagged anfractuosities and long rocky projections —the bays and headlands equally dangerous. The first bight is Macóca Bay, with its little river protected from all sides but the dangerous south-south-wester by two islets, the Tácuncanha, and a longer feature easily recognised by a split in the rock, a heap of dense and dark vegetation which supports two families. Beyond it are the Ponta de Tobatinga and two bluffs; here huge boulders line the shore, showing the violent send of the sea.

The next projection, Ponta Aguda, like most of these features, is a long neat's tongue, stony below, green above, grassy at the root, and clumpy with trees at the tip. Behind it lies the Bahia da Alagôa, a deep inlet with a sandy beach, showing at the bottom a large whitewashed house. Here there is often a tide rip, formed by a current from the north-east and a sea from the south-west. The bay and point "do Bananal" are shaggy hills with grassy clearings, and for a few furlongs the trend is from east to north-east. Off the Ponta do Cassão, where lie huge slabs of pink granite, the sea often breaks heavily, and the next inlet is divided into the Bahia da Lagoinha and the Bahia de Maranduba.

Our attention was then drawn to the Ponta da Fortaleza (fortress), a broad bluff, taking a name from its regular outlines, and fronted by a little insulated outwork of rock. Opposite it lies the Ilha do Malvirado (the "ill-turned"). All the other islets run parallel with the coast, but the lay of this is from north-west to south-east—considered to be the wrong direction. It is a caterpillar-like line with a central bulge and shaggy with the densest forest : consequently, it supports no inhabitants. Beyond it, a long deep sag, with shelving shore, forms a noted anchorage for small craft, and therefore is tolerably populous : it is divided into a multitude of minor baylets, and is bounded eastward by the Ponta de Sete Fontes, whose two prominent rocks are curiously split. We then pass a deep, somewhat shallow, and very safe bight with sands and houses backed by high and forested hills. The outer part is called Sacco do Flamengo, and the inner Sacco da Ribeira. Both are known to older writers as the Enseada dos Maramomís or Guaramomís (See the "Arte de Navigar" of Luiz Serrão Pimentel, No. 3, p. 229, Lisbon edit. 1681, quoted by Fr. Gaspar), then the only Indian permanent settlement on the coast between this and Itanhaem, south of Santos. The Guaramomís sought the society of the Portuguese, and were removed by them to Aldeâ Velha, a place one league north of the old Bertioga fort. Here, when José de Anchieta, the venerable Thaumaturgus of the Brazil, was praying in the chapel, the captain of the fort and his wife saw celestial lights and heard heavenly music. I must record a debt of gratitude to the Flamengo, one fierce black night when the crew could not haul in their sail, and when the canoe would not answer her helm. The ranch which sheltered us was, it must be confessed, populous with the Carrapato (the Ricinus or tick), yet, sleeping in it was far better than a wet berth among the fishes.

The Ponta da Enseada, a projection in the rocky continental beach, is divided from the Ponta do Boqueirão by a " gut " or passage some 160 feet broad. Due south of it is the Ilha dos Porcos—of pigs—an unsavory name found in Fr. Gaspar (p. 20), the people insist

e

upon turning it into "dos Portos"—of ports or ferries.
It is this crescent-shaped islet with the convexity turned
to the coast which makes the Saco do Flamengo so
safe. The main block, which has small outliers to the east
and north-east, rises in two peaks, the northern rounded
and the southern irregular; the latter, known as the Pa-
dra de Indajá, projects a low rib stretching south-west
towards the mainland, and forms a baylet which shel-
ters a dozen white houses, one of them large and conspicuous. The ground is cleared almost to the hill
summits and is renowned for coffee and manioc. In
olden times the islet was called Tapéra (ruin) de Cun-
habebe, the dreaded Cacique who, when Anchieta
returned from Iperoyg on his mission of reconciling
the Tamoyo tribes of Ubatúba and Larangeiras, carried
the reverend man in his canoe to São Vicente.

The Ponta do Boqueirão leads to the Bahia da Tonninha (of the Tunny), a wild shore where no man
anchors : it is known by a sandy beach in its peri-
phery and by a pair of rocky buttresses projecting
into the sea. Behind it is the Morro da Tonninha, a
well defined cone which, when clear, shows that an east
wind is imminent. And now after passing the bluff
and stony Ponta Grossa, the southern staple of Ubatúba
Bay, we turn from north-east to due west. The shores
appear quite worn out ; the herbaceous forest (Capoeira)
is thin and yellow, and the only conspicuous growth is
the Indajá palm (Attalea compta), with leaves on edge,
which fruits in December and January. *En revanche*
the seas are full of fish, as we could see by the host of
terns, the butterflies of the waters, hovering over every
wash.

Presently we passed the Ponto do Meirão at the inner entrance of the Barra de Ubatúba: the stony southern projection, bluff and with rocks honeycombed by the sea, like all its neighbours, fronts white cottages, some of them not unlike châlets, in clearings freshly fired for plantains and sugar-cane. We landed at the Ponta da Prainha, to the north-east of the settlement which lies at the bottom of the deep bay: here a rocky point stretches into the sea, and might easily become a pier. The clump of sheds and new whitewashed houses with shops on the ground-floor is faced with four wooden jetties, and there is the usual display of flags. The two small steamers which connect the place, very irregularly, with Rio de Janeiro, and are supposed to sail every four days, lie in four fathoms off the Sacco do Itaguá, on the south-east of the bay. The *Rade*, though defended to the north-north-east by the Ilha dos Côuves (of Cabbages), and sundry small outliers, is terribly affected by the east winds which roll in an awful sea. The gales are ever shifting, especially in August, making the beach very dangerous: the best season is from November to January, but it is also the wettest.

A walk of a few yards over a red hill of slippery clay leads to the Rua da Boavista, upon the shore where a single old gun lies. Ubatúba, by older writers called Ubatyba, derives its name from the quantity of tall cane (Ubá, properly Vubá, Arundo Sagittaria) which the indigenes used for arrows, and " tyba," place of growth or abundance : others prefer Obatyba, meaning manufactory of cloth (Oba). The air is said to

e 2

be exceptionally healthy, and the site is good ; it lies like Iguape upon a sandy flat ; behind it is a rolling subrange, bright green with cultivation and dotted with houses, whilst the back-ground is the wild Serra, darkly clad to the top and forming an arc. The usual ruddy thread shows the road to the interior : it is kept in fair order as far as the summit, but afterwards it becomes very foul. In the rear-curtain there is a Corcovado (hunchback hill) which, however, more resembles the Gavea of Rio de Janeiro, and behind it is shown a mamelon, rich, says the local legend, in gold and precious stones.

North of the town runs a winding stream, the Rio Grande, upon which lie boats and other gear. Though the mouth is only a few feet broad, the upper part spreads out far and wide : of the stone bridge only the piers remain, and the Troupeiros (muleteers) cross by a rough affair of timber 120 paces long. They complain that repairs are sadly wanted for the roads, and that they can hardly travel in safety to the northern port, Paraty, distant only a few miles. Yet a French engineer, M. Charles Bernard, and his assistant, M. Alphonse Boude, have been here two years endeavouring to mend matters.

Grass flourishes in the streets of Ubatúba as it does upon the shore. The town is deserted, like an African village at noon, or like Barège and Aranjuez out of the season : the long street may show a solitary old man. Yet there are signs of past prosperity when a single planter had his 600 head of slaves, in several heavy-eaved " Sobrados" (two storied houses) with Corinthian columns of plaster and statuettes, and in rooms neatly papered, furnished, and supplied with books, whilst each tenement has its Quintal (back yard) and garden. The best specimen, known by its coat-of-arms and Lisbon tiles, belongs to a Fazendeiro or planter, Sr. Balthasar. The smaller dwellings of wattle and dab are cleanly whitewashed, but when they fall, apparently, they are allowed to lie. In the south a chapel, Na. Sa. do Rosario, is in the last stage of neglect and decay ; the brick tower is unfinished, and the windows are torn off the hinges. Beyond it lies the Largo da Matriz, containing the Vicar's house, the Collectoria (octroi bureau), and a cathedral not yet christened—the white dickey, with the normal three windows and three doors, is painfully ornamented, and every line that should be straight is crooked, whilst the bricks behind are exposed ; of course there is no belfrey. The town ends south in a cemetery, also whitewashed. The best part is partitioned off and walled in for the use of the red-coated brotherhood of the "Santo Sacramento": here are some good marble tombs, whilst the walls intended to guard bodies from wet graves, as in New Orleans and parts of Spain, show the inscribed names of many a gentilhomme, prudhomme, and bonhomme.

In the Rua de Benavides there is an hotel, the "Bom Retiro," a thorough misnomer, kept by a Portuguese, Sr. Algarato. The "Gasthaus" in this part of the world is a study. The host probably combines inn-keeping with brokerage or some other matter : the mistress, if there be one, is far above her work, consequently from year to year nothing is washed or cleaned—it is worse than in Galway or Mullingar. The beds are bunks, the bed-rooms are stalls, hardly divided from one another by the thinnest of partition walls. The servants, a negro or two, know nothing and do nothing. Fresh meat is an event, lean chickens and "tainha" are the usual luxuries. The vilest stuff in the shape of beer and wine, bears the honoured names of Bass and Bor-deaux, being duly labelled at Rio de Janeiro. There is a billiard room, where the marker plays with himself; also a public room, which the presence of a stranger converts into a menagerie : it reminds you of the 'cute Chinaman who exhibited his British guest as a rare manner of beast. The people walk in, touch hat or not, sit down, expectorate, and indulge in a stare which, unbroken by a word, may last a quarter of an hour : when tired they rise slowly and lounge out of the room. Finally, the bill will show, that as in the depths of Ire-land, you are charged first-rate English prices for accommodation which no arithmetic can rate : your "addition" will be eighteen dollars a day instead of two, and a box of lucifers worth a penny will be modestly set down for nine pence.

The Brazilian Fazenda (plantation) shows much true hospitality : in these country towns, where an apology for an inn exists, there is as little as in Shetland or Italy. Moreover, we can hardly expect to be favourites after our late display of Palmerstonian gas—all fizz, and smell, and flare, without light—in the matter of slaves. I sent my introductory letter to the Juge de Droit, Virginio Henriques Costa, who returned the satisfactory

answer that he had received it. Hard upon a traveller
to be treated as a crypto-Palmerstonian, when he has
nought of sympathy with the vagaries of his eccentric
rulers! The Ubatúbans also have a bad name, they
are chiefly noted for swearing by "Gesu Christo", a habit
learned from the French, and for fighting and killing
one another. About six years before my time, the
Bishop of São Paulo visited the place, but soon left it
in disgust. Lately a murdered he-goat was hung at the
door of an unpopular official, with an inscription which
might have been written by "Sarah":

"Xarapim !
Vede que fazem a vos como fizerão a mim."[1]

He wisely left at once, knowing that the aggrieved
were perfectly capable of employing "Capangas," or
professional bravos, whilst the authorities were perfectly
incapable of defending him.

Ubatúba has seen better days. The treaty of
February 19, 1810, which, by the by, abolished the In-
quisition in Portuguese America, secured to England
the right of felling forest timber for her navy, and in
1817, when Rio de Janeiro became the capital of Portugal, establishments were set up here and at São
Sebastião. The effect was to render prices impossible,
and indeed it may be doubtful whether the operation
will pay anywhere—even at Camarones, opposite Fernando Po, where the finest of trees may be had for
the price of cutting. About 1820, the French immi-

[1] Anglicè—   Old goat !
Look out, or they'll treat you as they have treated me.

gration began : they were chiefly *colons de Saint Do-mingue*, although the people attribute the influx to the scattering which followed the downfall of the first Napoleon. The King, Don João VI, broke new ground, and freely granted "Sesmarias"—gifts of ground—where the new comers settled down for a time as planters, surrounded by multitudes of slaves. The sugar-cane, however, here, like that of the Beiramar (maritime region) generally, is poor and watery. A M. Robillard, originally a Parisian, after serving in the English navy, wasted some 500,000 francs. M. Millon, his managing man, died. M. Réné, son of a Breton gentleman, de la Jousselandière, had less money but no more luck. The brothers Jan, from Brittany, sold their lands and slaves at a profit and sensibly left the place ; the brothers Pierre and Louis Richet, also Bretons, unwisely stayed here and died. The Frères d'Herissey established a glass manufacture, which was subventioned by government—grass now overgrows the place where once 600 slaves worked. In 1848 M. Marquois, after wasting twelve years here, became Consul de France at São Paulo. M. Chaillot of Santo Domingo left two sons, Arsène and Carlos, who still grow coffee. There is also a French Vice-Consul, M. Réné, who lives at Colonia, distant two miles, and the list of notables may end with the local banker, Sr. Francisco de Castro, who was driven here by political feuds.

Ubatúba appears now ruined, the result of coffee disease, of deficient slave labour, and of emigration. The richest proprietor owns perhaps twenty-five head of negroes where he could work a thousand, and the largest fortune will not exceed £5,000. The thinness of the free population is mostly the effect of railways, which withdraw hands from these outlying districts to large centres, and to lines where transit and transport are cheap and easy. This is evidently a disadvantage to the townlets : on the other hand it is a great benefit to the Empire. We shall see the same things in Syria and other parts of Turkey, when that obese and lethargic land condescends to let the Giaour be up and doing.

I have now guided the reader over the hundred direct geographical miles of coast between Santos and Ubatúba, the scene of Hans Stade's travel and captivity. The details have been extended, perhaps, to a wearisome length, but they serve the purpose of placing the *mise-en-scène* before the reader's eye, and of showing what effect three centuries and a half have exercised upon these shores, where the Indian is now utterly extinct.[1]

---

[1] Throughout the Brazil not more than 250,000 "Indians" survive, according to the Census of August 1872. When the country was discovered, the total is supposed to have reached one million "Red-skins", or about two per square mile, and this, small as it is, compares advantageously with other wild parts of America. The slave population is numbered at 1,683,864, and the free white at 8,162,114—a grand total of 10,095,978 (in 1807, three millions), giving a revenue of under twenty shillings a head.

INTRODUCTION.

THE "INDIANS" OF THE BRAZIL.

NOTES ON THE AUTHOR-TRAVELLERS OF THE SIXTEENTH CENTURY. HANS STADE.

INTRODUCTION.

UNTIL the present age the anthropology of the native Brazilians was involved in error and misunderstanding. Various theories were afloat touching their origin : whilst some derived them from a southern focus, where modern Paraguay lies, others made them emigrants from the wilds and wolds of the northern continent. As regards their mutual relationship many, misled by the system of what appeared to be national names, distributed them into separate races, whilst a few, justly observing that the language was single and undivided, and that the same terms might be traced from Florida to the Rio de la Plata, determined the family to be one, without, however, explaining how and why each section seemed to claim a different and distinguishing title.

Upon the latter point it may be useful to enlarge. An immense confusion was caused by the old writers, whose books became the authorities upon the subject, such as Gabriel Soares (A.D. 1580-87), Yves d'Evreux (A.D. 1613-14), Gaspar Barlæus (A.D. 1647), Padre Simam de Vasconcellos (A.D. 1628), and Jaboatam (A.D. 1761). The authors who took from them, erudite Southey for instance, could not but perpetuate the evil, and it was not before the days of M. F. Adolfo de Varnhagen that we have anything like a sensible ethnological statement.

The error was simply that of dividing a single people into a multitude of different nations, each with its own name and *habitat*. For instance, Gaspar Barlæus in a copy of verses addressed to Count Maurice of Nassau, thus enumerates the "barbarians" subjected to the sway of the Netherlands :—

> "Nec barbara sperne
> Verba, Magayates et qui sibi lurida formant
> Tela, Tabajarres et pictos membra Tapujas
> Patagones et Canibales, pastumque cruore
> Humano deforme ; durosque Caëtas
> Tupiguas et Amizoceros sævosque Piryvos
> Et Tupinaquorum populos."

Hence the student applied himself to the study of such nationalities as the Pytiguaras, Putygoares, or Poti-guaras ; the Cayetés or Caitís ; the Tupynambas with their various divisions the Tupináens, Amoipíras Maracás, and Ubirajarás ; the Tupynamquis, the Papanás ; the Aymorés or Aímorés ; the Goaytacás, called Ouctanages by Abreu and Lima (Compendio da Historia do Brazil Rio de Janeiro, Lammaert), and Guaitacá (Plur. Guaitacazes) by Fr. Gaspar, with their subtribe the Papanazes ; the Tamoyos ; the Goayaná (Pl. Goayanazes or Guayanazes) ; the Carijós ; the Tapyiyas, commonly known as Tapuyas ; the Tobayaras or Taba-jaras, called Tabaîares by Yves d'Evreux, and many other similar distinctions. Under these great divisions were a multitude of clans, a list of whose names would fill pages. The huge list, amounting to at least seventy-six, was presently reduced to six nationalities, viz., Tobayaras, Potiguaras, Tapuyas, Tupinambás, Tamoyos, and Carijós. A further simplification included the three latter in the three former. After this, P. Simãm de Vasconcellos (Chronica da Companhia de Jesus, A.D. 1628) brought down the number to two, namely :

1st. The Tapuyas, *alias* Indios Bravos or Bravios (wild Indians, a vain term where all were wild) with their divisions, viz. Aimorés, Potentins, Guaiatacás, Guaramomís, Goarégoarés, Jeçaruçús, Amanipaqués, and Payeás.

2nd. The Indios Mansos (tame or settled), not including the Amazonian tribes. Their component items are Tobayaras, Tupys, Tupynambas, Tupynaquis, Tupigoares, Tupyminós, Amoigpirás, Araboyáras, Rarigoáras, Potigoares, Tamoyos, Carijós, and Goayanás.

Jaboatam (Fr. Antonio de Santa Maria) who wrote, in A.D. 1761, the "Novo Orbe Serafico brasilico ou Chronica dos Frades Menores da provincia do Brasil" (2nd edit. Rio de Janeiro, 1858) in his second "Digression" gives a list of the tribes on the seaboard of the Brazil, from Gran Pará to the Rio da Prata, and, like his predecessors, fails to solve the riddle. Yet the ethnological details of this work are so interesting that they might even now be offered in abridged translation to the public.

Southey ("History of Brazil," London, Longmans, 1810) found matters in this state, and left them as he found them, having no means of rectifying the "catalogue of barbarous and dissonant names." At length order grew out of the chaos in the "Historia Geral do

Brazil, by M. Francisco Adolfo de Varnhagen (Rio de Janeiro, Laemmert, 1854). I shall extract the substance from his eighth Secção or Chapter (vol. i. pp. 97- 108), as it is apparently unknown to English writers, and I shall take the liberty of adding a few notes.

These semi-nomades—the " Indians" of the Brazil— who were engaged in perpetual wars, apparently be- longed to one great family, that is to say, they had a com- mon origin, and all spoke dialects of the same tongue. For authorities see Gandavo,[1] Gabriel Soares (vol. i. pp. 13, 39, &c.), Padre João Daniel, and D'Orbigny : see also the " Revista " of the Institute of Rio de Ja- neiro, vol. iii. p. 175. This tongue was called " Lingua geral " by the first Portuguese colonists, and its area exceeded that of all the South American families of speech. The limits extended from the Amazonas River to the Porto dos Patos, and from São Vicente to the head waters of the Rio da Prata[2] (Ramirez, Letter of July 10th, 1858, Revista, xv. p. 27). In this vast ex- panse, however, there were sundry little isolated oases, if the expression be allowed, held by caravans which had migrated or fled their country : such were the

[1] This ancient author, for whom see the Introduction, seems not to have been free from the belief that there were truly national or *racial* differences ; yet he owns of the coast peoples, however much they had been divided, that, " Todavia na semelhança, con- dicaõ, costumes e ritos gentilicos todos saõ uns."

[2] Pero Lopes de Souza, in A.D. 1532, found on the Plata River a people speaking Guaraní, and calling themselves Nhandu, or the Emas (Struthio Americana). Many authors have assumed that " Guaraní" was the racial name of the Brazilian savages, whilst " Tupi" applied only to a certain section.

Aymorés or Botocudos (the modern Puris ?), the Cai-
riris and others. Thus we may explain the easy
progress of Portuguese conquest, and the identity
of geographical, botanical, and zoological expressions
which, with few exceptions, pervaded the Brazil.
The general name of the race known to itself, was
" Tupinambá":[1] from Pará to Rio de Janeiro, if you
asked an " Indian " who he was, his reply would have
been " Tupinambá." Abbeville is our authority for Ma-
ranhão ; Berredo for the Amazonas, Pará, and the To-
cantins ; Acuña (Nos. 22 and 69, folio 9, v. and 35)
for the Amazonas-races; Gabriel Soares for Bahia; and
for Rio de Janeiro Hans Stade, Thevet, and Jan van
Laet, whose " Novus Orbis" is partly borrowed from
Manuel de Moraes. The Tupinambá trunk put forth
a variety of new stems, branches, and offshoots, which,
however far-spread, never changed names.

This term, which has not been much discussed,
is derived from two words, " Tupi"[2] and " Mba." The

[1] Etymologically and literally Tupinambá (Tupi-anama-aba)
signifies " uncle warriors," or a "people related to Tupis". The
latter word may be written Tupi, or with the older writers Tupy.
I shall prefer the former, and similarly Guaraní (not Guaráni, as
in Southey) to Guarany. In the Brazilian tongue the terminal -y'
was pronounced mostly like the Greek "epsilon" and the French
"u". Thus " P'ty'," tobacco—whence the Brazilian words " Pitar,"
to smoke, and " Pitada," a pinch of snuff—was phonetically
written Betum and Pitun. It is, therefore, safer to use the " i."

[2] M. J. de Alencar, "O Guarany" (vol. i, p. 353), considers that
" Tupi" was used only by certain peoples, and that the great race,
which had conquered the country and had expelled, or absorbed
the older owners, was generically called Guarany. Hence he makes
the latter signify "Indigena Brasileiro".

f

latter was omitted when the clans ceased to be friends; and when on bad terms they insulted one another with "Tupi-n-aem," that is to say, "bad Tupis." As unfriendly neighbours they politely termed one another "Tupi-n-ikis," or "Tupi neighbours." "Mbá," the form in composition of "Abá," signified "vir," a chief or brave,[1] and their pride would concede this title to none but themselves—thus at times they would vaunt their own people as "Mbá-été," whence "Abá-été," meaning a "true brave." Sometimes, but rarely, when roused to fury by strife they would dub their former companions "Tupinambaránas," or wild savage "Tupinambás." When simply separated they called those from whom it was their boast to proceed "Tamoy," whence our "Tamoyos," signifying grandfathers, and consequently they became "Temiminós," grandsons[2] (*Dicc. Brazil*, pp. 17, 54 ; Thevet, Cosmogr. f. 914, v. writes Tominous). At other times they termed them-

---

[1] See *sub voce*, "Diccionario da Lingua Tupy, par A. Gonçalves Dias". Lipsia, Brockhaus, 1858.

[2] So Fr. Gaspar tells us that the Tamoyos of Ubatyba (Ubatúba), Larangeiras, and Angra dos Reis, offended by Portuguese pride, allied themselves with those of Rio de Janeiro, and in A.D. 1556 nearly annihilated the whites of São Vicente. Santo Amaro was the theatre of war, and we see in Hans Stade, the Fazendas and Casas Fortes were ravaged, whilst the fort of São Felippe was threatened. These troubles ended by the good offices of PP. Nobrega and Anchieta, whilst Men de Sá conquered the tribes of Rio de Janeiro. The same Fr. Gaspar tells us (p. 90) that the Tupins (plural of Tupi) lived between Itanhaem and Cananéa, and that the wild people (Selvajens) of São Vicente called their ancestors (Tapuy) a people from the north, and themselves their grandsons (Temiminós).

selves " Guayá " or "Guayá-ná," that is, "we, the esteemed," whence our "Guáiazes," or "Guaianazes," and
"Guiana," from the people near the Orinoco ; Southey
mentions other " Goayánases" (vol. i, note 28). Some
derive it from " Guáy," the esteemed, and "aná,"
people ; others from " Guaya," people, and "ná," esteemed, "Amoipiras" may signify distant relatives
(Tesoro Guarani, fol. 32 v., and 297 v.), and "Anacés,"
quasi-relations (ditto fol. 34 and 113 v).

Hence the confusion caused by applying different
names to the same tribe. This can be avoided only
by having recourse to the original language.

For instance, the clans who inhabited the captaincy
of São Vicente would call themselves primarily Tupinambás; when wishing to preserve their descent from
the northern " Tamoyos" they would be Temiminós ;
and when boastfully inclined, " Guayánás." Hostile
neighbours, as we find in Hans Stade, were termed
"Tupiniquins " (Tupi-n-ikis), or, by way of insult,
" Maracayás," *i.e.*, wild cats. At the same time the
colonists from Portugal would call these wild men
" Bugres," which means simply slaves, and " Caboclos,"
bald men, because the Indians, men and women,
plucked and scraped their hair from their faces and
bodies—the original pincers being a bivalve shell.
The latter word (Caboclo) was used in contradistinction
to "Emboaba," a fowl with feathered shanks, or a man
wearing nether garments.

Following out this analysis, we shall easily show
that the names, which ignorance and want of observation have represented to be national and racial, and

f 2

with which tedious catalogues have been filled, were simply epithets, in fact, nicknames often doubled and multiplied,[1] to express the mutual feeling of the clans. Hate was denoted by "Maracayás," wild cats; by "Nhengaibas" or "Nheengaibas," bad tongues;[2] and by "Tibiras" or "Tymbiras," the infamous. Respect appeared in "Tamoyos," grandfathers, and "Mbeguás," the peaceful. There were many which were simply descriptive, and generally ended in "iáras," "yáras," "uáras," or "járas," meaning lords or masters[3] (*Dicc. Brazil*, pp. 17, 71): such are "Ubira-járas,"[4]

[1] For instance, in the Captaincy of São Vicente, we find the people called by different authors Guaianás, Temimínós, Tupinambás, Tupiniquins, Maracayás, Bugres, etc., etc. Soares and Gandavo give the following list of tribes beginning from the south. In the actual provinces of Rio Grande do Sud and Santa Catherina, the "Carijós"; on the littoral of São Paulo, the "Guianás" (also called Goayaná, Guayaná, and Goaná, in the plural Goayanazes and Guayanazes); and to the north of them, according to the Jesuits, "Temimínós"; "Tamoyos" in Rio de Janeiro; "Guaitacazes" and Papanazes in Espirito Santo; "Tupiniquins" in Porto Seguro; "Aymorés" in the Ilheós; "Tupinambás", men related to Tupis) on the seaboard of Bahia; and "Tupináens", "Amoipiras", "Maracás", and "Ubirajáras", in the interior. Pernambuco had the "Caïtés", and further north were the "Petiguares" or "Potiguares". Finally, throughout the back-woods and unconquered interior were the so-called "Tapuia" nation, of old written "Tapuya" and "Tapyuya", which simply meant barbarians (Varnhagen's note, vol. i, p. 448).

[2] This corrects Southey (ii, 526)—"The Nheengaibas seem not to have been a Tupi race", etc.

[3] It exactly corresponds with the useful Hindostani affix— "Wálá", a man, and it also becomes in composition Guára, Goára, Pora, and so forth.

[4] Others translate the name "Warriors of the chief Poti" (*i.e.*, the Shrimp).

clubmen ; "Poty-uáras," shrimpers ;[1] for which others
prefer "Pety-uáras," smokers of tobacco (Petima, Purchas, v. 910); "Tába-járas," or "Tábaiáras," men who
inhabit "Tábas" or villages ;[2] "Guatós," canoers ;
"Guaita-cás" and "Guaiatacazes" ("Goatacáras" in
Dicc. Brazil, p. 28), walkers, scouts, runners, or
scourers of country; "Ca-iapós," bushrangers, robbers ;
" Cary-yós," descendants of the white men or the ancients ; Juru-unas, black-mouths, because their lips
were painted ; and "Temémbés" *(Abbeville*, f. 189) or
vagabonds, as opposed to the "Tába-járas." "Cama-
cans" may be from "Cuam-akan," signifying in this
case "heads rolled up."

" Purís" or "Purús," apparently corrupted to Orizes,
as applied to a people of the upper Amazonas, to a seaboard tribe still living south of Bahia, and to those who
held Taubate in A.D. 1645, means only cannibals.
(Tesoro Guarani, f. 319 v.) "Tagi-" (Ita-gy) "purús"
are men-eaters with stone hatchets ("Ita," stone, and
"gy," an axe). "Curúmará" proves that the wretches
who bore the name suffered from the itch—in fact,

[1] Near the Ubira-járas are supposed to have lived the ancient
" Amazons." Ubíra is also written Ybyra and Ymyra, meaning a
tree, wood, etc. Ybyra-pitanga, red wood, is that which gave a
name to the Brazil.

[2] According to P. S. de Vasconcellos, " Toba" means the face,
and "yara", lords : the whole meaning the "owners of the face of
the country", *i.e.*, the seaboard as opposed to the Sertão (back-
woods). A. Gonçalves Dias (Poesias, p. 418) preserves the transliteration " Tobajaras", but explains it Tábajáras, lords of villages.
Tába was the village composed of several Ocas (houses, the old
French "Carbets"); when the latter were isolated they took the name
of "Tejupab"or Tejupaba: for the latter word, see Note to chap. xxi.

were what we should call mangy. And, as might be expected amongst savages, there were not a few terms which decency absolutely forbids us to quote.

I may note, *en passant*, that these nicknames, so far from being confined to the Brazil, extended throughout South America. The Aymorés, more anciently written "Gaimurés" and "Gaimures," were so called by the Tupinambás from a poisonous fish. The "Aimáras," according to Captain Bernardo de Vargas Machuca (fol. 132), were so known from their sleeveless shirts; and in return they insulted their neighbours by calling them "Moxos" (Moksos), or "Molengas," sorry fellows. "Ottawas" ("Otauas"), in that widely-spread North American dialect which the French named Algonquin, meant no more than traders, and "Mascutinos" only signified inhabitants of river plains.

There was naturally in the Lingua Geral a general term applicable to absolute strangers, and thus corresponding with the Hebrew Goyi (Gentile), the Hindu Mlenchha (mixed or impure breed), the Greek βάρβαρος, the Latin Barbarus, and the Chinese Fan Kwei (foreign devil). Everyone not of the same race was "Tapuy."[1] Gumilla relates of the Caribs that, asked whence came their ancestors, they can but reply, "Ana cariná rote," *i.e.*, "we only are men," as a Jew would say "only we are Bashar" or human beings. According to Hervas (I, 270), many national names expressed nothing but

---

[1] The etymon is derived from Tába, a village, and "Puya", to fly; *i.e.*, those who fly the villages, barbarians, savages, enemies. So the Bedawin call themselves Ahl-bayt, tented men, opposed to the villagers, Ahl-hayt, wall-men, who inhabit houses.

men, people ; thus the Lules call themselves "Peles," the Peruvians "Runas," the Chiquitos "Naquiñones," the Darien Indians "Tule," and so forth. The same is the case with the Bube of Fernando Po.

Thus Tapuy presently became the "great Tapuya nation," when Tapuy Tinga, *i.e.*, white barbarian, was applied to their European allies, and especially to the French (*Dicc. Brazil*, p. 42). As regards the origin and true meaning of the word, we shall not agree with those who derive it from a country, and still less from a king, a great chief of that name who ruled the race when it was yet compact. The character of the people and of its language forbids us to consider it otherwise than as a collective root-noun, which the adjectives -mba, -iki, and -aem simply modified, and we refer to the Guarani dictionary rather than wander over a wild waste of conjectures.

Tupi or Tupy primarily means paternal uncle, and secondarily companion, comrade or fellow countryman. The connection in the popular mind is clear, when we remember that their relationship was only on the father's side, the mother being, as it were, but the nidus or cradle which lodged the child.[1] After the father the nearest of blood was the Tupi or father's brother, and they had scant regard for fraternity, so strong a tie amongst ourselves. Nor, perhaps, shall we err in considering that the title of uncle, still a

[1] The savages seem to have made a study of Monhang-pora, or the mysteries of generation ; hence they practised the Basque Gésine, or Couvade, which has now a literature of its own. This subject will presently recur.

favourite amongst the civilised peoples of Europe,
came in ancient times from the East. " Yá 'Ammi,"
" O my (paternal) uncle !" is heard every day amongst
the Arabic-speaking races. " Tio " is still general in
Portugal, and is applied to a negro in a kindly way,
nor have we yet seen the last of " Uncle Sam."

Other Tupis entitled themselves " Guaranís," meaning only "great braves."[1] Of the same breed were the
Caraïbes, Caraibes, or Caribes of Guiana, which suggests the Calybes of Xenophon, the tribe living about
Trebizond. According to D'Orbigny (*L' Homme Américain*, ii, 268, *et seq.*), these savages extended their
attacks to the Antilles. Enciso, treating of the same
islands in A.D. 1519, tells us that the cannibals of
Terra Firma used canoes to war amongst themselves,
and with foreigners. Gumilla (*Orinoco Illustrado*,

[1] I should rather say from Guára, an inhabitant, and therefore
lord of the soil, not subject to any owner. Padre Lacueva (D'Orbigny, *L'Homme Américain*, II, 313) derives from it " Guarayu",
i.e., " Guára", a people, and "yu", yellow. D'Orbigny considers
the terms Guarani, Guarayo, Caraïb, and Galibi, to be all synony-
mous with Carib, whence, probably, our cannibals, the " gluttons
of their foes' flesh." In Guarani, "Caruaybo" is applied to those
who support themselves miserably (R. de Montoya, Tesoro de la
lingua Guarani, f. 92, v.). Caryba (*i.e.*, Cary white, and Mbá, man,
whence Caraïba) or Caraybes (Alphonse le Xaintongeois) is translated by Yves d'Evreux, "Français, ou Chrétien". In the "Théogonie
Brésilienne, racceuillie en XVI Siècle," we find "Caraïbes ou Pageez"
(Pagé or priest), and Vasconcellos tells us that Caraïbe-bébé, in the
Southern Brazil, meant a powerful magician. From Cary, white,
is derived Caryoba, white (cotton) oba or shirt. Hence, too,
Carioca, the suburb of Rio de Janeiro, the Caraï-oca, or white man's
house, from the fort there built by Martim Affonso de Souza, and
mentioned by Men de Sá.

chap. 6) adds, "the prominent and dominant race in the eastern parts is the Cariba nation, which extends along the shores to Cayenne," and assures us that they have spread to the islands about Martinique. Other authors, knowing that Florida was occupied by them (Hervas, I, 389), suppose that they came from the north.[1]

In fact, the general opinion and traditions of the people, from the Amazonas to São Vicente, makes these invaders march southwards. The tenants of Bahia asserted that they came from the wilds beyond the Rio de São Francisco (Soares, ii, chap. 147). Cabo Frio (Thevet, *Cosmog.* f. 915) attracted to itself the Caraibes from northern Brazil. The wild men of São

---

[1] Not a few writers (for instance, Washington Irving, *Life of Columbus*) boldly derive the Tupis from the Apalachian mountains of the northern continent, across the Mexican Gulf—that New World Mediterranean, whose eastern shores are continuous archipelagoes—and the Caribbean Sea, to the shores of Paria, Guiana, and Amazonia. Another traditional account of their origin brings them up from the Paraguay River, the home of the Guarani language, of wild maize, and, according to Saint Hilaire, of the Ombu fig. It has been well remarked that in the Old World, whilst emigration went from east to west, the course of conquest was from north to south; that is to say, from cold to heat, from the poorer to the richer lands, from the harsher to the milder climate. In the southern hemisphere, however, the bleak south represents our north. I do not believe in "dense forests" ever being the *vagina gentium*; on the contrary, as the history of the world everywhere tells us, high and comparatively barren plains have most often sent forth hordes of conquerors. Therefore, if authorities are equally balanced, I should prefer to derive the Tupi-Guarani from the regions of La Plata. On the other hand, the voice of tradition amongst the red tribes pointed to the north—their Scandinavia.

Vicente considered those of Rio de Janeiro their forefathers. The emigration swept downwards in succes-
sive surges, driving all before it, successively dislodging
the possessors of the soil, and "leaving no more mark
behind it than the sounding wave which breaks upon
the shore."

It is possible that the cradle of the great nation,
which included the Tupis, the Guaranis, and the Oma-
guás, might have been in the glades and forests that
clothe the Amazonas' banks. Between this stream and
the mighty Orinoco, which are not unconnected, they
might have lived as an agricultural race, till, finally be-
coming navigators, and, emboldened by voyages upon
the inner waters, they went forth in their canoes, extending northwards to the islands of the American
Mediterranean, and southwards to the furthest confines
of the Brazil. From the Jarupá to the Rio Negro, the
ground, cut by natural canals, supported a large population; thus Acuña (No. 38) alludes to the crowded
state of the Amazonas' banks, and especially to a Tába,
or village, about a league long, which furnished his
expedition with more than five hundred measures
(fanegas) of manioc flour. Hence there might have
been an exodus to the southern parts of the continent,
and the conquerors would carry with them not only
their canoes, but their primitive agriculture, the planting and rearing of maize and manioc, of beans and
"squashes" (Aboboras or Jurimús), and their knowledge
of simples and poisons.

These Tupis, therefore, were the Jasons of Brazilian
mythology, the Phœnicians of her ancient history, and

the Norman invaders of more modern ages. They owed the facility of their conquests to an overpowering fleet of war canoes, whilst the barbarous tenants of the land possibly ignored this weapon, like the Aymorés, of whom mention has been made. They brought with them a perpetual state of warfare, habits adverse to population, such as earth-eating, and poisoning, and excesses of debauchery hardly to be expected in an uncivilised race. Their society reminds us of Spenser's "Sans Foy, Sans Loy, and Sans Joy," to which we may add Sans Roy, and thus they never took the first step towards the aristocratic monarchy of Peru. In fact, we may apply to them the

"Soy même est sa Loy, son Sénat et son Roy,"

of Ronsard, who ends, like J. J. Rousseau, with singing, "Je voudrois vivre ainsy."

So far M. Varnhagen.

We cannot be surprised that, in the days when philanthropy had not become a profession, travellers said hard things of their wild "brethren." "They are very treacherous: all they do is with deceit" (Luiz Ramirez). "They live like pigs in a stye" (cevados em chiqueiro); "quorum Deus est venter (as Saint Paul says) semper mendaces, malæ bestiæ, ventres pigri," etc. "They are people without honour—without any virtue when they have not fear, and servile in all things when they have" (Vargas). "They have rarely real and sincere friendship" (Bandeira). "They are vicious and inconstant in every sense of the word ; .... very light and very ungrateful, light, disloyal, envious,

. . . stained with vice, . . . disorderly and indolent"
(Voyage of a Brazilian). "False and faithless . . .
very suspicious, ignoring pity, without ideas of healthy
morality arising from sentiments of shame and sensi-
bility, which respects decorum and good faith; they
are stupidly brutal, and their phlegmatic tempers are
hard to move" (Varnhagen). All dwell upon their
inordinate love for tobacco, their ravenous "agriopha-
gous" hunger, their practice of cannibalism, and their
religious observance of revenge. The ethnology is not
without its romantic and fabulous side (Southey, I,
685); but here we have no room to consider the
western types of the Amazons, the Pigmies, the Mono-
culars, and so forth. Our authors prefer the picturesque
aspect of the subject—

> "Such of late
> Columbus found the American, so girt
> With feather'd cincture, naked else and wild
> Among the trees, on isles and wooded shores."

At last a papal bull, "Veritas ipsa quæ nec falli nec
fallere potest" (Paul III.), in A.D. 1536, and the Council
of Lima, A.D. 1583, were found necessary, ordering
Christians to believe that these wild men-beasts are
descended from "Adam."

There are not many printed works of travel, contemporary with the savages, which describe the race
in all its vigour, and of which it may be said, "L'homme
du lieu auquel le Brésil croist, est tel qu'ici à l'œil il
apparoit." Hence the value of Hans Stade.

The following *Bibliotheca Americana* contains the
principal eye-witnesses during the 16th century, the

Brazil having been discovered in A.D. 1499. The names are chiefly taken from Note A upon the "Reflexões criticas sobre o Escripto do Seculo XIV, impresso con o Titulo de Noticia do Brasil, no Tomo 3° da Collecção de Not. ultr., accompanhadas de interessantes Noticias bibliographicas, e importantes Investigações historicas por Francisco Adolfo de Varnhagen, Socio correspondente da Academia (pp. 73-78, vol. v. Collecção de Noticias para a Historia e Geografia das Nacões ultra-marinhas que vivem nos dominios Portuguezes ou lhes saõ visinhas : Publicada pela Academia Real das Sciencias, Lisboa. Na Typografia da mesma Academia, 1836).

1. The letter of Pero Vaz (Vaas in older writers) Caminha addressed to El Rei D. Manuel from the Terra de Santa Cruz (the Brazil), on May 1, A.D. 1500. The original is in the Real Archivo (Drawer 8, Bundle 2, No. 8). It was first printed, very incorrectly, as a note to the Corografia Brasilica of Ayres do Cazal, Rio de Janeiro, 1817. The Royal Academy of Sciences (Lisbon) then edited it, with some emendations, in the Noticias above alluded to (vol. iv., No. 3). A French translation appeared in 1822.

This curious document is most valuable as the production of an eye-witness, who gives all the required details. It was poetised by the fertile imagination of the historian De Barros. A French writer declares that, after a scrupulous examination, he finds no contradictions in the version of the latter, nor in those of Goes and Osorio : a little more care would enable him, with the indefatigable Cazal (Corografia, etc.), to detect a host of inaccuracies.

2. The "Viagem as Indias Orientaes" of the Florentine Giovanni da Empoli, factor of a Portuguese ship, A.D. 1503, who touched at Vera Cruz (the Brazil,) so called from the invention of the Holy Cross, May 3rd (*Noticias Ultramarinas,* vol. iii. No. 6).

3. The "Relação da Viagem de Cabral," published in the Collections of Ramusio ("Delle Navigazione e Viaggi racolti da M. C. B. Ramusio; Vinegia, Giunti, 1550"), and of Gryneus (Novus Orbis), and translated in the *Noticias Ultramarinas* (vol. ii.).

4. The voyage of the ship *Hope,* of Honfleur, which begins in June 24, 1503, and ends in 1505. The commander, Captain Gonneville, declares in his áccount that he had been preceded some years (dempuis aucunes années en ça) by other French voyagers. M. d'Avezac, who published this interesting little volume from a MS. in the Arsenal library, claims to have established the fact that French seamen discovered the Brazil before the Spaniards and Portuguese. His reasons are these. "Some" years must mean at least three ; *therefore* Frenchmen had touched on the coast, probably for dye-wood, before the various companions of Columbus — Alonzo de Ojeda, Vincent Yañez Pinzon of Palos, Diego Lope, and Pedro Alvares de Cabral, Lord of Azureira in Beira, who was cast upon the southern continent on April 24, or second octave of Easter (Jaboatam and Fr. Gaspar) in the same year (A.D. 1500). This assertion requires more definite evidence ; it is hardly possible to get so much out of a vague "some".[1]

[1] The first commander who reached the Brazil was Alonzo de

5. The two letters of Amerigo Vespucci, who travelled by order of the King in the ships of Gonçalo
Coelho (May 10, 1501, and May 10, 1503), and pub-

Ojeda, who, with Amerigo Vespucci on board, touched at Cape Saint
Augustine about the end of June A.D. 1499. The second was
Pinzon (A.D. 1500), and the third was Diego Lope, about one
month after Pinzon ; whilst Pedralves (Pedro Alvares) Cabral was
the fourth.

It is not a little curious that the Brazilian historians give a sub-
ordinate rank to the discovery of Pinzon, who struck Cape St.
Augustine, which he believed to be India, on January 28th (26th?),
A.D. 1500, three months before his Portuguese rival, to whom all
the glory is assigned. The latter Capitão Mór started with thirteen ships from Belem, on March 9th, 1500, lost his way to India,
and accidentally made Monte Pascual, south of St. Augustine ;
thence he ran down to Porto Seguro, where he arrived on the 3rd
of May with twelve ships, having sent one to Portugal. Were the
Brazilians Portuguese, we could see the reason of this injustice;
but they have no love for the Lucitanians, and surely one's enemy's
enemy should be one's friend.

This is but the official discovery of Brazil which had certainly
been visited often before. Doubtless many Portuguese *en route*
to India were cast upon the coast. Without mentioning the pilot
Sanchez, who died in the house of Columbus at Porto Santo—a
subject of considerable dispute—I may instance the João Ramalho, alluded to in my preface. This worthy declares that he had
been ninety years in the Brazil, in a will duly drawn up on May
3rd, 1580, by the notary Lourenço Vaz, with the aid of the Juiz
Ordinario, Pedro Dias, and four witnesses (notes of the Villa of
São Paulo). He must then have been wrecked in A.D. 1490, or
two years before the first voyage of Columbus. On the other
hand, João Ramalho's memory may have failed him. .

I have elsewhere attempted to show that what civilization belonged to the barbarians of the Brazil was introduced by the European castaways thrown on shore by the famous equatorial current,
which carried Cabral to the New World, and thus to explain the fact
of the coast having been missionarised by St. Thomas, the unbelieving
Apostle. The ancients have also claims to the discovery. According to Silva Lisboa (*Annaes do Rio de Janeiro*), at the Villa das

lished, it is said, for the first time, in A.D. 1504.[1] A
Portuguese translation will be found in the *Noticias
Ultramarinas* (vol. ii. No. 4). These letters have
caused an immense controversy—it would be impossible here to give even an abstract of it.

6. The Diario de Pero Lopez de Souza,[2] alluded to

Dôres, two leagues from Montevideo, a stone covering a brick tomb
was found to bear in Greek characters the name of Macedonian
Alexander, and beginning " 'In these places Ptolemy'. . . . There
was also found the shell of a sword-hilt, showing the effigy of
Alexander, and a helmet upon which Achilles was dragging the
corpse of Hector." Meanwhile, we would ask, where are these
most important relics ?

Again, we recently hear from Dr. Ladislao Netto, Director of
the Museum, Rio de Janeiro, that a stone has been found at
Parahyba containing " eight lines of the most beautiful Phœnician
characters, without separation of words, without vowel points and
quiescent letters." The purport of the inscription is, that the
Canaanites, as they call themselves (?), left Eziongeber (Akaba),
and sailed for eleven (twelve ?) novilunes (lunar months) along the
land of Egypt (Africa). The well-known words Alonim w'alonat
(Superi, superæque) are said to be legible. Unfortunately, Dr.
Netto, who, not knowing Phœnician, borrows all from Gesenius, did
not see the stone, and does not know where it is. The slaves of
Sr. Joaquim Alves da Costa found the stone at the farm of Pouso
Alto, near Parahyba (north or south ?), and brought it to their
master. He copied the characters and forwarded his work to the
Marquis de Supucahy, who in turn forwarded it to Dr. Netto.
May we ask why the latter does not publish a fac-simile ?

[1] Damião de Goes, in his *Chronica de El Rei D. Manoel*, expressly says that Gonçalo Coelho set out with six ships on June
10th, A.D. 1503 (not 1501). And Southey (i, 24) makes Amerigo
Vespucci command the expedition of 1501 ; yet, in the next page,
he finds the *savant* controlled by the Naviprætor or Navi-
præceptor (Gryneus, p. 156).

[2] In 1550 appeared a German translation of the letters of Cortes,
entitled " Ferdinandi Cortesii von dem newen Hispanien so im

in the Preface ; the cruise occupied three years from December 3, 1530.

7. The relation of a Frenchman from Dieppe, concerning various voyages which he made to Newfoundland, to the Brazil, to Guinea, etc. First published in Italian by Ramusio (19 of vol. iii).

The author speaks with rancour about the Portuguese inviting his compatriots to invade and occupy the Brazil, of which he offers a short description. He is supposed to have written in A.D. 1535, from these words: "The Brazil was partly discovered by the Portuguese *about thirty-five years ago*. Another portion was discovered by a Frenchman called Denis de Honfleur, and French ships subsequently voyaged here." The Dieppe pilots, who claim priority upon the Guinea coast, are supposed to have explored the Maranham shore in A.D. 1524 ; and Alphonse le Xaintongeois, whose cosmography in the original MS. is preserved by the Bibliothèque Impériale of Paris, entered the mouth of the Amazonas river in A.D. 1540, and wrote in A.D. 1543 (Ferdinand Denis, p. viii; Introduction to Père Yves d'Evreux).

8. The letter of Gonsalo Fernandes Oviedo to Cardinal Bembo, on the navigation of the Amazonas River, dating January 20, 1543, and printed in the collection of Ramusio.[1]

9. " La Déduction de la Somptueuse Entrée" (fol-

Meer gegen Niedergang, zwei lustige historien erstlich in Hispanischen Sprache durch himselbsts beschrieben und verteuscht von Xysto Betuleio und Andrea Diethero." Augsburg, in fol.

[1] The existing state of geographical knowledge, as regards the

g

lowed by the "Cérémonial de France") by Maurice
Sève, Sceve, or Sæve, published at Rouen, December 9,
1551, by M. Fred. Denis, under the title of "Une fête
Brésilienne, célébrée à Rouen en 1550, suivie d'un
Fragment du XVIme. Siècle roulant sur la Théogonie
des anciens peuples du Brésil et des poésies en langue
Tupique de Christovam Valente." Paris, Techener,
1850, gr. in 8vo.

10. The magnificent Portulan of Guillaume le Testu,
A.D. 1555. The author, a Protestant, was one of the
most able pilots in the days of Charles IX, navigated
the African and American seas, and was killed in
action with the Spaniards.

11. The history of Hans Stade, concerning which
more details will be offered at the end of this Introduction. In the same year (A.D. 1557) was printed at
Evora the "Relaçam do que ho adiantado da Florida,
dom Fernãdo de Souto passou em conquistar," and the
volume, in 8vo, was lately reproduced by the Academy
of Sciences, Lisbon. It appeared in an English dress
in A.D. 1563, and was translated into French by
M. D. G., A.D. 1685.

12. The "Copie de quelques lettres sur la navigation du Chevalier de Villegaignon," etc. Paris, A.D.
1557.

The celebrated Chevalier Nicolas Durand de Villegaignon, Vice-Admiral of Brittany, is said to have
composed the Vocabulary of De Lery amongst other

New World and Africa, is resumed in A.D. 1518 by the cosmographer Fernandez de Enciso, Suma de Geographia. He popu-
larised the thoroughly inaccurate expression "West Indies."

valuable opuscules. He involved himself in the atrocious quarrels between the fervent Catholics and the furious Calvinists or Huguenots, who gave him the title "Cain of America". In due course of time, "Villagalhão," as he is still called in the Brazil, and Viragalham in old books, will doubtless undergo "une réhabilitation." Already men begin to quote Ronsard:[1]

> "Docte Villegaignon, tu fais une grande faute,
> De vouloir rendre fine un gent si peu caute."

13. The "Discours de Nicolas Barré sur la Navigation du Chevalier de Villegaignon en Amérique." Paris, A.D. 1557.

14. "Les Singularités de la France Antartique, autrement nommée Amerique," etc. Par André Thevet, published in 8vo, at Antwerp (Paris?), A.D. 1558,[1] and in Paris in 4to.

This travelling Cordelier, who became cosmographer to Henry III of France, is exceedingly interesting, especially at the present time, on account of the careful study which he bestowed upon the savages and their "gentilismo". An Italian edition, in 4to, appeared at Venice in A.D. 1584, and was used by the Abbade Barbosa to prove that the author, André de Teive, was a Portuguese.

15.[2] The "Histoire des choses mémorables advenus

---

[1] Lacroix du Maine supposed that Thevet published in 1556, but he was certainly in error.

[2] In A.D. 1560, Father José de Anchieta wrote his "Epistola quamplurimarum rerum naturalium; quæ S. Vincentii (nunc S. Pauli) Provinciam incolunt, sistens descriptionem. Exaratum *Sancti Vicentii* quæ ultima est in India Brasilica vergens ad Aus-

en la terre du Brésil, partie de l'Amérique Australe, sous le Gouvernement de M. le Chevalier de Ville-gaignon," etc. A.D. 1561. 1 vol., 12mo. This work is also a diatribe against " Cain." Of a similar nature is the book of the Protestant minister who visited the Brazil in A.D. 1556 : "Petri Richerii lib. duo apologe-tici ad refutandas naenias, et coarguendos blasphemos, detegendaque mendacia Nicolai Durandi, qui se Ville-gagnonem cognominat." Printed in A.D. 1561 (no place). Small 4to.

16.[1] The "Historia da Provincia de Sancta Cruz" (an unauthorised change from Vera Cruz), "a que vul-garmento chamamos Brasil." Lisbon, A.D. 1576, 1 vol., 4to, by Pero de Magalhãens de Gandavo, the first regular Portuguese historian of the country, whose work, had it not been of the rarest, would have been much used by modern writers. It was lately trans-lated into French (Archives des Voyages) by H. Ternaux Compans, and the Academy of Sciences, Lis-bon, announced a re-impression.

17. The "Tratado da Terra do Brasil, no qual se

trum Lusitanorum Habitatio, Anno Domini 1560, sub finem mensis Maii. Minimus Societatis Jesu." Published in tom. i, Nos. 1, 2, and 3 of the *Noticias*, before alluded to. It bears the traces of its age ; for instance, § xvi : " Inveni columbrum justa viam jacentem in spiras collectum, quem, signo crucis prius munitus, percussi baculo et interfeci." This is not included in the list, as it cannot properly be called a book of travels.

[1] Meanwhile, two MSS. are mentioned : 1st. The " Summario das Armadas e Guerras ho Rio Parahiba"; and, 2nd. The " Tra-tado da Conquista do Cabo Frio", by Antonio Salema (Gabriel Soares, Part I, chapter lv). Of course there are many others.

contem a informação das cousas que ha nestas partes, feito por Pero de Magaglhães" (sic): an abridgment of Gandavo, published in A.D. 1576, and reprinted by the Academy in the *Noticias Ultramarinas* (vol. iv, No. 4).

18. The "Roteiro da Jornada de João Coelho de Sousa ao Rio de S. Francisco," referred to by Gabriel Soares, Part I, chapter xx).

19. The " Histoire d'un voyage fait en la terre du Brésil, autrement dit Amérique, donnée par Jean de Lery. À la Rochelle, A.D. 1578." 1 vol., 8vo.

De Lery is called by Auguste de Saint Hilaire the "Montaigne des vieux voyageurs." He travelled to Rio de Janeiro in the days of Villegaignon (A.D. 1556). I believe the first edition was published at Rouen in A.D. 1571. Many subsequent issues of the book appeared, the 5th in A.D. 1611.

20. "A letter written to Mr. Richard Staper by John Whithall from Santos (in Brazil), the 26th of June, 1578." It was republished by Southey (*Supplementary Notes to History*, I, pp. xxxii-xxxiv), from Hakluyt, and I reproduce it here.[1]

---

[1] Copy of a letter written to Mr. Richard Staper by John Whithall, from Santos, the 26th of June, 1578—

" Worshipfull sir, and welbeloued friend, Mr. Staper, I haue me most heartily commended unto you, wishing your health euen as mine owne.

" These few words may bee to let you understand, that whereas I wrote unto you not many dayes past by the way of Lisbon, howe that I determined to bee with you very shortly ; it is in this country offered mee to marry, and to take my choice of three or foure, so that I am about three dayes agoe consorted with an

21. The "Relacion y derrotcro del Viaje y descu-
brimiento del estrecho de la Madre de Dios, antes

Italian gentleman to marry with his daughter within these four
dayes. This, my friend and father-in-law, Signor Joffo Dore (Doriâ),
is born in the citie of Genua, in Italy; his kindred is well knowen
amongst the Italians in London ; also hee hath but onely this
childe, which is his daughter, which he hath thought better bestowed upon mee than on any Portugal in this country, and doeth
give with her in marriage to me part of an Ingenio which he hath,
that doeth make euery yeare a thousand roues of sugar. This
my marriage will be worth to mee two thousand duckets, little
more or lesse. Also Signor Joffo Dore, my father-in-lawe, doeth
intende to put into my haunds the whole Ingenio, with sixtie or
seuentie slaues, and thereof to make me factor for us both. I give
my liuing Lord thankes for placing me in such honour and plenti-
fulnesse of all things.

"Also, certaine dayes past I talked with the Prouedor and Captaine, and they haue certified me, that they haue discouered certaine mines of siller & gold, & looked every day for masters to
come to open the said mines ; which, when they be opened, will
inrich this countrey very much. This place is called S. Vincent,
and is distant from you two thousand leagues, and in 24 degrees
of latitude on the south side of the equinoctial line, and almost
under the Tropike of Capricorne, a countrey it is very healthfull,
without sicknesse.

" Moreouer, I haue talked with the Captaine and Prouedor, and
my father-in-lawe, who rule all this countrey, for to have a ship
with goods to come from London hither, which have promised mee
to give mee license, saying that nowe I am free denizen of this
countrey. To cause a ship to come hither with such commodities
as would serve this their countrey, would come to great gaines,
God sending in safety the profite and gaines. In such wares and
commodities as you may ship hither from London is for every one
commoditie deliuered here three for one, and then after the proceed may be employed in white sugar at four hundred reis the
roue (acroba).

" I meane, also, to have a friend in London to sende me a ship of
60 or 70 tunnes, little more or lesse, with such commodities as I

llamado de Magaleanes por Pedro Sarmiento de Gamboa." Published in A.D. 1580.

An unworthy attempt to rob the great Magellan,

shall give advise for. If you and Master Osborne will deale here, I will deale with you before any other, because of our old friendly friendship in time past. If you haue any stomake thereto, in the name of God, do you espie out a fine barke of seuentie or eightie tunnes, and send her hither with a Portugal pilot to this port, S. Vincent, in Brazil, bordering upon the borders of Peru.

" Also I herewith write unto you in what forme and maner you shall furnish this voyage in commodities and otherwise.

" First, you must lade in the same ship certaine Hampshire & Devonshire karsies; for the which you must let her depart from London in October, and to touch in the Canaries, and there to make a sale of the said karsies, and with the proceed thereof to lade fifteene tunnes of wines that be perfect & goode, & sixe dozen of Cordovan skinnes of these colours, to wit: orange, tawnie, yellow, red, & very fine black. I think you shall not finde such colours there; therefore, you must cause them that go upon this voyage to take saffron with them, to cause the same skinnes to bee put into the said colours. Also, I thinke you shall finde oyles there. Three hogsheads of sweete oyle for this voyage are very necessary, or a hundred and fifty canes of oyle. Also, in London you may lade in the said ship these parcels of commodities or wares, as followeth :

: " Imprimis, Foure peeces of hollands of middle sort.
" Item, One piece of fine holland.
    Four hundred elles of osenbriges, very fine.
    Four dozen of scizzors, of all sorts.
    Sixteene kintals of pitch, of the Canaries.
      &c.   &c.   &c.
" These be such sort of wares as I would you should send, if you meane to deale, or send any ship hither. Have you no doubt, but, by the helpe of God, I shall put all things in good order according to your contentment and profit; for my father-in-lawe, with the Capitaine and Provedor, doe rule this country. My father-in-law and I shall (God willing) make a good quantitie of sugar every yeere, which sugar we intend to ship for London from

who was naturally distasteful to the Spaniards, of his right to the Straits.

22. The "Narrativa Epistolar de uma Viagem e

henceforth, if we can get such a trustie and good friend as you to deale with us in this matter. I pray you presently after the receipt of this my letter to write me answere thereof, and send your letter to Mr. Holder to Lisbone, and he will convey it to me out of hand.

"Besides the premises, send six yards of

Skulef parchment lace of diuers colours.

Six yards of crimosin velvet.

Six yards of crimosin satten.

Twelve yards of fine puke blacke.

"Here, in this countrey, instead of John Whithall, they have called me John Leitoan; so that they have used this name so long time, that at this present there is no remedie, but it must remaine so. When you write unto me, let the superscription be unto John Leitoan.

"Thus I commit you, with all yours, to the Holy Ghost for ever.

"If you send this ship, I would have you give this order, that she touch in no part of the coast of Guinea nor any other coast, but to come directly hither to the port of S. Vincent, and from the Canaries let her be dispatched in my name, to wit, John Leitoan.

"Also a dozen shirts for my wearing let be sent, if you send the ship.

"Item, six or eight pieces of sayes for mantles for women, which is the most necessary thing that can be sent.

"By your assured friend,

"JOHN WHITHALL."

Santos, p. 359. —" It was my chance," says Knivet, "going up and down from cell to cell in the College of Jesus, that I looked under a bed standing in a dark hole, where I found a little chist fast nayled, & the seames thereof were white with wheat flower. I drew it forth, &, finding it of great weight, broke it in pieces, wherein I found 1700 riels of eight, each whereof containeth four shillgs Eng. This hole I took for my lodging, and no man new of my good purchas: cloth, shirts, blankets, & beds, and such stuffe no man regarded."

Missão Jesuitica pela Bahia, Ilheos, etc. Escripta em duas cartas ao Padre Provincial em Portugal." The Jesuit Fernão Cardim, who was superior of the Jesuits in 1609, lived at Bahia and Ilheos, and visited the southern "Indians" A.D. 1583-1618. His excellent work, which is compared with those of Jean de Lery and Yves d'Evreux, was edited by Varnhagen, Lisbon, 1847. 1 vol., 8vo (123 pages).

23. The "Tratado Descriptivo do Brazil em 1587, obra di Gabriel Soares de Souza, Senhor de Engenho da Brazil, nella residente dozesete annos, seu Vereador da Camara." It is generally known as the Roteiro[1] Geral.

The author concluded in A.D. 1587 a work composed of two parts : 1. Description of the Coast ; 2. Of the Notable Things in the Brazil: almost contemporary with Yves d'Evreux, he was wrecked, and died upon the inhospitable shores of the southern continent in A.D. 1591. Judicious readers prefer it in some points, especially in the description of native tribes, to all the works of the 16th century upon the same subject.

---

[1] There was long a mystery about this anonymous " Roteiro geral com largas informaçoēs de toda a costa que pertence ao Estado do Brasil, e descripcão de muitos lugares delle, especialmente de Bahia de Todos os Santos", dedicated to Christovam de Moura in 1587. The Ácademy of Sciences, Lisbon, recognising the importance of the anthropological and ethnological portion of the contents, published it in the *Noticias Ultramarinas* (vol. iii, Part I, of 1825). Varnhagen, after the collation of many MSS., which bore different titles, at length determined that it was composed in A.D. 1587 by Soares, and printed it under the name of *Noticia do Brazil.*

"This precious chronicle" (says M. Ferdinand Denis)
"contains more facts upon the subject of the ancient
races inhabiting the Brazil than any other contempo-
raneous work." It was lately published by Varnhagen,
in Rio de Janeiro. 1 vol., 8vo.

24.[1] The "Strange Adventures of Andrew Battel,
of Leigh, in Essex, sent by the Portuguese prisoner to
Angola, who lived there and in the adjoining regions
near eighteen years" (*Purchas his Pilgrims*, vol. ii;
Pinkerton, vol. xvi). "The author," an ignorant
man, and an authority only as to what he actually
saw, "fetched the coast of Brazil" in A.D. 1589,
went to the Plata river, visited the "Island of Saint
Sebastian, lying under the Tropic of Capricorn," on
his return northward, and was sent from Rio de
Janeiro to Angola. All his notices of the Brazil are in
chapter i.

25. The "Voyage Round the World" of Antonio
Pigafetta, of Vicenza, who accompanied Magalhaens
on the first circumnavigation, touched at the southern
shores of the Brazil and, after three years' absence, returned to Seville in A.D. 1522. An abridgment of his
travels was published by Ramusio, in the Raccolta di
navigazione e viaggi, fol., Venice, A.D. 1550.

26. The "Libro universal de derrotas, alturas,
longitudes e conhencenças de todas as Navigações,
etc.," ordinado por pilotos consummados nesta scien-
cia e virtudes de aproveitar em serviço de Deos.

---

[1] Here come the Historiarum Indicarum Libri XVI, Florentiæ,
1588, which give a short account of the Brazil, and the MS. of
Domingos d'Abreu de Brito.

Manuel Gaspar, March 1st, A.D. 1594. One volume, 4to, with plates, exists, according to Snr. Doutor Rivara, as far as the 83rd page, in the "Bibliotheca Publica Eborense."

27. The "Arte da Grammatica da lingoa mas usada na costa do Brazil," by José de Anchieta Coimbra, 1595, very rare. This venerable ecclesiastic, who travelled to the Brazil in 1553, and died there in 1597, wrote several other works. The first is the "Epistola quamplurima-rum rerum naturalium, etc.," published by the Academy in 1799, and incorporated in the Memorias do Ultramar (vol. i, 4to, A.D. 1812). The second is the "Brasilica Societatis Historia et vitæ clarorum Patrum qui in Brasiliâ vixerunt", mentioned by Sebastião Beretario. The life of this ecclesiastic was written in Portuguese by Pedro Rodrigues, and printed by Beretario in 1617; also by Estevan Paternina, who translated the biography of Anchieta from Latin into Spanish, and printed it at Salamanca, A.D. 1618, 1 vol., 12mo ; and by P. Simam de Vasconcellos, Lisbon, A.D. 1672.

28. The "Roteiro de todos os Sinaes, comhecimentos, fundos, baixos, alturas e derrotas que ha na costa do Brazil desde o Cabo de Sãto Agostinho até o Estreito de Fernão de Magalhães."

In this respectable list probably the most remark-able work is that of Hans Stade of Hesse, although Varnhagen characterises the earliest written account of the Brazil as "un tanto pintoresca." It was printed for the first time in German at Marburg (A.D. 1557), and it has become very rare; many writers on the Brazil have failed to find copies. Even in 1586 Theodore Turquet

explained a part of it to Jean de Lery, who had never
seen it. Translated into Latin, it was included in the
(Jean) " de Bry Collection," for which the reader can
consult the Dissertation published by Camus in 1802.
This is the edition used by Southey, who (vol. ɪ,
chapter vii), after his wont, succeeded admirably well
in " tearing the entrails out of the work." Some
writers are of opinion that the illustrations of Hans
Stade's book have been adopted by Thevet and De
Lery. Most of them are purely fanciful, and seem
borrowed from some book on Turkey. In chapter ix
we have domes and crescents; in chapter xii, scimitars
and turbans; and in chapter xxviii, an armed elephant.
Hans Stade is noticed in the Collection of M. Ternaux
Compans (p. 269); in the Revista Trimensal (vol. i, p.
299); and in the Magasin Pittoresque of 1850 (an
article written by M. Ferd. Denis).

Hans Stade would have sunk into the oblivion
which shrouds his tormentors, but for the rude, truthful, and natural volume which he has left to posterity.
His style, though simple and full of sincerity, is a poor
contrast with the graceful and charming garb which
distinguishes P. Yves d'Evreux[1] and the later writers.

[1] See " Voyage dans le nord du Brésil, fait durant les années
1613 et 1614, par le Père Yves d'Evreux. Publié d'après l'exem-
plaire unique conservé à la Bibliothèque Impériale de Paris. Avec
une Introduction et des notes par M. Ferdinand Denis, conser-
vateur à la bibliothèque sainte Geneviève. Leipzig et Paris,
Librairie A. Franck, Albert L. Herold, 1864." Admirably edited
and well printed, this number of the " Bibliotheca Americana"
forms a text-book for students, who can rely with confidence
upon the judgment and the learning of M. Denis.

His vile transliteration of foreign words requires the especial notice of an editor. His piety is essentially that
of the age when the Jesuits spat on children by way
of baptism, and saved the dying by surreptitiously
sprinkling them with holy water. Like the common
order of man, he has queer ideas about St. Elmo's fire,
and he dreads being eaten more than being killed.
His superstitions are manifold : the Tupis see "the
Devil", and are providentially punished for pulling up
his crucifix; the Almighty "works wonders" for his
especial benefit ; his prayers are heard, and all his
enemies come to a well-merited bad end. He pro-
phecies in hope of saving his life ; ' he threatens his
enemies with the "Man in the Moon", adding, however,
"God forgive me this!" and he especially avoids en-
lightening them when the savages believe that storms
and fair weather are sent in answer to his supplications.
In fact, it is curious to mark the narrowness of the
border-line between the belief of the Brazilian cannibal
and that of the Christian European of the sixteenth
century. And, although the latter does not eat his
enemies, he foresees for them a far worse fate : he
has the grace to ejaculate "May God forgive them!"
but it is plainly evident that he does not. He is
especially vindictive against the ship which would not
receive him on board, and against the young Frenchman who nearly caused him to be devoured, although
the latter did at last try to make amends for his former
act of barbarity. And yet he behaves nobly by remaining with the Christian captives when he might
have effected an escape. Finally, this fellow-country-

man of the late lamented Dr. Barth of Tinbuktu shows
uncommon powers of acute observation : it is certain
that he could not have taken notes, yet his descriptions of the fauna and flora, of the trade and manu-
factures, and of the customs and polity which fell
under his inspection during a captivity of seven and a
half years are, as far as they go, excellent.

Southey is the first to own that the adventures of
Hans Stade form an interesting part of his history.
He devotes a whole chapter (i, 7) to the analysis of
the little volume, and he ends by saying, with ample
justice : "The history of his adventures is a book
of great value, and all subsequent accounts of the
Tupi tribes rather repeat than add to the information
which it contains."

BIBLIOGRAPHY.

THE first edition of the remarkable narrative of Hans Stade is that of 1557, published at Marpurg, from which the present translation, edited by Captain Burton, has been made. It is entitled " *Warhafftige Historia unnd beschreibung einer landtschafft der Wilden, Nacketen, Grimmigen, Menschfresser Leuthen in der Newen Welt America gelegen...Da sie Hans Standen von Homburg."* The book is a small quarto of 165 pages (unpaged), with numerous quaint woodcuts. In the same year, another edition, also in small quarto, appeared at Frankfort-on-the-Maine, which is very scarce. There is a good copy in the Grenville Library.

The next edition was a · Flemish translation, published at Antwerp in 1558 : " *Waragtighe Historiœ ende Beschrijving eens landts in America ghelegen ...... Beschreven door Hans Staden, 'Tantwerpen,* 1558. 8vo."

In 1567 the work of Hans Stade was, for a third time, published in German, at Frankfort-on-the-Maine, in the third part of the " *Dieses Weltbuch von Newen erfunden Landtschafften durch Leb. Francke."*

In 1592 the narrative of Hans Stade was again published in folio, at Frankfort-on-the-Maine, in the collection of voyages of De Bry.[1] It was translated into Latin.[2] The second edition of this Latin version of Hans Stade appeared in 1605, and the third in 1630.

A fourth edition of the original German edition appeared in folio, at Frankfort, in 1593 ; and a Dutch translation was pub-

---

[1] See *Struvius Mesuel. Biblioth. Hist.,* III, Pt. ii, p. 49 ; and the *Mémoire de Camus,* p. 56. Also *Biblioth. Heber,* tom. VI, No. 442.

[2] The translator, under the name of *Teucrius Annœus,* was a fellow townsman of De Bry.

lished at Amsterdam, in 8vo, in 1630. "*Hans Staden von Hom-burgs Beschryringhe van America.*" A second edition of the Dutch version appeared at Amsterdam in 1640 ; and a fifth edition of the German at Frankfort in 1631, in folio. A sixth German edition, in quarto, was published at Oldenburg in 1664.

Then followed two more Dutch editions. In 1686 one appeared at Amsterdam, in quarto, with viii and 72 pages, illustrated with woodcuts ; and in 1706 a version appeared in a collection of voyages published, in 8vo, at Leyden. "*De vooname Scheeps-togten van Jan Staden van Homburg in Hessen, na Brazil gedaam, anno* 1547 *en* 1549." In "*Naauherrige Versameling der Gedenk Waardigste Zee in Land Reysen.* Vol. 52 : door Pieter Vander Aa. (Leyden, 1706)."

The fifth Dutch translation of Hans Stade was published at Amsterdam, in quarto, in 1714. "*Description de l'Amérique par Jean Stade de Homburg, en Hollandais.*" This edition is men-tioned by Boucher de la Richarderie, in the "*Bibliothèque Univer-selle de Voyages.*" Tom. v, p. 503. (Paris, 1806). The sixth and last Dutch edition appeared, in folio, at Leyden, in 1727 ; being a second edition of Pieter van der Aa.

A French translation was published in the collection of voyages of M. Ternaux Compans (vol. iii. Paris, 1839. 8vo). "*Véritable Histoire et Description d'un Pays habité par des hommes sauvages situé dans le nouveau monde nommé Amérique, par Hans Staden de Homberg in Hesse.*"

The most recent German edition appeared at Stuttgart in 1859. It is entitled "*Warhafftig Historia under Beschreibung einer Londtscheft der Wilden, Nacketen, Grimmegen Menschfresser Leuthen in der Newen welt America gelegen...Da sie Hans Staden von Homberg:*" reprinted in the "*Bibliothek des Liberischen Vereins in Stuttgart.*" Band xlvii. (Stuttgart, 1859. 8vo.)

Hans Stade has never before been translated into English ; but Southey, in his *History of Brazil*, gives a full abstract of the old German traveller's adventures, taken from the Latin version in De Bry.

C. R. M.

VERITABLE HISTORIE

And description of a country belonging to the wild, naked,
savage, man-eating people, situated in the
New World, America;

Unknown in the Land of Hesse before and since Christ's birth, until
the two past years, after the day when Hans Stade, from
Homberg in Hesse, has, through his own experience,
learned them, and now, by means of the press,
brings them to light.

DEDICATED TO HIS SERENE HIGHNESS,

The high-born LORD H. PHILIPSEN, Landgrave of Hesse, Count of
Catzenellenbogen, Dietz, Ziegenhain, and Nidda,
his gracious Lord.

WITH A PREFACE

BY

DR. JOH. DRYANDRI, CALLED ZYCHMAN,

Ordinary Professor of Medicine at Marpurg.

To the Serene and Highborn Prince and Lord, the LORD
PHILIPSEN, *Landgrave in Hesse, Count of Catzen-*
ellenbogen, Dietz, Ziegenhain, and Nidda, etc.,
my gracious Prince and Master.

————

MERCY and peace in Christ Jesu our Saviour, Gracious
Prince and Master! So speaks the holy and kingly prophet
David in the hundred and seventh psalm: " They that go
down to the sea in ships, that do business in great waters;
These see the works of the Lord, and His wonders in the
deep. For He commandeth and ariseth the stormy wind,
which lifteth up the waves thereof. They mount up to the
Heaven, they go down again to the depths: their soul is
melted because of trouble. They reel to and fro, and stag-
ger like a drunken man, and are at their wit's end. Then
they cry unto the Lord in their trouble and he bringeth
them out of their distresses.

" He maketh the storm a calm, so that the waves thereof
are still.

" Then are they glad because they be quiet; so He
bringeth them unto their desired haven.

" Oh that men would praise the Lord for His goodness,
and for His wonderful works to the children of men.

" Let them exalt Him also in the congregation of the
people, and praise Him in the assembly of the elders."

In this manner do I thank the Almighty Creator of
Heaven, Earth and Sea, his son Jesus Christ, and the Holy
Ghost, for the great mercy and compassion which, among
the savage people of the country Brazil, called the Tuppin

Imba,[1] who ate men, and whose prisoner I was for nine months, and amidst many other dangers, were through their Holy Trinity quite unexpectedly and wonderfully vouchsafed to me, and that after long misery, peril of life and body, I am again, after past travels and sea voyages, in the Grand Duchy of Hesse, my much beloved fatherland, where I dutifully announce myself without delay. Would Your Highness, at your leisure, allow to be read to you this narrative about the by me traversed land and sea, on account of the wonderful deeds that Almighty God vouchsafed

---

[1] For Tupinamba, see the introduction. The author of the "Somptueuse Entrée," etc., writes "Toupinabaulx": Thevet calls them " Toupinambaux" (plural); Jean de Lery, Tooupinambaoults, meaning a "noble people of God"; the diphthong " aou" denoting " admirable"; Malherbe softened the word to Topinambous, adopted in the age of Louis XIV. Claude d'Abbeville (early in the seventeenth century) prefers Topynambas; Yves d'Evreux (chapter vii et passim), Topinambos and Tapinambos.

Pero Lopes (A.D. 1531) when at Bahia saw an action amongst these people of fifty canoes on each side, and averaging sixty men in each (300 + 300) : the braves, who had pavoises or large shields painted after the European fashion, fought from noon to sunset. The prisoners were tied with cords, put to death with much ceremony, roasted and eaten. Hans Stade extends them from Rio de Janeiro to the great province of São Paulo. In the Caramurú of Fr. Rita Durão (x, 22) we find them upon the Bahian seaboard. Southey (1, 42, 429), following d'Abbeville and Yves d'Evreux assigns to them a habitat from Pará and Maranham to Bahia, where they held the islands of the Bay of All the Saints, and they are spoken of in other captaincies. The introduction has explained these discrepancies by showing the word to be used by themselves and their friends, not by their enemies.

Part 2 of Hans Stade's volume is devoted to describing their manners and customs. It must be noted that he says nothing of the artificially flattened noses of the infants, described by Jean de Lery, Claude d'Abbeville and other old travellers in the Brazil.

The Tupinambas sided in early times with the French against the Portuguese. They boasted to be the principal tribe, planted manioc, and had better wigwams than their neighbours. Yet they were cannibals, like the Mpángwe (Fans) of the Gaboon river, a comparatively civilised negro tribe, and they ate their enemies slain in battle, probably for the usual superstitious reasons.

me in my distress ? That Your Highness may not doubt
me, and suppose that I put forward untrue things, I would
personally offer you a passport to assist this recital. To
God alone be in all Honour and Glory !

And I herewith hasten to express my humble submission.

Dated Wolffhagen, the twentieth day of June,
Anno Domini, Fifteen hundred
and fifty-six.

The born subject of Your Highness Hans
Stade from Homberg in Hesse,
now citizen of Wolffhagen.

To the Highborn Lord, the Lord Philipsen, Count of
Nassau and Sarprück, etc., his Gracious Prince, sends D.
Joh. Dryander much greeting, with offer of his services.

Hans Stade, who now through the press publishes this
book and history, has begged me that I will look through
his work and writing of these stories previously to printing,
correct them, and, if necessary, improve them. To this,
his wish, I have from several causes assented. Firstly, I
have known this author's father now for more than fifty
years (for he and I were born and brought up in one city,
namely, Wetter), and not otherwise the same, at home and
in Homberg of Hesse, where he now resides, than as an
upright, pious and honest man, who was also learned in
good arts. As a well known proverb says, "the apple
always tastes of the trunk," and, as may be expected, Hans
Stade, this honest man's son, is reported to be like his
father in virtue and piety.

Moreover, I accept the task of correcting this little book
with the more pleasure and satisfaction, inasmuch as I
willingly occupy myself with those matters which concern
mathematics, such as cosmography, that is, the description
and measurement of counties, cities and roads, some of
which are in many ways brought forward in this book. I

most willingly look into such matters, when I find that
any one uprightly and truly reveals and brings to light the
things which he has undergone, and I now noways doubt
that this Hans Stade writes and makes known an account
of his history and travels, not from the statements of other
men, but thoroughly and correctly from his own experience
without falsehood, the cause being that he therein seeks
no glory or worldly fame, but alone God's honour and
praise, and gratitude for favours and deliverances vouchsafed to him. And it is his principal object to make
known this history, that all may see how mercifully and
against every hope our Lord God has delivered this Hans
Stade from out of so much peril, because he called unto
Him, and rescuing him from the ferocity of those savage
peoples (by whom he for ten months daily and hourly had
to expect that he would be unmercifully struck dead and
eaten), again allowed him to return to his beloved fatherland, Hesse.

For this inexpressible mercy of God he would wish, as
much as lies in his limited power, to be duly thankful to
Him, and for His praise to disclose openly the favours
vouchsafed him. And in fulfilling this pleasant task, the
order of events leads him to describe the itinerary and the
different things that happened during the two years whilst
he was out of his own country.

And as he tells his tale in a simple manner, and not with
flowery style, or fine words and arguments, this gives me
great belief that it is authentic and veritable; nor could he
derive any benefit even if he preferred lying to telling the
truth.

Besides, he is now settled, together with his parents, in
this country ; and he is not, as is the usage of rovers and
liars, accustomed to vagabondize, gipsy-like, from one country to another. Therefore he must expect, that should
other travelled people who have been in the islands arrive
here, these would (presently) prove him a liar.

And this is to me a sound argument that his account and the description of this history is truthful, inasmuch as he states the time, country and place where Heliodorus,[1] son of the learned and widely known Eoban of Hesse, who has now been long absent on discovery in foreign lands, and was by us here believed to be dead, was with this Hans Stade in the country of the savages, and saw how pitifully he was captured and led away.. This Heliodorus, I say, may sooner or later (as is hoped shall happen) return home, and if Hans Stade's story be false or lying, he will put him to shame and denounce him as a worthless man.

From these and similar strong arguments and conjectures towards defending and sustaining the truthfulness of Hans Stade, I will now turn aside, and further briefly point out the reasons for which this and similar such-like histories gain but little credence and belief.

Firstly, travellers have, with their unlimited lies and spreading of false and invented stories, brought matters to such a pass, that but little belief is accorded, even to those honest and truthful men who come from foreign lands. Moreover, it has become a general saying: "Whosoever would lie, let him lie about things far off and out of the country," for nobody will go thither to verify his statements, nay, rather than take this trouble he (the listener) will believe them.

Nothing, however, is gained by discrediting truth on account of lies. Here it is to be noted that though to the

---

[1] Also mentioned in the conclusion of this book as " one of the sons of the late Eoban of Hesse." Helias (originally Elias, a Jew) Eoban, born in A.D. 1488, died in A.D. 1540, was a German poet of distinction in his day (Southey 1, 45 note and 191), but as he wrote in Latin, he was presently forgotten. According to Monsignor Pizarro (Memorias historicas do Rio de Janeiro, viii, 309), the son of this Eliodoro Ebano was Theodoro Ebano Pereira, captain of the war canoes, who, after reestablishing Rio de Janeiro founded Iguápe of São Paulo in A.D. 1554, and Coritygbe, the modern Curitiba, capital of the province of Paraná.

commonalty many recounted matters appear impossible, yet
when those matters are laid before men of knowledge, and
are well weighed, they are found to be correct and consis-
tent, and they also prove themselves so to be.

This observe from one or two examples taken from astronomy. We people who live here in Germany, or near by,
know from long experience how long winter and summer,
as well as the other two seasons, autumn and spring, endure;
therefore how long and how short are the longest day in
summer and the shortest day in winter, and through this,
also, what the nights are.

Now, for instance, when it is said that there are certain
parts of the world where the sun for half a year does not
set, and where the longest day with those people is six
months, that is half a year long; likewise that places are
found in the world, where in one year the " quatuor tem-
pora," that is, the four seasons, are doubled, therefore that
two winters and two summers certainly exist there in one
year. Likewise that the sun with all the stars, small as
they appear to us here to be, yet that the smallest star in
the heavens is larger than the whole earth, and that there
are innumerably many of them.

Now when the comman man hears these things, he greatly
despises them and he believes them not, and considers them
as things which are impossible. Yet these matters are so
thoroughly proved by astronomers, that those having knowledge of the science do not doubt them.

Therefore it must not on this account follow, that because
the mass consider these things untrue, they are really so ;
and how badly would the art of astronomers fare, if they
could not demonstrate these heavenly bodies, and foretell
from certain causes the eclipses, that is, the darkenings of
the sun and moon, for fixed days and hours when they shall
occur. Yes, men have announced them even some hundred
years beforehand, and they have been found by experience

to be correct. " Yes," say they, " who has been in the heavens, and has seen these things, and has measured them ?"

Answer : Because daily experience of these things agrees with the demonstration. One must consider them true, even as it is true that if I add together the figures three and two, these will make five.

And from certain reasons and clear proofs in science, it happens that man can measure and calculate how high it is to the moon's firmament, and from there to all the planets, and, last of all, to the starry heavens. Yea, also the dimensions and size of the sun, the moon, and the other heavenly bodies; and from the study of the heavens, or astronomy, with geometry, we can even calculate how wide, round, broad and long the earth is. Yet these things are unknown to the unlearned man, and are considered by him as unworthy of belief. Ignorance would also be pardonable in the common person, as he has not studied much in philosophy. But that the highly important and the almost learned should doubt those things which are proved true is shameful and also harmful, as the ordinary man looks up to these, and their error being thus confirmed to him, says : " If this were true, then it would not have been contradicted by this or the other writer." Ergo, etc.

That St. Augustine and Lactantius Firmianus, the two most learned, holy, and well-experienced men, not only in theology, but also in other arts, doubt and will not admit that the antipodes can exist, viz., that men are found who on the opposite side of the earth, and under us, walk with their feet towards us, and therefore have their head and body hanging underneath them and against the heavens, and yet do not fall off, etc. This sounds strange, and yet it is everywhere held by scientific men to be so, and that it cannot be otherwise, and it is found true, however much the holy and highly learned authors mentioned above have denied it. For this must be the positive fact, that those who live ex diametro per centrum terræ must be "antipodes," and a true proposition is the following : Omne versus cœlum vergens ubicunque locorum sursum est. And we need not travel to the New World to seek the antipodes, for these antipodes are also here in the upper hemisphere of the globe. For if we compare and place against each other the extreme country of the west, which is Spain and at Finisterre, with the east where India lies, these extreme nations and inhabitants of the earth will almost give a sort of antipodes.

Several pious theologians pretend to prove that the prayer of the mother of the sons of Zebedey (Zebedee) had become true, when she begged the Lord Christ, that of her sons one might sit on his right hand and the other on his. left. This, it is said, really so happened, inasmuch as James is supposed to have been buried at Compostela, not far from Finis Terræ (Finisterre), which is commonly called Finstern Stern, and is held in honour. And that the other apostle rests in India, or towards the rising of the sun. That therefore the antipodes have long existed, and that even without considering that at the time of Augustin the new world America, under the earth, had not been discovered, they would yet in this way have existed. Some theologians, and especially Nicolaus Syra (who otherwise is respected as an excellent man), assert that whereas the earthball, or the world, for the half part lies and floats on the water, therefore that the hemisphere upon which we live projects above the waters, yet the other part underneath us is in such a manner surrounded by water that no beings can exist there, all which is against the science of cosmography, and has now, moreover, through the many voyages of the Spanish and Portuguese, been found to be far different; that the earth is everywhere inhabited, yea even in the subtorrid zone, which our forefathers and writers never would admit. Our generally used spices, sugar, pearls, and many similar wares, are brought to us from these countries.

This paradox of the antipodes and the before mentioned measurement of the heavens, I have purposely brought forward to support the previous argument. Many other things might perhaps be here mentioned if, with my long preface, I wished to be tedious to you.

But many similar arguments will be read in the book written by the worthy and learned Magister Casparus Goldworm, Your Highness's diligent superintendent at Weilburgh, and Predicant, which book, in six parts, treats of many miracles, wonders and paradoxes, such as in former times and the present have happened, and will shortly be put in print. To that book, and to many others, which describe these things, such as the " Libri Galeotti de rebus vulgo incredibilibus", I wish to direct the attention of the indulgent reader, if he wishes to know more of these matters.

And may it be herewith sufficiently asserted, that it is not necessarily straightway a lie when something is stated which to the common man appears strange and unusual, as in this history, where all the people in the islands go about naked; and having no domesticated animals for food, and no such things in usage as we have for preserving life, such as clothes, beds, horses, pigs or cows, nor wine or beer, etc., must live and exist in their own way.

In order to make an end to my preface, I will briefly show what induced this Hans Stade to put his two voyages and travels in print. Many may interpret this to his disadvantage, as if he wished hereby to gain glory and to make a transient name. I know him far differently, and I believe truly that his mind is framed in a very different manner, as may also here and there be noticed in his history.

Because, having passed through so much misery, and suffered so much adversity, in which his life was so often in peril, and he was without hope of being liberated and of ever returning to the home of his parents, yet, God in

whom he always trusted, and prayed to, not only delivered
him from the hands of his enemies, but was also moved by
his faithful prayers to show among the godless men that the
veritable and true God, strong and powerful, still existed.
It is known that to the prayers of the faithful God never
places limit or time, but it here has pleased God, through
this Hans Stade, to show his miracles among the godless
savages. This I should not know how to gainsay.

It is also known to everyone that troubles, sorrow and
sickness, etc., generally so turn men to God, that they in
adversity cry to Him more than before. Some hitherto
according to popish ways, perhaps pledge themselves to this
or the other saint with pilgrimage or penance, so that they
may be helped in their distress, and these vows are generally strictly kept, except by those who think to defraud the
saints of their vows. Erasmus Roterodamus describes in
his Colloquies concerning shipwreck, that one in the ship
vowed to St. Christopherus, whose picture in a church at
Paris stands some ten yards high, like a great Poliphe-
mus, that if he helped him out of his troubles, he would
burn to him a wax taper as large as the saint. His
next neighbour, who sat near him, knew of this man's
poverty, and rebuked him for such vow, and said, that
even if he sold all his goods on earth, yet could he not
bring together wax enough to make so large a taper.
Answers him upon this the other, whispering that the saint
might not hear it, and said: " When he has saved me from
this danger, I will scarcely give him a common farthing
candle."

And the other story of the knight who was in a shipwreck is also similar. This knight when he saw that the
vessel was about to sink, called upon St. Nicholas to help
him in his need, and that he would offer him his horse or
his page. Then his serving man rebuked him, saying, that
he should not do thus, whereon would he then ride ? quoth

the knight to his servant, whispering, that the saint might

the knight to his servant, whispering, that the saint might
not hear: "Hold thy peace, when he has helped me out
of these straits, I will not give him the tail of my horse."
In such manner thought each of the twain to cheat his
saint, and so soon to forget vouchsafed benefits.

Now that this Hans Stade may therefore not, after God
has helped him, he considered as one of such who forget
mercies, he has determined by this book and description to
praise and to glorify God, and from a Christian spirit to
make known and to bring to light, wherever he can, the
wonders and mercies He has shewn him. And if this was
not his intention, (which is honourable and just) he would
much rather be spared the trouble and labour, and also save
the not small expense which this type and printing have
cost him.

As this history has been by the author submissively dedicated to the Serene and Highborn Prince and Lord, the
Lord Philipsen, Landgrave of Hesse, Count of Catzenellenbogen, Dietz, Ziegenhain and Nidda, his Prince and
gracious Master, and in the name of His Highness has
caused this to be published; and has long before been by
His Highness our gracious Lord, and in my presence and in
that of many others, examined and thoroughly questioned
upon all points of his shipwreck and imprisonment, and of
which I have often spoken and narrated to Your Highness
and to other Lords; and as in Your Highness I have long
seen and observed a remarkable lover of such and similar
astronomical and cosmographical sciences; so I have desired
submissively to write this my preface or introduction to
Your Highness, which Your Highness may graciously
accept from me, until I shall publish something more
weighty in the name of Your Highness.

Commending myself herewith humbly to Your Highness.

Date, Marburg, Day of St. Thomas, year MDLVI.

CONTENTS OF THE BOOK.

I.

Of two voyages completed by Hans Stade in eight and a-half years.[1]

The first voyage was made from Portugal, and the other from Spain to the New World.[2]

II.

How in the country of the wild tribe named Toppinikin[3] (who are subject to the king of Portugal) he was employed as a gunner against the enemy.

Lastly, taken prisoner by the enemy and led away, he was ten and a-half months in danger of being killed and eaten by the enemy.

III.

Also, how God mercifully and miraculously released this prisoner in the before-mentioned year, and how he returned again home to his beloved fatherland.

All given in print for the glory of God and in thankfulness of His kind mercy.

---

[1] The original says "in neundthalb jaren." This can only mean eight years and a half, and is evidently intended to cover the time between first leaving home and last returning to it.

[2] The first voyage lasted sixteen months, from April 29, 1547, to October 8, 1548.

The second lasted about six years, from the fourth day after Easter, 1549, to February 20, 1555.

Thus the total was, in round numbers, seven years and a half.

[3] The Tupiniquins (Tupi-n-ikis), meaning limitrophe or contiguous Tupis or Tupi neighbours, are called by Jean de Lery Tooupinamkiy, and by Gabriel Soares Tupy-namquis, and are often alluded to in these pages (chapters 14, 44, 50). They are located about the captaincies of the Ilhéos, Porto Seguro and Espirito Santo, and de Laet gives them the character of being most vindictive and destructive. They fought against the Aymorés: as will presently appear, they were friendly with the Portuguese, and on terms of deadly hatred with the Tupinambás and the French, who were then bent upon converting the Brazil into a France Méridionale or a France Antarctique.

THE CAPTIVITY OF HANS STADE.

CAPUT I.

What helps the watchers in the town,
The mighty ships that plough the main,
If God doth not protect the twain?

I, HANS STADE from Homberg in Hesse, resolving, if it should so please God, to visit India, travelled with that intention from Bremen to Holland, and found in Campon ships which purposed loading salt in Portugal. Thither I sailed with them, and on the 29th day of April, 1547, after sailing on the waters for four weeks, we arrived at a city called Sanct Tuual.[1] Thence I proceeded to Lissebona, which is five miles from Sanct Tuual. In Lissebona I went to an inn, the host of which, a German, was called the young Leuhr; with him I remained some time. This same innkeeper I informed that I had left my country, and asked him when I might succeed in sailing to India. He said that I had delayed too long; and that the king's ships which sailed to India, had departed. I then begged him as I had missed this voyage, to help me towards another, as he knew the language, and that I would in my turn be of service to him.

He took me to a ship as a gunner. The captain of the vessel was named Pintado, and he intended sailing to Brazil for the purpose of trade, and also he had orders to seize such ships as commerced with the white Moors of Barbary. Also whenever he found French ships trafficking with the

---

[1] The name of Setubal has fared badly at the hands of foreigners: here it is Sanct Tuual, and English seamen still persist in calling it Saint Ube's.

savages in Brazil, they were to be taken as prizes. Besides this he was also commanded by the king to conduct to that country certain prisoners who had deserved punishment; these being spared for the purpose of peopling the new countries.[1]

Our ship was well furnished with all such warlike contrivances as are used at sea. We were three Germans in her, one named Hans von Bruckhausen, the other Heinrich Brant of Bremen, and I.

Caput II.

Description of my first voyage from Lisbon out of Portugal.

We sailed from Lisbon with another small vessel, which also belonged to our captain, and first we arrived at an island called Eilga de Madera,[2] belonging to the king of Portugal; it is inhabited by Portuguese, and is fruitful of vines and sugar. There, at a city named Funtschal[3] we took into the ship more victuals.

Thereafter we sailed from the island towards Barbary, to a city named Cape de Gel,[4] belonging to a white Moor king,

---

[1] These "degradados" (convicts) were a "boa droga ou semente para fazer novas fundaçoens e colonias," remarks old Jaboatam. Yet we did the same in the United States and Australia, and other European nations follow our example to the present day.

[2] Ilha da Madeira, the island of wood, from the Latin "materia," so called because it was found covered with virgin forests. The same was the case with the Madeira affluent of the Amazons. "Materiam cædere" (Vitr.) means to fell timber, "materiarius" was a woodman or wood worker, and Cæsar describing Britain says: "Materia cujusque generis ut in Gallia est; præter fagum et abietem."

[3] Funchal, the field of fennel (funcho), a weed which overran the site upon which the city now stands.

[4] Arzilla, a small port about thirty miles from Tangiers, once in the possession of the Portuguese (Lempriere's *Morocco*, chapter 1). Schiririffe is for Sherif, a descendant of Mohammed the Apostle.

named Sehiriffe. This city was formerly occupied by the
king of Portugal, but had been taken from him by the said
Sehiriffe. It was here that we thought to come upon the
above-mentioned ships which were trading with the infidels.
We arrived there finding many Castilian fishermen near the
shore, and these giving us information that many ships were
near the city, we sailed past it, when a ship came well
laden out of the harbour. This we pursued and overtook,
but the crew escaped us in their boats. Then we perceived
an empty boat lying ashore which would serve us well for
boarding the captured vessel, so we sailed to it and
fetched it.

The white Moors came riding up hard to protect it; but
they could not succeed against our guns. We took it and
sailed with our booty, which was sugar, almonds, dates,
goatskins and gum arabic, with which the ship was well
laden, back again to the Eilga de Madera. Thence we despatched our small ships to Lisbon, to report such news to
the king, and to learn how to proceed with the said prize,
as Valentian and Castilian merchants were among the
owners.

We were answered by the king that we were to leave the
prize there in the islands, and continue our voyage, meanwhile His Majesty would thoroughly sift the matter.

We acted accordingly, and again sailed to Cape de Gel,
to see if we could obtain more prizes. But our undertaking
was in vain, and we were prevented by the wind, which near
the coast became contrary to us. The night before All
Saints' Day, we sailed from Barbary with a strong gale
towards the Brazils. Now when we were at sea, four hundred
miles from Barbary, many fishes came about the ship, these
we caught with fishhooks. Of these some which the sailors
named albakore, were big, some bonitte, were smaller, and
some were called durado.[1] Also were there many fish as

---

[1] The well known Albacore mackerel; the bonetta, bonito or striped

large as herrings which had on both sides wings like a bat, these were much pursued by the big ones ; when they perceived these behind them, they raised themselves out of the water in great numbers and flew about two fathoms high above the sea, some of them nearly as far as one could see. Then they again fell into the water. We found them often in the morning lying in the ship, where they had fallen in whilst flying during the night. And they were called in Portuguese language, pisce bolador. Thereafter we came under the equinoctial line, where there was great heat, for the sun stood straight above us, when it was noon ; there was no wind for several days,[1] then in the night came oftentimes great thunderstorms with rain and wind, they arose quickly and they subsided as quickly. We had to watch diligently that these should not overtake us when under sail.

But as now winds returned, blowing storms during some days, and against us, we conjectured that if they continued long, we should suffer hunger. We prayed to God for favourable wind. Then it came to pass, one night when we had a great storm and were in great trouble, many blue lights appeared to us in the vessel, of which I had seen none before. Where the waves rolled into the forepart of the ship, there the lights also appeared.[2] The Portuguese

tunny (Thymbus pelamys, Cuv.), a voracious animal, very fond of the peixe voador or flying fish, here called pisce bolador, and the dorado of which Martial writes—"Non omnis pretium laudemque aurata meretur" (Lib. 13).

[1] These "doldrums" in the calm latitudes of the Atlantic, followed by furious squalls, are chronicled by every old voyager.

[2] Commonly called Saint Elmo's, or San Telmo's Fires ; the Dioscuri (Castor and Pollux) of the ancients, which "in navigiorum summitatibus visuntur"; known to the middle ages as Sancti Germani Sidus and Corpus Sanctum, whence our Corposant or Corpuzance, through the Italian Corpo Santo or the Spanish Cuerpo Santo ; dedicated to Saint Nicholas and to Santa Clara, as well as to St. Elmo (Pigafetta lib. 1) ; the Peaceable Fires of Nieuhoff's *Voyages and Travels into Brazil* (A.D.

said, that the lights were a sign of coming good weather, especially sent by God to cheer us in our peril. We thanked God therefore in a general prayer. Then they disappeared again. And these lights are called Santelmo or Corpus Santon.

Now when the day broke, the weather became fine, and a fair wind arose, so that we visibly saw that such lights must be a miracle of God.

We sailed along through the ocean with good wind; on the 28th day of January (1548), we caught sight of land, part of a cape called Cape de Sanct Augustin.[1] Eight miles therefrom we arrived at the haven named Brannenbucke.[2] And we had been eighty-four days[3] at sea without seeing land. There the Portuguese had established a settlement called Marin.[4] The commander of the place was

1640, Pinkerton, vol. xiv), and the Will-o'-the-Wisps and Davy Joneses of the English seaman.

[1] This cape is mentioned by Amerigo Vespucci on his voyage of A.D. 1501. The Rostro Hermoso or Beautiful Face of Pinzon (?), it was called Cabo de Consolacion by the second captain who made South America, and it was the first landfall usually affected by the early navigators (Angelo and Carli, A.D. 1666). It lies in S. lat. 8 deg. 20 min. 41 sec. and W. long. (G.) 34 deg. 56 min. 42 sec., about thirty-three direct geographical miles nearly due south of Pernambuco.

[2] See Caput III.

[3] Not eighty-eight as Southey says, vol. i, p. 55.

[4] Marin or Marim is a corruption of Mayry, any city, from Mayr, Mair, Maïr, Maire, or Maïre, a stranger, often used by Thevet and De Lery, and applied to any European settlement, as opposed to the tabas (wigwam villages) of the natives. Others derive it from Mari or Mairy, the name of a fruit. Southey (i, 252) thinks Maire to be a corruption of Maistre, Magister, which it certainly was not. It was applied to superior beings and even to Christians: thus Ruiz de Montoya (*Tesoro de la Lengua Guarani*) explains it by mâ-râ?—"what is it?" "what is there?" an allusion to some mysterious being. This, however, like "Tupa" (see part 1, chap. 20) is by no means satisfactory. On this site, which formerly belonged to the Tabayarás (village men), afterwards rose the fair city of Olinda. The Recife, called by strangers "Pernambuco", was at first its port, the "base town" of Sir James Lancaster (A.D. 1595).

named Artokoslio;[1] to him we delivered the prisoners, and also discharged sundry goods, which they kept there. We transacted our matters in this harbour, wishing to sail further, where we expected to load.

Caput III.

How the savages of the place Prannenbucke[2] had become rebellious, and wanted to destroy a settlement of the Portuguese.

It so happened that the savages of the place had become rebellious against the Portuguese; they had not been so before, but they now began to be so on account of the Portuguese having enslaved them. We were, therefore, begged for God's sake, by the governor of the land, to occupy the settlement called Garasu,[3] five miles from the harbour of Marin, where we lay, and which the savages had dared attempt to take. The inhabitants of the settlement Marin could not go to help them, for they conjectured that the savages would also set upon them.

We therefore went to the aid of those in Garasu with forty men from our ship, sailing thither in a small craft. The settlement lay on an arm of the sea, which extended

[1] Elsewhere called Artokoelio and in De Bry, Artus Coelho (Southey). The captain general of Pernambuco was then Duarte Coelho. Hans Stade abounds in these corruptions, like his countryman Schmidel, the great authority further south.

[2] The Prannenbucke of chapter 3, and the Bramenbuche of part ii, chapter 2—B and P being Teutonically confounded. The French make it Fernambouc, and some have derived it from Fernam (Fernando) and bourg. The etymology is Paraná-mbok or-mbo " sea-arm", and it was picturesquely and accurately so called by the Indians from the gap in the natural wall which here fringes the coast, hence the Portuguese " Mar Furado" (*Noticia de Brazil*, p. 24). Pernambuco, in the province of that name, lies in S. lat. 8 deg. 4 min. 7 sec., and in W. long. (G.) 34 deg. 52 min. 44 sec.

[3] The name of the factory is Iguaraçu, from " Igara," a canoe, and " assu," big.

two miles inland. Our force in defence might consist of about ninety Christians. Besides these, were thirty Moors and Brazilian slaves, who belonged to the inhabitants. The savages[1] who besieged us were estimated at eight thousand. We in our beleaguered state had only a palisade[2] of rails around us.

Caput IV.

How their fortifications were constructed, and how they fought against us.

Round about the settlement in which we were beleaguered was a forest, wherein they had made two forts of thick trees, to which they retreated at night, and if we attacked them,

[1] These people were the Caetés (from caa, a bush and ete, good), also written Caytés, Calhetés, Cahetés, Cayetés, Caités, and in many other ways. Some derive from them Cattéte, a suburb of modern Rio de Janeiro, which, however, is properly Caitetú, a peccary. According to Gabriel Soares, they occupied the seaboard of Pernambuco, north of the Potyguaras, and they extended for a hundred miles of coast from northern Parahyba to the great Rio de S. Francisco. On the occasion mentioned in the text, they rose against the Tabayarás, who were allied with the Portuguese. P. Yves d'Evreux (pp. 302-304) speaks of their idols as rudimentary statues, possibly borrowed from the French, and to these sacrifices were offered. They were barbarians passing into the first stage of progress, agriculture, and the jangada or catamaran still used at Pernambuco is borrowed from them. Fond of music and the dance, they were as warlike as they were false, and their cannibalism was notorious. According to Vasconcellos (1, 32), on June 16, 1556, they killed and devoured that saintly prelate, D. Pedro Fernandes Sardinha, first bishop of Bahia; the procurator of the Royal Treasury at the same city; two canons of the see; two pregnant women, and over a hundred persons, men, women and children, who when returning to Portugal in a French brig were wrecked upon the shoals of the S. Francisco River. The crime was punished by the successors of Duarte Coelho, who, aided by the Tupinambás and the Potyguaras, nearly annihilated the Caetés.

[2] Varnhagen gives an illustration of these stockades (*History*, vol. 1, p. 116), probably borrowed from our author's descriptions scattered over the book. Southey (1, 55) makes the savages "pile up two rude

there they would remain. Close by they had sunk pits in the ground round the settlements, in which they lay during the day, and out of which they came to skirmish with us. When we fired at them, they all fell down, thinking to duck from the shot. They had besieged us so thoroughly that we could neither move to nor fro; they came close to the settlement, they shot many arrows in the air,[1] intending them to fall and hit us in the settlement; they also shot arrows at us whereon they had tied cotton and wax, and these they ignited, purposing to set fire to the roofs of the houses, and they threatened how they would eat us when they had got us.

We had still a little food, but it soon ran out. For it is in that country the custom to fetch fresh roots every day or every other day, and to make meal or cakes thereof; but we could not get at such roots.

Now when we saw that we had to suffer from want of victuals, we made with two barks for a settlement named

bulwarks of trees" instead of planting them, and he justly remarks that eight thousand men against ninety Europeans and thirty slaves, some of whom were negroes and others natives, is probably an exaggerated number, which Abreu e Lima (*Compendio*, p. 38) further exaggerates to "doze mil".

[1] These savages had two ways of shooting, one direct, the other called "atirar por elevação": in the latter they lay on their backs, placed their feet against the bow and drew the string with both hands. The same is the practice with some tribes in Bhootan. For their art in "tirer leur flèches en haut", see Yves d'Evreux (p. 29); and Hans Stade, part 2, chapters 7 and 26, for their general skill and their fire arrows, which Garcilasso mentions in *Peru* (iii, 36). They could kill a fish jumping out of water, and were fatal shots at the distance of four hundred feet. The savages of the Brazil still shoot by elevation, and some are said to be so expert that they can choose a man out of a crowd, or make the arrow fall from the air within a few inches of their own toes. Old travellers navigating the Brazilian rivers defended themselves by awnings and curtains of hide. According to Nieuhoff, the bow was called guirapara or virapara, the string, usually of the tucum-palm or the pita-aloe, was guirapakuma, and the arrows of ubá cane (Alencar, *O Guarany*, i, 363) were termed Huí.

Tammaraka[1] to fetch victuals. But the savages had laid
large trees over the water-channel, there were many of them
on both sides of the shore, intending to prevent our voyage.
We broke these again by force and about midway we remained high and dry. The savages could do us no harm in
the ships, but they threw much dry wood from their fort
between the shore and the ships, thinking to burn it, and
they hove their pepper which grows in that country, so as
to drive us by the smoke out of the ships. But they did
not succeed, and meanwhile the tide returned; we sailed to
the settlement Tammaraka, the inhabitants gave us victuals,
wherewith we sailed back to the besieged place. They had
again thrown obstacles in our passage, they had laid trees
as formerly across the channel, and they lay thereby upon
the shore; they had all but felled two trees a little from
the ground, and at the top they had tied things called
Sippo,[2] which grew like hops, but which are thicker. The
ends they had made fast in their forts, as it was their intention when we came, and wanted again to break through,
to pull the Sippo, that the trees might suddenly break and
fall on the ships.

We sailed past, and broke through the first tree: it fell
towards their fort, the other fell into the water close behind
our small ship. And before we began to burst through the
impediments, we called to our companions in the settlement,
that they should come to our aid. When we commenced to

---

[1] Itamaraca, a well known island, was conquered, together with the
Terra Firma adjoining, by the Portuguese in A.D. 1531. It afterwards
became one of the eight captaincies. The author of the *Noticias de
Brazil* (1589) calls it " Tamaraqua", and it is described at great length
by Nieuhoff.

[2] Cypó or Cipó means "flat root" and Cipo-îm is the salsapa-
rilla. The generic Tupi term for llianas has been naturalised in the
Luso-Brazilian tongue, and it corresponds with the West African
"bush-rope" and " tie-tie." The stratagem alluded to in the text was
familiar to the Payaguás of the Paraguay river.

shout, the savages shouted also, so that our besieged friends might not hear us, for they could not see us on account of a wood which lay between us. But otherwise we were so near them that they might well have heard us, if the savages had not shouted in such manner.

We brought the victuals into the settlement; and when the savages then saw that they could accomplish nothing, they desired peace and again departed. The siege lasted nearly a month, of the savages several remained dead, but of the Christians none.

When we saw that the savages had again become peaceable, we departed once more for our great ship, which lay before Marin; there we took in water, also mandioca meal for food. The commander of the settlement Marin thanked us.

CAPUT V.

How we sailed from Prannenbucke to a country called Buttugaris,[1] came upon a French ship, and engaged it.

Thence we sailed forty miles off to a harbour, named Buttugaris, where we purposed to load the ship with Brazil wood, and also to pillage some victuals from the savages.

[1] As has been said in the introduction, Potyguaras would mean shrimpers (Jaboatam uses Pytiguaras) and Petyguaras tobacco smokers. Alencar (*Iracema*, p. 167) finds difficulty in explaining the word, which he says is corrupted from " iby-tira", a highland (*i. e.*, iby land + tira, high), and yara, owner of. Thus Pytiguara from Ibyticuara would be the Lord of Highlands, which their enemies changed to shrimp-eater, from poty, a shrimp, and uara, eater. Others write Pytagoares. Gabriel Soares assigns to his Pytiguaras a hundred leagues of coast between Parnahyba and the Jagoaribe or Rio Grande. Others locate them between the Parahyba do Norte and the Rio Grande do Norte, and give them as headquarters the Serra de Copaoba. Fierce and savage, they were much feared by their neighbours, and they are said to have numbered from twenty thousand to thirty thousand bows. They were held to be next in dignity to the Tabayarás, with whom they had implacable feuds, because the latter took part with the Portuguese, and, allying

When we arrived there we found a vessel from France, loading Brazil wood, we attacked it, intending to capture it, but they destroyed our mainmast with one shot, and they escaped us : several belonging to our ship were shot dead, while others were wounded.

After this we agreed to return to Portugal, for we could no longer get to wind-ward of the harbour, where we intended to obtain our victual. The wind was against us, we sailed with a small stock of provisions to Portugal, and we suffered great famine, some of us eating goatskins, which we had in the ship. To each of us daily was given one small cup of water, and a little Brazilian root meal (cassava) ; we were one hundred and eight days on the water, and on the 12th of August we came to some islands, called Losa Sores,[1] belonging to the king of Portugal. At that place we anchored, rested and fished, and there we saw a ship at sea, to which we sailed to learn what ship it was. It proved to be a pirate, and prepared to resist us, but we gained the upper hand and took the vessel from them, they escaping from us in the boat to the islands. The ship contained much wine and bread, wherewith we refreshed ourselves.

Hereafter we encountered five ships, belonging to the king of Portugal, which were to await at the islands the arrival of the ships from India, to convoy them to Portugal. We remained with them ; and helped to pilot an Indiaman, which arrived at an island called Tercera, and there we remained. Many ships, which had all come from the new countries, some bound for Spain, others for Portugal, had met at the island. We sailed from Tercera nearly one

themselves with the French, they went to war with the Caetés and the Tapuyas.

[1] Los Açores (the Kites), the well known Azores or Western Islands. Terceira is the chief of the nine forming the Archipelago, and its city, Angra, represents the capital.

hundred vessels in company, and arrived at Lisbon about the eighth day of October, 1548, having been sixteen months on the voyage.

After this I rested some time in Lisbon, determined to sail with the Spaniards to the new countries which they occupy. I sailed with that intention from Lisbon in an English ship to Castile, to a city called Porta Sancta Maria.[1] There they purposed loading the ship with wine, and thence I travelled to a city called Civilien,[2] where I found three ships fitting out, to sail to a country called Rio de Platta,[3] in America. This region with the rich gold-country named Pirau,[4] which was discovered some years ago, and Brazil, all form one continent.

To conquer this land forthwith, several ships had been sent some years before, and one of them returning (home) requested more assistance, saying how rich it was in gold. The commander of the three ships was named Dohn Diego de Senabrie,[5] he was on the part of the king to become governor of the country. I repaired to one of the ships, which were well equipped; and we sailed from Civilien to Sanct Lucas,[6] where the Civilien river enters the sea, there we lay awaiting a favourable wind.

[1] Porto de Santa Maria, the most southerly island of the Azores, is in N. lat. 36 deg. 58 min., and in W. long. (G.) 35 deg. 12 min. 33 sec.

[2] Seville.   [3] Rio de la Plata.

[4] Peru.

[5] In 1549 D. Juan de Senabria (Southey, i, 133) accepted the captaincy of Paraguay, but died in Spain before the expedition was ready to sail. He was succeeded by his son Diego.

[6] San Lucar (here by mistake Lucas) do Barameda is the harbour at the mouth of the Guadalquivir river (Wady el Kabir, the great Fiumara), about forty miles S.S.W. of Seville.

Caput VI.

Description of my other voyage from Civilien, in Spain, to America.

Anno Domini 1549, the fourth day after Easter, we sailed out of Sanct Lucas, and the wind being against us, we took refuge at Lisbon. When the wind became favourable we sailed to the Canary Isles, and anchored at an island called Pallama,[1] where we took in some wine for the voyage. There also the pilots of the vessels agreed, in case we were separated at sea, upon which part of the land they would meet again, namely in twenty-eight degrees on the south side of the equinoctial line.

From Palma we sailed to Cape Virde,[2] that is, the green headland, which lies in the land of the black Moors.[3] There we had nearly suffered shipwreck. From that place we sailed our course, the wind was against us, beat us several times back upon the coast of Gene,[4] where the black Moors also dwell. Thereafter we arrived at an island, called S. Thomé, belonging to the king of Portugal; it is an island rich in sugar, but unhealthy. In it live Portuguese with many black Moors, who are their slaves. Having taken in

---

[1] Palma (Canarian Archipelago), in N. lat. 28 deg. 43 min. and W. long. (G.) 17 deg. 45 min. It is described by George Glas (lib. iii, *History of the Canary Islands*, 1 vol. 4to, London 1764), who says that the natives called it Benahoare, meaning "my country." See part 2, chap. 1.

[2] The Portuguese Cabo Verde and our Cape Verd, in N. lat. 14 deg. 43 min. 25 sec. and W. long (G.) 17 deg. 30 min. 45 sec.

[3] The Black Moors are the modern Joloffs or Yoloffs, the Kru-men or Kru-boys, and possibly the Mandingas. Hans Stade does not confine the name to Mahometans after the fashion of later travellers.

[4] Guinea, here meaning Upper Guinea from Cape Mesurado (N. lat. 6 deg. 18 min. 30 sec.) to Cape Palmas (N. lat. 4 deg. 24 min.) It is better known as the Grain Coast, from the Cardamom, formerly called Guinea Grains and Grains of Paradise. This weed, now universally neglected, gave the main impulse to English exploration.

fresh water at the island, we sailed further. In a storm at night, we had lost sight of our two companion ships, so that we sailed alone. The winds were much against us, for they have the peculiarity in that sea, that when the sun is on the north side of the equinoctial line, they blow from the south.[1] In the same manner when the sun is on the south side, they come from the north, and they are wont to blow stiffly during five months from one quarter. They prevented us for four months from sailing our proper course. Then when the month of September arrived, the winds began to be northerly, and we directed our course south-south-west towards America.

Caput VII.

How, in twenty-eight degrees latitude, we arrived at the Continent of America, and could not make out the harbour, whither we had been directed ; and how a great storm arose on the coast.

Thereupon it happened that one day, which was the eighteenth November, the steersman took the sun's height, and found that we were in latitude twenty-eight degrees :[2] we then sought land to the west. Thereafter on the twenty-fourth of the said month we saw land. We had been six months at sea, and had often been exposed to great danger. Now as we came hard by the coast we knew not the harbour, and could not find the mark which the head steersman had given us. Also we hardly dared enter unknown harbours, and therefore we tacked up and down the coast. It began to blow hard, till fearing that nothing would save us from perishing on the rocks, we lashed

---

[1] Or, in modern parlance, the winds follow the sun.

[2] South latitude. This would be about seven miles and a half south of the Punta de Naufragados, the southernmost extremity of the Ilha de Sta. Catharina in the modern province of that name.

several barrels together, put powder therein, stopped up the bung-holes, tied our weapons upon them, so that if we suffered shipwreck, and any of ours escaped therefrom they might find their weapons on land, as the waves would throw the barrels on shore. We then tacked with the intention of sailing away from the land again, but it availed us not, the wind drove us upon the rocks which lay hidden in the water at a depth of about four fathoms, and we were obliged on account of the great waves to sail right on to the shore, thinking that nothing could save all from perishing together.

But God ordained that, as we came close upon the rocks, one of our companions saw a haven into which we sailed.

There we saw a small ship which had escaped before us, and had sailed behind an island, so that we could not see it, and could not know what ship it was. We did not follow it further, but we lowered our anchor, and praised God that he had helped us out of our peril, rested and dried our clothes.

It was about two o'clock in the afternoon, when we anchored : and towards evening there arrived a large boat full of savages alongside of our ship, and desired to speak with us. But none of ours could well understand the language; we gave them some knives and fishhooks after which they again sailed away. The same night another boatful came, and among them were two Portuguese who asked us whence we came. We then told them that we were from Spain, they said that we must have a skilful pilot to have so entered the harbour, for they knew the harbour well, but that with such a storm as that with which we had entered, they knew not how to make it. Then we told them all the circumstances, how the wind and waves would have brought us to a shipwreck. How whilst we were expecting nothing else, than that we should perish, we had suddenly sighted the harbour, and that therefore God had helped us unexpectedly, and had saved us from shipwreck, and also that we knew not where we were.

When they heard this they marvelled and thanked God, and told us that the harbour in which we were was called Supraway,[1] and that we were about eighteen miles[2] away from an island called Sancte Vincente,[3] belonging to the king of Portugal, and that they lived there, and those whom we had seen in the small ship had made off, because they had thought that we were Frenchmen.

We also asked of them, how far from there was the island of Sancte Catharina,[4] for that we were bound thither. They said it might be about thirty miles (leagues) to the south, and that there was a nation of savages there called Carios,[5] of whom we should be well on our guard, and they

[1] Superaqui is the long tongue of land which, with the Ilha Peças, forms the northern passage into the bay and harbour of Paranaguá. The latter is in S. lat. 25 deg. 34 min. 8 sec., and in W. long. (G.) 48 deg. 26 min. 50 sec.

[2] The reader must bear in mind that Hans Stade's miles are North-German *meilen*, which may be assumed as equivalent to long leagues. More correctly, it is one fifteenth of a degree=4·606 English statute miles=8,106 yards. The Flemish league is 6,869 yards; and the Dutch, which is probably the measure here used, is only 6,480 yards.

[3] St. Vincent, for whose name see preface, is the well known island, harbour and town, in the province of São Paulo, S. lat. 24 deg. 1 min. 11 sec., and W. long. (G.) 46 deg. 30 min. 20 sec. The settlement was founded by Martim Affonso de Sousa in A.D. 1532, and is first described in the *Epistola* of P. Anchieta. Being exposed to storms and harassed by pirates, it was superseded in A.D. 1543 by Santos, so called " Ex ejusdem vocationis nosochomio ibi constituto," and this is now the chief if not the only port of export in the province of S. Paulo. For further details see chapter 38.

[4] Santa Catharina, in S. lat. 27 deg. 35 min., with S. Sebastian and S. Francisco, are the principal islands of southern Brazil. The chief settlement is Nossa Senhora do Desterro, called by the natives Jurume-rim or Jururémerim (Varnhagen, i, 38). Here there was a British Consulate before it was removed to Santos. See chap. 9.

[5] The Carijós are repeatedly alluded to in the following pages (*e. g.*, chapters 9, 18, 30, and Part II, chapter 2). They were southerners in-

said : The savages of this harbour were called the Tuppin Ikins, and were their friends, from them we had nothing to fear.

We inquired in what latitude this said land lay, they told us, in twenty-eight degrees, which is correct. They also gave us indications by which we could recognize the land.

CAPUT VIII.

How we then again sailed out of the harbour, in search of the country to which we were bound.

Now when the east-south-easterly gale had subsided, the weather became fine, and when the wind blew from the north-east, we got under sail, and went back again to the before-mentioned country. We sailed for two days seeking the haven without being able to make it out. But we per-ceived by the shore, for the sun was so darkened that we could not take our observations, that we must have sailed past the harbour. We could not return on account of the wind, which opposed us.

But God is a helper in need. As we were at our even-ing prayers, begging for His mercy, it so happened, before

habiting a comparatively cold country, and extending, according to Gabriel Soares, along some seventy miles of coast, from the Rio Cananéa to the Porto dos Patos ; they occupied the littoral of Rio Grande and Sta. Catharina, and the Manga (channel) between that island and the main. They destroyed an expedition of eighty men sent in 1533 by Martim Affonso to explore the interior of Cananéa, and to prospect for gold mines. A warlike race, they fought in the open field, and when worsted they fled to the bush, where their enemies did not follow them. Their food was fish, game, and manioc, and they were not cannibals. To keep out the cold, which is sometimes severe in those regions, they built their houses of taipa (swish), roofed with tree-bark, and they wore two skins of the beasts killed for food, one before and the other behind (Jaboatam).

it became night, that dull clouds arose in the south, whither the wind was driving us. Before we had ended our prayers, the north-easterly wind fell and blew so that it could hardly be felt. Then the south wind, which does not often prevail at that season of the year, began to blow, with such thunder and lightning as to cause us fear, and the sea became very rough, for the south wind met the waves of the north wind. It was also so dark that we could not see, and the fierce thunder and lightning made the crew waver, till no one knew where he should lend a hand to shift the sails. We therefore expected that we should all be drowned that night. God, however, caused the weather to change and to improve, and we sailed back to the place whence we had that day come, and again we sought the harbour. Yet we could not find it, for there were many islands near the mainland.

Now when we again arrived at twenty-eight degrees (of south) latitude the captain ordered the pilot to steer us in among the islands, and to let go an anchor, in order to see what country it was. Then we sailed in between two coasts, where we found a fine port ; then we anchored, and resolved to set out in the boat that we might further reconnoitre the harbour.

CAPUT IX.

How some of us sailed with the boat to examine the harbour, and found a crucifix standing on a rock.

And it was on Saint Catharine's Day,[1] in the year 1549, that we lowered our anchor, and some of us, well armed, sailed off in the boat further to examine the harbour. We

[1] New style, May 5: for old style we must reckon back eleven days.

came to think that it must be a river, which is called Rio de S. Francisco,[1] which lies in the same province, for the further we went up it, the longer the river appeared. And we now looked around again and again, to see if we could perceive any smoke, but we saw none. Then we thought that we sighted some huts near a wilderness, and in a ravine. We sailed thither, but they were old huts, and we perceived no men therein; so we went further, till it became evening, and there lay before us in the river a small island, for which we made, in order to pass the night, supposing that there we could best protect ourselves. When we came to the island it was already night, and we could scarcely venture to repair on shore to spend the night there. Some of us went round about the island to see if anybody was in it, but we perceived no one. Then we made a fire, and cut down a palm-tree, and ate the pith of it.[2] There we passed the night, and early in the morning we sailed further into the country, for our intention was to discover if there were people there, inasmuch as when we had seen the old huts, we thought the land must be inhabited. Now as we so sailed onwards, we saw from afar a piece of wood standing upon a rock, which seemed like a cross. Several of us

[1] This must not be confounded with the great Rio de S. Francisco, further north. Behind the island of S. Francisco is a deep and winding indenture, into which a number of small waters fall, the largest being known as the S. Francisco. It is a disappointing stream. The northern entrance is called the Barra de S. Francisco, and João Dias Point is in S. lat. 26 deg. 6 min. 33 sec. Within the broken bay is now the large German colony of Joinville.

[2] Southey (i, 186) quoting Pedro Cieza de Leon (chap. vi, see the excellent translation by Clements R. Markham, C.B., printed for the Hakluyt Society, London, 1864), informs us that the cabbage-palm would probably have been extirpated had it not been so difficult to fell. " It was the hard work of half a day for a man with an axe to get the tree down and cut off its head." This is not the case in the Brazil, where the young palm is preferred : I have felled half a dozen " palmitos" in half an hour. Almost all the palms, it may be noted, bear an edible cabbage, but some species are much preferred to others.

D

thought, who could have placed it there? We passed it, and found it was a large wooden cross, secured with stones to the rock, and to it was tied a piece of the bottom of a barrel, upon which letters were cut. But we could not easily read them, and we wondered what ships those could have been that had erected it there, still not knowing whether this was the harbour where we were to meet.

Thereupon, we again sailed further in from the cross, to seek other land further on: the bottom of the barrel we took with us. As we so sailed along, one of us sat down, and reading the letters on the bottom of the barrel, began to understand them. The following was carved thereon in the Spanish language: Si vehn por ventura, eckila armada desu majestet, Tiren uhn Tire ay Averan Recado.[1]

That is to say in German: "If peradventure any of His Majesty's ships should come here, they may fire a gun, when they will receive further information."

And we sailed forthwith back to the cross, and fired off a falconet, and proceeded to sail further into the country.

As we so advanced, we sighted five canoes full of savages, that came rowing straight down upon us, our guns being in readiness. Now when they came near us, we saw a man who wore clothes and had a beard. He stood in the forepart of the canoe, and we perceived that he was a Christian. Then we called upon him to stop, and to come in a canoe for parley with us.

When he drew near in such a manner, we asked him in what country we were, and he answered, "You are in the harbour of Schirmirein,[2] so called in the savage tongue."

---

[1] This would be "Si ven (viniera) por ventura aqui la armada de Su Majestad, (que) tiren un tiro y averan (habran) recado."

[2] Shir-merim (see chapter 7) or Xerimerim (Varn. *Hist.* i, 38, who however confounds it with Meyembipe or St. Sebastian) is the Carijó name of Santa Catharina. Southey (iii, 647 note) identifies "Schirmirein" with the island of Juru-Mirim, "which Vasconcellos interprets the *Little Mouth*, I know not from what fancied similitude." The epithet

Moreover he said, "that you may therefore know ·it, it is called St. Catherine's harbour, which name has been given to it by the first discoverers."

Then we were glad, for that was the harbour which we sought, and in which we were although we had not known it, also we had arrived there on St. Catherine's Day. Know ye hereby how God helps and saves those who are in trouble, and who call earnestly to Him.

Then he asked us whence we came. We said that we were the king's ships from Spain, and we purposed sailing to the Rio de Platta,[1] also that there were more ships on the way, and we hoped (if it pleased God) that they would also soon arrive, for here we intended to meet. Then he declared himself well pleased and thanked God, for he had three years previously been in the province of Rio de Platta and had been sent from the place called La Soncion,[2] held by the Spaniards, down to the coast, which is some three hundred miles journey, in order to induce the tribe known as Carios, and who are friends of the Spaniards, to plant roots called mandioca, so that the ships might there again (if it happened that they were in want) obtain provisions from the savages. Such had been the orders of the captain who took the last news to Spain; he was named

is still applied to many debouchures of streams in the Brazil. The *Noticia* (chapter 66) mentions the Jumirim as the name of the (southern) S. Francisco. The maps show a Sahy-merim or Lesser Sahy (the Sahy Guassú or Greater being a little north), a stream whose mouth, in S. lat. 26 deg., divides the modern provinces of Paraná and Santa Catharina.

[1] Rio de la Plata.

[2] The capital of Paraguay, Asuncion, whose name has often been · before Europe during the five years' war which ended in the heroic death of President Lopez. Old authors sometimes confound the Assumption of the Virgin (N. S. August 15), when the place was taken from the Carijós by Juan de Ayolas, with the Ascension of the Saviour kept in May, the last Thursday but one before Whitsunday.

Capitan Salaser,[1] and had also returned with the next ship.

We sailed with them to the huts where he (the Portuguese) lived among the savages, and the latter entertained us after their manner.

CAPUT X.

How I was sent with a boat full of savages to our large ship.

Thereupon our captain begged the man whom we found among the savages, that he would cause a canoe to be manned, which should be conducted by one of us to the great ship, so that this also might proceed there.

Then the captain sent me off with the savages to the ship; we had been absent three nights, and those in the ship did not know what had become of us. Now when I fired an arquebuss from the boat, on approaching the vessel, they made a great alarm and prepared for defence, and would not permit me to approach nearer with the boat, but called out to me, asking what had happened, where the rest of the crew remained, and how I so came alone with the boat-full of savages. I remained silent and gave no answer, for the captain had commanded me to look sorrowful, in order to observe what those in the ship would do.

Now as I answered them not, they said among themselves, "the affair is not altogether right, the others must be dead, and they come with this one; perhaps they have others in the rear with whom to seize the vessel." And they were about to fire. Yet they called out once more to me, then I began to laugh, and said, " Be comforted, good news! let me come nearer so that I may give you ac-

[1] In chap. 12 Salasar, a certain Juan de Salazar, a follower of the Adelantado Mendoza.

count of it." Upon this I told them how matters stood ; at which they were exceedingly glad, and the savages sailed home again in their boat. We arrived with the great ship close to where the savages dwelt, when we let go an anchor, lay there and waited for the other vessels which had parted from us in the storm, and which had yet to arrive.

And the village where the savages live is called Acuttia,[1] and the man whom we there found was called Johann Ferdinando,[2] a Buschkeyner from the town of Bilka, and the savages who were there were called the Carios. The latter brought us much venison and fish, for which we gave them fish-hooks.

Caput XI.

How the other ship of our fleet, in which the head pilot was, and of which we had lost sight at sea, arrived.

After we had been there about three weeks, arrived the ship in which the head pilot was. But the third vessel had perished and of it we heard nothing more.

We again prepared to sail on ; having collected six months' victual, for we had still some 300 miles to proceed by water. When we had all things ready, we one day lost the great ship in the harbour, so that the voyage was in such manner prevented.

We lay there during two years running great danger in the wilderness, and we suffered great hunger, having to eat lizards, field-rats, and other strange animals such as we could procure, also the shell-fish which hung to the rocks,

[1] Possibly Cutía (not to be pronounced Cutiá, "white"), the agouty or "cautious animal", from acuty, to await or to look out. Near the city of S. Paulo, there is still a village of the same name, variously written Cotía, Cuttía, and Coteya. See part 2, chap. 10.

[2] Juan Hernandez, a Vizcaino, or Spanish Basque (Buschkeyner) of Bilbao (Bilka), vulgarly called Bilboa, and in Basque Ibaizabel, the capital of the Biscay or Viscaya Province.

and similar unusual food. The savages who at first brought us provisions enough, when they had obtained sufficient wares, withdrew from us for the most part to other places : we also dared not rely entirely upon them, so that it grieved us to remain there and perish.

We therefore agreed that the greater part should travel overland to the province called La Sumption, which was three hundred miles off. The others were to proceed thither with the remaining ship. The captain kept several of us by him, who were to proceed with him by water. Those who went by land carried provisions with them for their march through the wilderness, and taking some savages they set forth. But many perished with hunger, and the others arrived at their destination, as we afterwards learned : as to the rest of us, our craft was too small to put to sea with.

Caput XII.

How we agreed to sail to Sanct Vincente, where the Portuguese possess the land, intending to freight another ship from them wherewith to end our voyage, and how we suffered shipwreck in a great storm, not knowing how far we were from Sanct Vincente.

Now the Portuguese have taken possession of an island close to the mainland called S. Vincente (in the savage tongue Urbioneme[1]). This same province lies about seventy miles (leagues) distant from the place where we were. Thither it was our intention to sail and to see whether we could freight from the Portuguese a ship in which to make the Rio de Plata, for a craft such as that still left us was too small for all of us to sail therein. To seek information about this, some of us sailed with the captain named

---

[1] In chapter 14 called Orbioneme. This probably is the origin of the corrupt " Orpion", or " Morpion", which Thevet and d'Abbeville make the native name of St. Vincent Island.

Salasar to the Island S. Vincente, and none of us had been there, except one called Roman, who thought that he could find out the place again.

We sailed out of the harbour called Inbiassape,[1] which lies in thirty-four degrees south of the equinoctial line, and we came after sailing about two days to an island called Insula de Alkatrases,[2] about 40 miles (leagues) away from whence we sailed. Then the wind became unfavourable, so that we were obliged to anchor. On the said island were many seabirds, which are called Alkatrases, these are easy to catch, and it was at the time they rear their young.[3] There we landed and sought fresh water in the island, and found still there some old huts, and fragments of pottery of the savages who had formerly lived in the island, and we came upon a small fountain on a rock. Then we struck dead many of the above-mentioned birds, and also taking their eggs with us to the ship, we cooked the birds and the

[1] In chapter 13, called Byasape. The position is confused. The author has just told us that he was 70 *meilen* (= 280 geographical miles=4 deg., 40 min.), from St. Vincent. This would place him in S. lat. 28 deg., 41 min., but he expressly says, " xxxiiii gradus sud-west equinoctial."

Many small ports in the Brazil are called from the Piaçaba palm. Inbiassape may be the Biguassú River which falls into the bay behind the island of St. Catherine, in S. lat., 27 deg., 29 min. On the other hand, there is Porto de Piaçabussú on the mainland west of St. Vincent : I believe it to be a mongrel word composed of Pai, Padre or priest, Sabia wise and Ussú great.

[2] Assuming Hans Stade to have been a little way south of St. Catherine, the Ilha dos Alcatrases, the Pelican Islands alluded to in the Preface, lying in S. lat. 24 deg., 6 min., 15 sec.; and long. (G.) 45 deg., 46 min., 32 sec. ; about five miles south of the parallel of the Barra de Santos, are those used as trigonometrical points by Captain Mouchez in the hydrographical survey of 1856-64.

[3] At the Lage, or Rock Isle, south-south-east of Santos, there is a " gull fair", and the birds are as tame as those described in the text, allowing men to lift them off their nests. There is also a spring called Agua Agria (the sour water), supposed to have healing properties. Capt. Napier, R.N. and I visited it on May 9th, 1865.

eggs. Now when we had eaten, a great storm arose in
the south, so that we could scarcely retain our anchor, and
feared greatly that the wind would cast us up on to the rocks.
Already it was almost evening, and we still hoped to enter a
harbour called Caninee.[1]

But before we got there it was night, and we could not
enter, but sailed away from the land in great danger, thinking not otherwise but that the breakers would beat the ship
to pieces, for it was near a promontory of land, where the
waves are still larger than in the midst of the sea far from
land.

And we had during the night got so far away from land,
that in the morning we could not see it. But after some
time we again sighted the land, and the storm was so
heavy that we could hardly maintain ourselves longer,
when he who had been into the country, came to the conclusion, as he saw the land, that it was Sanct Vincente,
and we sailed there, but we found it so covered with fog
and clouds that we could not recognize it. We were
obliged to heave into the sea everything of very heavy
weight, in order to make the ship lighter, and because of
the large waves we were in great fear. Still we sailed on,

[1] Cananéa, or settlement of the Cananean woman—"La pauvre Chan-
anée reputée pour chienne." Martim Affonso de Souza touched here,
erected a Padrão, or stone cross, which still exists, and sent his ill-fated
expedition to prospect for gold. It lies in S. lat. 25 deg., 1 min.,
4 sec. ; and W. long. (Rio de Janeiro), 4 deg., 49 min., 4 sec., or
60 direct geographical miles south-west of the Barra de Santos. The Ilha
de (bom) Abrigo, a detached lump of rock masks the entrance, and in
rough weather adds greatly to the danger. In the cloudy and foggy
season, the entrance to the sea-arm, called Mar Pequeno, may easily be
mistaken for that of Santos, and I know by experience the risk of making
it in a small craft, when the water is not very smooth. Cananéa is one
of the many little ports belonging to the Province of S. Paulo : of late
years there has been a rumour about ceding it to the adjoining Southern
Province of Paraná. Its name has been heard in England on account
of the singular folly or knavery of attempting to stock the land with
British peasants, the meanest of races.

expecting to find the harbour in which the Portuguese lived. But we were mistaken.

Now when the clouds had broken a little, so that the land could be seen, Roman said that he thought the harbour was before us and that we were to steer straight to a rock, behind which lay the harbour. We sailed to it, and as we came close upon it, we saw nothing but death before our eyes, for it was not the harbour, and we were obliged to sail straight upon the land on account of the wind, and to suffer shipwreck. The waves dashed against the shore, causing horror. Then we prayed to God for mercy and salvation for our souls, and did as beseems seafaring men, who are about to be shipwrecked.

As we came where the waves broke upon the coast, we rose so high on the waters that we looked down upon a steep as from a wall. The first shock with which the ship went aground, broke her to pieces. Then several sprang out and swam at once for the land, some of us arrived on shore upon the fragments. In such manner God helped us all, one with another, alive on the coast, and it blew and rained so hard that we were truly cast away.

CAPUT XIII.

How we discovered in what country of the savages we had suffered shipwreck.

Now when we had reached the shore, we thanked God that he had permitted us to reach land alive, and yet we were also sad, for we knew not where we might be, inasmuch as Roman did neither quite recognize the country, nor could tell whether we were far from or near to the Island of S. Vincente, also whether savage men dwelt there, from whom we might suffer harm. And it happened that one of our companions named Claudio (who was a Frenchman) ran

along the strand in order to get warm, and saw behind
the forests a village, the houses of which were built in
the Christian manner. Thither going he found it to be a
settlement wherein Portuguese live, and known by the
name Itenge Ehm,[1] situated two miles (leagues) from Sanct
Vincente. Then he told them how we had been shipwrecked there, and that the crew suffered much from cold
and that we knew not whither to go. When they heard
this, they came running out, and took us with them to
their houses, and clad us. There we remained several days
until we had recovered ourselves.

Thence we travelled overland to Sanct Vincente, where
the Portuguese did us all honour, and gave us food for
some time. After this each one began something by
which to maintain himself. As we there saw that all our
vessels had been lost, the captain sent a Portuguese ship
after the rest of our crew, who had remained at Byasape,
in order to bring them, which also happened.

---

[1] Itanhaem of modern days; some explain the word " bad rock";
others (preferably) " Pedra que falla", stone that speaks, *i.e.*, echoes
Southey (i, 189) remarks, " If Fray Gaspar da Madre de Deos" (the
monographer of Santos) " had perused these Travels he would have seen
that there was a Portuguese settlement at this place in 1555...which he
denies."

For a short time Nossa Senhora da Conceição de Itanhaem, as it is
now called, became under the Counts of Vimeiro (and Ilha do Principe),
Capital of the Captaincy of St. Vincent, now the Province of S. Paulo.
It lost this rank in 1679, the harbour being found useless. According
to local tradition, the port was spoiled by the Dutch, and the same is
related of St. Vincent; but in both cases, the shallowness of the modern
bars which choke and block up the little rivers, seems to denote a secular
upheaval of the shore-level. The chief peculiarity of this place is the
high rock, a huge lump of the granite common to all the coast, upon
which its church is built. The streamlet can harbour only canoes, and
consequently there is no trade. Itanhaem lies ten direct geographical
miles from Santos harbour. The only road, a long round, is by the
shore, and when I left the country in 1868, the local government was
preparing to bridge the S. Vicente river.

Caput XIV.

How Sancte Vincente is situated.

Sancte Vincente is an island, which lies close to the main-land, therein are two hamlets. One is called in the Por-tuguese language S. Vincente, but in the savage tongue Orbioneme, the other lies about two miles therefrom, and is called Uwawa Supe. Besides these there are also in the islands sundry houses called Ingenio,[2] and in these sugar is made.

And the Portuguese who live therein have for allies a tribe of Brazilians who are called the Tuppin Ikin,[3] and the territory of this nation extends some eighty miles inwards, and about forty miles along the sea-coast.

This tribe has on both sides enemies, on the south side and also on the north side. Their foes on the south side are called the Carios, and those on the north side are known as the Tuppin Imba. They are also called by their enemies

[1] In Purchas (v, 1242), we find the island of St. Vincent called Warapisuma, which Varnhagen (1, 53) explains by the Guará, Ibis Rubra, or Tantalus Ruber (Linn.), there common (see also H. Stade, chap. 19). The historian (1, 141) seems to identify Uwawa, or as he writes it, Iwawasupe with Enguaguaçú, "signifying the Monjôlo, or great mor-tar, a name taken from one of the primitive sugar-plantations there es-tablished". Fray Gaspar also writes "Engua", which should be "Indoá", and makes the rim of the fanciful mortar—it is now called by a name more expressive but less polite—to consist of the hills of Santos Island, and the tall semi-circular ridge of the coast range (Serra Acima) which appears almost to encircle the islet. Uwawa Supe may have occupied the site where Santos afterwards rose, the first tenement being a Casa de Misericordia, built by Braz Cubas in 1543.

[2] Engenho throughout the Brazil means a sugar-plantation and its works, which, as an old author remarks, truly denote the genius and the ingenuity of man. The word is explained by the author in chapter 18.

[3] Southey (1, 189), remarks upon this passage, "It seems that the Goaynazes had left the country." But possibly this tribe is included under the Tupiniquins, or Tupi neighbours.

Tawaijar,[1] as much as to say, enemy; these have done much injury to the Portuguese, who to this day remain in fear of them.

Caput XV.

How the place is named from which they suffer most persecution of the enemy, and how it is situated.

Five miles from Sancte Vincente lies a place called Bri-kioka,[2] to which place their enemies the savages first arrive, and sail through between an island called Sanct Maro, and the mainland.

To intercept the passage of the savages several Mam-meluck[3] brethren were stationed there. Their father was

---

[1] These are the Tabayarás (owners of Tabas or villages, opposed to Tre-membés, nomades); the name is also written Tobayarés, and is differently explained by Jaboatam, from toba, a face, and yara, lord, *i.e.*, lords of the face, or front of Earth, that is to say, the seaboard in contradistinction to the interior, and especially Bahia, the foremost or best of dwelling places. These people occupied Pará, Maraham, Northern Parahyba, Pernambuco, Bahia, Espirito Santo, and S. Paulo. They are the Ta-baiares of Yves d'Evreux, the first Brazilian tribe which in the north allied itself with the Portuguese, and opposed the French with bitter animosity. It produced the famous Poty (Camarão, or the Shrimp), and his brother Jacaúna, with the chiefs Itabyra (vulg. Tabyra), Itagiba, Pyragiba, and others who supported Jeronymo d'Albuquerque against La Ravadière.

[2] In chapter 32 Brickioka, from the Buriqui or Biriti monkey, "huma especie de macacos" called Pricki in part 2, chapter 29. When Hans Stade informs us, chapter 18, that the "Island of Sancte Vin-cente" is five *meilen* from "Sancte Maro", he means that the settlement of Saint Vincent was at that distance from the Bertioga Fort, on the mainland. I have described the actual state of the latter in the preface.

Southey (i, 189) is unusually incorrect, when he assures us "There is an island called Bertioga, about five miles from St. Vicente, half-way between the mainland and St. Amaro."

[3] Also written "Mammaluck". The word is corrupted from the Arabic Mamlúk (مملوك one bought, *i.e.* a slave), and was probably derived from the Egyptian Mamelukes, who were Kurds till about A.D. 1244, when Sultan Salah el Din (Saladin) preferred Turco-Circassians. Charle-

a Portuguese, and their mother was a Brazilian woman, the same were Christians, skilled and experienced in customs and languages both of the Christians and the savages. The eldest was called Johan de Praga, the other Diego de Praga,[1] the third Domingus de Praga, the fourth Francisco de Praga, the fifth Andreas de Praga, and their father was called Diago (Diego) de Prage.

The five brothers had, about two years before I arrived, undertaken together with the friendly Indian people, to build a fort there against their enemies, according to the customs of the savages : this they had also so carried out. Consequently several Portuguese had joined them, and had settled there, as it was a fine country. This their enemies the Tuppin Imba had discovered, and had prepared themselves in their country, which begins about twenty-five miles (leagues) off. They had arrived there one night with

voix (book vi) in 1618 says, that these Mestiços (Metis) were so called, because they resembled the ancient slaves of the Egyptian Soldan ; and the Jesuit writers of the 18th century attribute the successes of the Dutch at Pernambuco to their toleration of these half-castes. Fray Gaspar says, that the mules produced by whites and " Indians" were called " Mama-culos " ; he ignores the derivation of the word, but declares that it did not come from Egypt, a country here unknown. It was a name of fear, and became even more terrible in the 18th century, when the brave and sanguinary Mamalukes of São Paulo began their raids upon the Province of La Guayra, and the Spanish Missions to the west. Yet as Varnhagen remarks, it is curious to find the horror excited by these Paulista "Commandos", intended to captive " Indians", when 300 years ago, Europe supported the right of putting to death prisoners of war (Grotius *De Jure Belli et Pacis*, lib. iii, chapter 7). Mamalucco meaning the offspring of a white man by an " Indian " woman, is now obsolete in S. Paulo, where Caboclo (see introduction) has taken its place. The *Naturalist on the Amazons* (i, chapter 1, p. 35) tells us that Mameluco is the son of an Indian and a white, while the civilised Indian is called Tapuyo or Caboclo. In Pará the original term " Curiboca " is still retained for the issue of African and " Indian."

[1] There is more about these men in chapter 41. Praga is of course the Teutonic form of Braga, as Pricki for Buriqui, and Presillig for Brasilig.

seventy canoes, and had attacked them at daybreak as is their custom.[1] The Mammalucks together with the Portuguese had run into a house, which they had built of earth, and defended themselves. The other savages had also kept together in their huts and defended themselves whilst they could, so that many of the enemies had remained dead. At last, however, the foe had gained the upper hand, had set fire to the place of Brikioka, and had captured all the savages, but to the Christians of whom there might have been about eight, and the Mammelucks in the house, they had not been able to do any harm, for God intended to preserve them. The other savages, however, whom they had taken there, they had at once separated and divided, and thereupon they had returned to their own country.

Caput XVI.

How the Portuguese rebuilt Brikioka, and afterwards raised a fort in the island of Sanct Maro.

Upon which the authorities and community thought it advisable that the said place should not be abandoned, but that it should be strongly fortified, for at that point the whole country could be defended. This they had done.

Now when the enemies perceived that the Brikioka settlement was too strong for them to attack, they during the night passed by water immediately above the place, and captured whomever they could seize about Sanct Vincente. For those who lived in the interior thought they were in

---

[1] The practice of all savage peoples, who rely upon the drowsiness of the attacked when enjoying the " beauty sleep " before dawn, and who want the day soon to break, so that after darkness has covered the attack, they may have light to pursue the fugitives, and to drive away or to carry off their slaves, cattle, and other booty. See part 2, chap. 26.

no danger, as the neighbouring settlement had been built up and fortified, and for this very reason they suffered harm.

Thereafter the inhabitants thought well to build a house close to the water, on the Island of Sanct Maro, which lies immediately opposite Brikioka, and to place therein guns and men, in order to prevent the passage of the savages. Thus they had begun to build a bulwark on the island, but they had not finished it, the cause being, as they informed me, that no Portuguese gunner would venture to remain therein.

I went there to see the place. Now when the inhabitants heard that I was a German and knew something about gunnery, they begged me to remain in the house on the island, and there help to watch the enemy. They offered to procure me other companions, and to give me good pay. Also they said, that if I did this, I should be rewarded by the king, for the king was wont to be a particularly gracious master to those who in such new countries give their aid and advice.

I agreed with them that I should serve in the fort four months, when an officer on the part of the king would arrive there in ships, and build up a stone blockhouse, which would then be stronger, as it also came to pass. During most of the time I was in the blockhouse with three others, having some guns with me, but I was in great danger on account of the savages, for the house was not strong, we had also to keep watch diligently, that the savages might not pass by secretly during the night, as they several times attempted, yet God helped us to perceive them during our watches.

Several months afterwards came the officer of the king, for the community had written to the king how great was the insolence displayed by the enemies to the country from the before-named side. Also (they reported) how fine a country it was, and that it was not advisable to abandon it. In order to amend this, the Colonel, called Thome de Susse,[1] came and examined that part of the country, and the points which the community desired greatly to have fortified.

Then the community informed the officer of the services which I had rendered them, by repairing to the house when no Portuguese would venture therein, as it was so badly fortified.

This pleased him greatly, and he said that he would bring my conduct before the king, if God helped him back again to Portugal, and that I should be rewarded.

The time which I had agreed to serve the community, namely four months, was past, and I asked leave. But the officer together with the community desired that I would remain some time longer in the service. Whereupon I gave my assent to serve two years more, and when the time was over they should, unless certain circumstances prevented it, allow me to sail in the first ship which I could find, to Portugal, when my services should be rewarded. To this effect the officer gave me on the part of the king my " privilegea" (commission), as it is also customary to give to such of the king's gunners who demanded it. They built the stone-fort and they placed several pieces of cannon inside. I was commanded to keep vigilant watch and look out in the fort with the guns.

[1] The well-known Thomé de Souza appointed, by D. Joao III, the first Governor-General of the Brazil, where he landed on May 29th, 1549. This energetic officer, who took out with him the Jesuits, then a highly educated and progressive order, founded (S. Salvador da) Bahia, and after thoroughly organising his viceroyalty, returned home in 1553. He was succeeded by Duarte da Costa.

Caput XVII.

How and from what cause we had to expect the enemy more at one time
of the year than at another.

We had, however, to be especially on our guard more than
usual against them, during two seasons, particularly when
they proposed invading with violence their enemies' country. And these two periods are, the one in the month of
November when a fruit becomes ripe, which is called in their
language Abbati,[1] from which they make drink called Kaawy.[2] Therewith they have also the Mandioka root, of which

[1] This word is written Abaty, Abatij, Abaxi, Abashi, and Ubatim
(*Noticia do Brazil*); it is applied to the Milho de Guiné, in old Portuguese
Zaburro, Zea Mays, Maïs, or Maize, a Haytian word which Yves d'Evreux
writes " May", and explains blé de Turquie. St. Hilaire believes it to
grow wild in Paraguay. The liquor made from it was called Abati-yg,
millet water, beer, the African pombe, much like the Cornish stuff which
Dr. Andrew Boorde described to be " white and thick as though pigges
had wrastled in it." Southey (i, 191) is thus greatly in error when he
explains *Auati* (de Bry for Abbati), as " probably the Acayaba of Piso
and Marcgraff, which bears the *Acajou*, or Cashew nut."

[2] The similarity of this word and the Otaheitan Kava is merely super-
ficial. Kaawy, Cau-y, Caöi, or vulgarly Cauim (in chapter 18, Kawewi,
and in chapter 28 Kawawy), is properly Acaju-yg, or Caju-yg, Cashew-
nut water (fermented), generically applied to all fermented liquors, even
of manioc-root. Hence the old French coined the substantive, Caouïnage
drinking bout, and the verb Caouïner. Whilst the North American tribes
had no fermented liquor, Bacchus, say the old authors, seems to have
made his home in the Brazil. Marcgraff gives nine kinds of fermented
liquors, the best being that called Nandi by Nieuhoff, the juice of the
pine-apple (Nana-Vyg, whence our Ananas). They prized that of the
Cashew, which once grew wild over the land, and whose nuts, often cast
upon the Cornish shore, suggested a western world. They also made
wine of the Jabuticaba Myrtle, and the Pacoba, or plantain (Pecou-yg).
The chief materials, however, were the manioc-root, of two kinds, the
poisonous and the harmless (Aypim, or Macachera). Of these were the
Payuaru, the Cauï-Caraçu, and the Cauï-Macachera. From the Tapioca
or sediment, they made Tapiocu-yg (Nieuhoff's Tipíaci) and from Beiju
or Manioc cakes (Beiutingui Nieuhoff, p. 869). They ignored the grape, but

E

they also mix up some in order to make the drink when the Abati is ripe. Returning from war they would have some of the Abati for brewing the drinks with which to eat their enemies, when they have caught any, and to rejoice a whole year thereat when the Abati time (again) comes.

We had also to expect them in August, when they go in search of a certain kind of fish which passes from the ocean into such fresh waters as flow into the sea, in order to lay its spawn therein. The same are called in their language Bratti,[1] the Spaniards call them Lysses. About the same period they are accustomed to sally forth together and make war, in order that their expedition may be better assisted by supplies of food. And of these fish they catch many with small nets, also they shoot them with arrows; they take home with them many fried, and they also make therefrom a flour which they call Pira Kui.[2]

not the vinho de mel, the classical mead of Scandinavia: its name, Garápa, is now applied to the fermented juice of the sugar-cane.

[1] The well-known Paraty, a term applied by some writers to the Sparus or Tainha, which the annotator of Father Anchieta says is a white mullet (Mugil Albula Linn.) Southey (ii, 635) erroneously writes the word Talinhas. In chapter 41 we find that the Portuguese name of the Bratti (Paraty) or Lysses (Lissa) is " Doynges" (Tainhas), which are described to be as large as a good-sized pike. According to Nieuhoff, the Dutch of Pernambuco called these fish " Herders."

[2] P. Anchieta writes (Epistola quam plurimarum rerum naturalium quæ S. Vincentii, nvnc S. Pauli, Provinciam incolunt, sistens descriptionem, § vii) Pirâ-iquê, i.e., piscium ingressus, the spawning season when the fish, which his annotator compares with herring-shoals, repair to fresh water. In chapter 41, and part 2, chapter 26, we find this signification given to Pirakaen, which must not be confounded with Pira-caem (" fish badly roasted "). Pirá or Pyrá is the generic Tupi word for fish whereas Píra or Pýra is the itch. The Piracemas of S. Paulo were shoals of fish, chiefly the Saguairú, left upon the grassy banks by the sudden falling of the floods. Anchieta (loc. cit. § iii) translates Piracêma, piscium exitus, and tells us that it happened twice a year, in September and December, that is just after the height of the rains.

Caput XVIII.

How I was captured by the savages, and the way in which this
happened.

I had a savage man, of a tribe called Carios ; he was my
slave, who caught game for me, and with him I also went
occasionally into the forest.

Now it happened once upon a time, that a Spaniard from
the island of Sancte Vincente came to me in the island of
Sancte Maro, which is five miles (leagues) therefrom, and
remained in the fort wherein I lived, and also a German by
name Heliodorus, from Hesse, son of the late Eoban of
Hesse, the same who was in the island of Sanct Vincente
at an ingenio, where sugar is made, and the ingenio belonged to a Genoese named Josepe Ornio.[1] This Heliodorus was the clerk and manager of the merchants to whom
the ingenio belonged. (Ingenio, are called houses in which
sugar is made). With the said Heliodorus I had before had
some acquaintance, for when I was shipwrecked with the
Spaniards in that country, I found him in the island of
Sancte Vincente, and he showed me friendship. He came
again to me, wanting to see how I got on, for he had
perhaps heard that I was sick.

Having sent my slave the day before into the wood to
catch game, I purposed going the next day to fetch it, so
that we might have something to eat. For in that country
one has little else beyond what comes from the forests.

Now as I with this purpose walked through the woods,
there arose on both sides of the path loud yells such as the
savages are accustomed to make, and they came running

[1] Giuseppe Adorno, a scion of the well-known Genoese family, which
settled in the Brazil, and especially at S. Paulo (Fray Gaspar). According to Vasconcellos, this man outlived a hundred years. In 1589-90, he
established with a donation the Carmelites at Santos, whence they passed
to Rio de Janeiro.

E 2

towards me; I knew them, and found that they had all surrounded me, and levelling their bows with arrows, they shot
in upon me. Then I cried, "Now God help my soul;" I had
scarcely finished saying these words when they struck me to
the ground[1] and shot (arrows) and stabbed at me. So far
they had not (thank God!) wounded me further than in one
leg, and torn my clothes off my body; one the jerkin, the
other the hat, the third the shirt and so forth. Then they
began to quarrel about me, one said he was the first who
came up to me, the other said that he had captured me.
Meanwhile the others struck me with their bows. But at
last two of them raised me from the ground where I lay
naked, one took me by one arm, another by the other,
and some went behind me, and others before. They ran in
this manner quickly with me through the wood towards the
sea, where they had their canoes. When they had taken me
to the shore, I sighted their canoes which they had drawn
up from the sea on to the land under a hedge, at the distance of a stone's-throw or two, and also a great number
more of them who had remained with the canoes. When
they, ornamented with feathers acccording to their custom,
saw me being led along they ran towards me, and pretended
to bite into their arms, and threatened as though they would
eat me. And a king paraded before me with a club wherewith they despatched the prisoners. He harangued and
said how they had captured me their slave from the Perot[2]

[1] Usually the sign of capture was to place the hand upon the shoulder,
a rite retained by the modern bailiff. "Tu ne m'as pas mis la main sur
l'epaule en guerre ainsi qu'a fait celuy qui m'a donné à toy pour me
reprendre" is the speech which Yves d'Evreux (p. 45) puts into the
mouth of a "red" man.

[2] Southey (i, 58) writes, "I have sometimes suspected that ... the Brazilians meant to call their enemies *dogs, perros*". The word is Spanish,
not Portuguese, yet Camoens uses *Pero*. Juan de Lery has Maïr et
Pero for Français et Portugais, and it has elsewhere been seen that
Maïr and its cognate forms mean a stranger generally. Possibly it was
applied to the Portuguese as a corruption of Pedro, as we say "Sawney"

(so they call the Portuguese), and they would now thoroughly revenge on me the death of their friends. And when they brought me to the canoes, several of them struck me with their fists. Then they made haste among one another, to shove their canoes back into the water, for they feared that an alarm would be made at Brikioka, as also happened.

Now before they launched the canoes, they tied my hands together, and not being all from the same dwelling-place, those of each village[1] were loath to go home empty-handed, and disputed with those who held me. Some said that they been just as near me as the others, and that they would also have their share of me, and they wanted to kill me at once on that very spot.

Then I stood and prayed, looking round for the blow. But at last the king, who desired to keep me, began and said they would take me living homewards, so that their wives might also see me alive, and make their feast upon me. For they purposed killing me " Kawewi Pepicke,"[2] that is, they would brew drinks and assemble together, to make a feast, and then they would eat me among them. At these words they left off disputing, and tied four ropes round my neck, and I had to get into a canoe, whilst they still stood on the shore, and bound the ends of the ropes to the boats and pushed them off into the sea, in order to sail home again.

Sobáy or Çobáy being the name by which Portugal was known. Ayres de Cazal believes that it took its origin from a Portuguese blacksmith who settled amongst the savages of Maranham—but those were days of scant intercourse. Dr. Moraes e Mello has also explained it (p. 440). In the conclusion of Part 2, Perott appears to be the name of an individual (Pierot?).

[1] Aldêa is the Portuguese word here used.

[2] Southey (i, 193) explains this " as we say, a Michaelmas goose, or Christmas ox". In chap. 28, Kawaway means wine (see p. 49); in Part 2, chap. 25, Pepicke seems to signify revenge.

Caput XIX.

How, when they were sailing back again with me our people arrived, purposing to retake me from them, and they turned and faced them and skirmished with them.

There lies a small island close to the island where I had been captured, in which rest certain water-birds called Uwara,[1] having red feathers. They asked me if their enemies the Tuppin Ikins had that year also been there, and had caught the birds with their young. I said "Yes," but they nevertheless determined to see for themselves. For they esteem greatly the feathers which come from the birds, almost all their ornaments being made of feathers. And a peculiarity of the said birds Uwara is that when they are young, the first feathers which they grow are whitish grey; the next however, when they become fledged, are of a blackish grey, with these they fly about a year, after which they become as red as any red paint.[2] And they sailed to the island, expecting to find the birds. Now when they had proceeded about the distance of two musket-shots from the spot where their canoes had been, they looked back, when it

[1] See chap. 14 and Part 2, chap. 34, where the Uwara-pirange (for piranga, i.e., red ibis) is very well described. Yves d'Evreux calls this brilliant phenicopter Courlier rouge—red curlew. The modern orthography is Guará; Alencar, however, writes Gará, deriving it from yg or ig, water, and ara a macaw, which it resembles in its glowing colours. Guará must not be confounded with Guára, the Brazilian wolf (Canis Brasiliensis), derived from "u", to eat; "g", relative, and "ára", the desinent—G-u-ára, the eater, and G-u-ára-ã, the great eater.
The islet alluded to in the text is evidently the Ilha do Arvoredo, a rocky lump some eight miles S.S.W. of the Barra da Bertioga, and close to the shore of Santo Amaro. It need hardly be remarked that the ibis is not a sea-fowl.

[2] These words are evidently copied by A. Gonçalves Dias, when he says of the ibis, "Nasce bianca, torna-se preta e por fim de um encarnardo vivissimo". The feathers were used for the Acangátaras, or dress coronals and the kilts of the Tupi savages.

was seen crowded by the Tuppin Ikin savages, also some Portuguese among them, for a slave who was following me when I was captured, escaped them and raised an alarm as they took me. These intended to release me and called out to my captors, that if they were brave they would come to them and fight. And they turned back with the canoes again to those on shore, and these shot with blow-pipes[1] and arrows upon us, and those in the boats back again to them; and they untied my hands once more, but the ropes round my neck still remained firmly bound.

Now the king in the boat, in which I was, had a gun and a little powder, which a Frenchman had bartered to him for Brazil wood. This I was compelled to fire off at those on shore.

When they had so fought for some time, they feared that the others might perhaps be reinforced by boats and pursue them; and they sailed away, after three of them had been shot. They went about the distance of a falconet-shot past the bulwark of Brikioka, wherein I used to be, and as we so passed, I was obliged to stand up in the boat that my companions might see me, and they from the fort fired at us two large guns, but their shot fell short.

Meanwhile several canoes from Brikioka came sailing after us, and thought to overtake us, but they paddled away too quickly. When my friends saw this and that they could effect nothing, they again made for Brikioka.

[1] The well-known Sarbacan, of which Varnhagen (i, 114) says, " No Amazonas faziam uso da *Zarabatana* hervada". It is the Sampat of Java, used to kill birds, and a toy of the kind has been introduced into Europe. In Brazil recondite poisons were remarkably common, hence we are again disposed to postulate a higher civilization than that of the Tupis.

Caput XX.

What happened on the return voyage to their country.

Now when they were about seven miles (leagues) away from Brikioka towards their own country, it was, reckoning by the sun, about four o'clock in the afternoon, and it was on this same day that they had captured me.

And they sailed to an island and drew their canoes on shore, and intending to remain there the night, they took me from out of the canoe on to the shore. When I got on land I could not see, for I had been struck under my eyes ; also I could not walk well, and had to remain lying on the sand on account of the wounds which I had received in my leg. They stood around me and threatened how they would eat me.

Now when I was in such great terror and misery, I thought over what I never before contemplated, namely the sad vale of sorrow wherein we here live, and I began with tearful eyes to sing from the depth of my heart the Psalm :[2]

" Out of the depths have I cried unto Thee," etc.

Then said the savages, " Hear how he cries, how he laments !"[3]

Thereupon it seemed to them that there was no good encampment to be made on the island, for the purpose of remaining there passing the night, and they sailed away

[1] The Tupinambás would make for their own country as directly as possible, and twenty-eight nautical miles to the N.N.E. would land them upon the rock-stack called Montão de Trigo.

[2] De Profundis clamavi, Psalm cxxx, 1 :—
    " Dum vita medio convertitur anxia luctu,
        Imploro superi Numinis æger opem."

[3] A great disgrace amongst the savages of South, as well as of North, America.

again to the mainland, whereon were huts, built at a former time. It was night when we arrived there, and they drew the canoes ashore, and made a fire, and then led me to it. There I had to sleep in a net which in their language they call Inni,[1] which are their beds, and are tied to two posts above the ground, or if they are in a forest they make it fast to two trees. The ropes which I had round my neck, they lashed to a tree above, and they lay during the night round about me, mocking me and calling me in their language, " Schere inbau ende", Thou art my bound beast.

Before the dawn broke they put off again, and rowed the whole day, and when the position of the sun indicated about vesper time, they were yet two miles (leagues) from the place where they purposed encamping for the night. Then a great black cloud arose and came behind us, of terrible aspect, and they rowed quickly, that they might reach land and escape the clouds and wind.

Now when they saw that they could not escape them they said to me, "Ne mungitta dee. Tuppan do Quabe, amanasu[2] y'an dee Imme Ranni me sis se." That is as much as to say, " speak with thy God,[3] so that the great rain and wind may

[1] In Part 2, chap. 6, it is called " Ini", from " in", to be lying down (A. Gonçalves Dias), or Inimbó, thread, string. The hammock (a Haytian word) was more generally known as Maquira, Kysaba, or Kiçava (*Chrestomathia da Lingua Brasilica* pelo Dr. Ernesto Ferreira França, Leipzig, Brockhaus, 1859). Invented to escape vermin, it was woven by the women from the fibre of the Murity palm, which was soft as cotton-thread. Nieuhoff tells us that the Tapuyas had hammocks twelve to fourteen feet long, which lodged four sleepers. In the Brazil there are still two kinds, the small and the large or double: the latter enables the occupant to lie " athwart ship", and thus his head and feet are not tilted up.

[2] Aman-usu, great wind, or rain. As has been said in the Preface, I navigated these seas in a canoe during mid-winter, and I can well realise the wish of the savages to exorcise the storm.

[3] The Tupi word is Tupá, which Dobrizhoffer (ii, 77) and Ruiz de Montoya explain as Tû! exclamation of astonishment, and Pa? interrogative particle. This would reduce it to the formula "'! ?" a decidedly

do us no harm." I remained silent and made my prayer to God, as they demanded it from me, and said: "O Thou Almighty God, Thou heavenly and earthly Lord, who from the beginning hast helped and hast heard those who among the godless call upon Thy name, vouchsafe me Thy mercy, so that I may perceive that Thou art still with me, and that the savage heathens may see, that Thou my God hast heard my prayer!"

I lay bound in the canoe so that I could not turn round to see the weather, but they looked constantly behind them, beginning to say, "Oqua moa amanasu." That is; "The great tempest passeth away."[1] Then I raised myself a little and looking back, saw that the great cloud passed off, upon which I thanked God.

Now when we came to land, they did with me as they had done previously. They tied me to a tree, and they lay around me during the night, saying that we were now near their country, and that we would arrive there against the evening of the following day—whereat I did not much rejoice.

ingenious style of defining the "Unknowable". (See Mâ-râ, note to chapter 2). Tupá meant simply the "thunderbolt"; the thunder was known as Tupá-ci-nunga, or noise of Tupá, and lightning as Tupá-berábá, light of Tupá. The discharge of electric fluid appeared to these savages, who had no Deism, as Varnhagen seems to think, but abundant diabolism, a destructive being over their heads. "C'est un nuage dans lequel est Dieu, mais dont il ne sort pas encore" quotes M. Ferd. Denis. The pious and the credulous transferred Tupá to the name of the Almighty, and translated it "Excellencia espantosa". It was adopted by the Jesuit missionaries, who called the church Tupan-Oca or Tupaóca (House of Tupá), and the congregation Tupá-tayra (son of Tupá—a Christian). And in 1656 the disciples of Loyola got into trouble by designating God as Tupá, and God the Father as Tuba—"both being the names of infernal spirits" (*e.g.*, Tubuel and Tubuas). See Southey (ii, 444-447).

[1] Of course it was a common "tornado" blowing off shore.

Caput XXI.

How they behaved to me on the day when they brought me to their habitations.

On that same day about vesper time, reckoning by the sun, we beheld their habitations, having therefore been three days on the return voyage. For the place I was led to was thirty miles (leagues) distant from Brikioka. Now when we arrived close to their dwellings, these proved to be a village which had seven huts, and they called it Uwattibi.[1] We ran up on a beach which borders the sea, and close to it were their women in the plantations of the root which they call Mandioka. In this said plantation walked many of their women pulling up the roots ; to these I was made to call out in their language : " A junesche been ermi vramme," that is : " I, your food, have come." Now when we landed, all young and old ran out of their huts (which lay on a hill), to look at me. And the men with their bows and arrows entered their huts, and left me in the custody of their women, who took me between them and went along, some before me and others behind, singing and dancing in unison, with the songs which they are accustomed to sing to their own people when they are about to eat them. Now they brought me before the Iwara huts,[2] that

[1] The distance of 30 leagues (= 120 miles = 2 deg.,) from the Bertioga, allowing for the windings of the coast, would place the author at the modern Ubatúba Merim, or the Lesser. In chapter 41 we are told that there are two Uwattibis, and there are still two Ubatúbas. I prefer the eastern, or smaller settlement, because in chapter 40 we are told that Uwattibi is only 8 *meilen* from Rio de Janeiro, whereas the greater Ubatuba is nearly 120 miles.

[2] The Tupi " Oca " is badly translated by the German *Hutten*. Pigafetta (book 1) calls the house " Boi ". As amongst the Cowitchans of Northern America (Captain Wilson, *Trans. Ethno. Soc.*, New Series, vol. i), these tenements were 60 or 70 feet long, divided into rooms for the

is the fort which they make round about their huts with great long rails, like the fence of a garden. This they do on account of their enemies.

As I entered, the women ran to me, and struck me with their fists, and pulled my beard, and spoke in their language : " Sche innamme pepicke a e." That is as much as to say : "with this blow I revenge my friend, him whom those among whom thou hast been, have killed."

Thereupon they led me into the huts, where I had to lie in a hammock, whilst the women came and struck and pulled me before and behind, and threatened me how they would eat me.

And the men were together in a hut, and drank the beverage which they call Kawi, and had with them their gods, called Tammerka,[1] and they sang in praise of them,

several families by rush mats, and provided with a central fire whose smoke passed through the roof. Some of them contained 200 head. The French more sensibly applied to their long reed granges the Guiana word "Car-bet", and in the colonial language of the seventeenth century, carbeter meant to hold a council, or pow-wow. The village (Taba), which contained several of these huge wigwams (Ocas), lasted some four years. The open central space between the Ocas, where prisoners were slain and public business transacted, was called Ocára—it corresponds with the "Palaver-house" of the Central-African villages. The palisade here termed Iwara, is mostly known as Cahiçára, Caiçara, or Caiça. The rails were usually trunks of the Gissara, a thorny palm, or of the Taboca, a Brazilian bamboo, and in chapter 28 we are told how the huts were fronted by the impaled skulls of eaten enemies. Varnhagen (i, 116) describes the village at some length, and further details of dimension and shape will be found in Hans Stade, Part ii. Southey (ii, 476) does not understand " Tujupàr de Pindoba "—it means a ruinous hut of palm leaves.

[1] In other parts of the volume this Tammerka is written Tamerka, Tammaraka, Miraka, and Maracka, which approaches nearest to the correct modern form Maracá. A. Gonçalves Dias (sub voce) accents it Maráca, which is unusual. The word, which also means a rattlesnake, is usually applied to a calabash (Crescentia Cujete), adorned with feathers and full of pebbles, which, when rattled and assisted by ven-triloquism, or some equally easy fraud, gave prophetic answers. The

for their having so well prophesied that I should be captured by them.

This song I heard, and for half an hour none of the men came near me, but only women and children.

Caput XXII.

How my two masters came to me and told me that they had presented me to one of their friends, who was to keep me and kill me, when I was to be eaten.

I knew not then their customs so well as I have since learned them, and I thought "Now they prepare to kill thee." After a little while those who had captured me, named Jeppipo (Yeppipo) Wasu, and his brother Alkindar Miri, came to me and told me how they had, from friendship, presented me to their father's brother Ipperu Wasu,[1]

Tupi race had no other visible object of worship. Cabeça de Vaca found the Maracá in Florida, and according to P. Andrès Perez de Ribas, the Mexicans called it Ayacaztli. Pedro Cieza de Leon tells us that when the people about Anzerma first saw Spaniards, they called them Tamaracas, great idols or superior beings. As the Tupi race seems to have adored thunder and lightning, this implement may have been its symbol.

So universal was the worship of the prophetic rattle, that some authors have net hesitated to ascribe to it the easier adoption of the continental name of America—the land of the Maracá. Its use has survived in the Matraca board-rattle of the modern Brazilian churches, at times when bells may not be rung. In Dahome it becomes simply a musical instrument : the gourd with its bunch of feathers mounted upon a stick, and partly filled with maize, or pebbles, acts castanets.

[1] Yperuguassú would mean the great shark, "ism bi'l musammá"—a name suiting the named, as the Arabs say. Southey (i, 196) quotes Harcourt (*Harleian Miscellany*, 8vo, vol. iii, 184) touching a chief called "Ipero" in the Aracoory country, and subjoins, "Here then is the Tupi language extending into Guiana". He might safely have prolonged it far into the northern continent. The shark is known in the Brazil by two names, Tubarão and Mero.

who was to keep me, and also to kill me, when I was to be eaten, and thus to gain a new name with me.

For this same Ipperu Wasu had a year before also captured a slave, and had as a sign of friendship presented him to Alkindar Miri.   Him he had killed and thereby he had gained a name ;[1] so that Alkindar Miri had in return promised to present Ipperu Wasu with the first whom he might capture.   And I was the first.

Further the two above-mentioned who had taken me said, "Now will the women lead thee out to the Aprasse :"[2] this word I understood not then, but it means dancing.   Thus they dragged me along with the ropes,[3] which were round my neck, from out of the huts on to an open place.   Then came all the women who were in the seven huts, and seized hold of me, and the men went away.   Several of the women led me along by the arms, and several by the ropes which were bound round my neck, so roughly and tightly that I could hardly breathe.   In this manner they went along with

---

[1] "The Tupi names were usually derived from their flora or fauna. They changed them after slaying an enemy, as the Arab when the first son is born to him, showing that in the former destructiveness, and in the latter philo-progenitiveness are the ruling passions. Women also followed the example when their husbands had distinguished themselves by an "act of bravery." The adjective, Guaçú or Guasú, and its euphonical modifications (açu, uçu, waçu, etc.) almost always entered into the title, and even the Portuguese were not ashamed of being called, for instance, Mandú-açú, Manecco-Grande, or Manuel the Great (a certain M. Rodriguez). Dr. Lery tells us that he was greatly respected because Leri-assú means the Great Oyster. See misprint of *Noticia*, chap. 140, " Keriasu").

[2] Aiporaçei is to dance, and Poraçeia is the dance, vulgarly Aprassé, Purassé, and Poraçé. It is applied peculiarly to the performances which preceded the human sacrifice and the cannibal feast. According to Nieuhoff (p. 873), the common dance was known as Guau, and there was a third style, Urucapi ; another, much affected by children, was the Curupìrâra, and besides that were the Guaibipaié and the Guaibiquaib uçu.

[3] The cotton ropes with which the prisoners were bound for death are called Mussurána ; hence the colonial phrase Indios da Corda, namely, those condemned to die.

me, and I knew not what they intended doing to me, upon which I remembered the sufferings of our Lord Jesus Christ, and how he suffered innocently at the hands of the vile Jews, whereby I consoled myself and became more resigned. Then they brought me before the huts of the king, who was called Vratinge Wasu, which means in German, the Great White Bird.[1] Before his huts lay a heap of freshly dug earth, whither they led me and sat me down thereon, and some held me, when I thought nothing else but that they would dispatch me at once. I looked round for the Iwara Pemme,[2] wherewith they club men, and asked whether they were going to kill me then, when they answered, " not yet." Upon which a woman came from out of the crowd towards me, holding a fragment of a crystal, set in a thing like a bent ring, and with this same piece of crystal shaved off my eyebrows, and would also have cut the beard from my chin, but this I would not suffer, and said, that they should kill me with my beard. Then they replied, that for the present they would not kill me, and left me my beard. But after some days they cut it off with a pair of scissors, which the Frenchmen had given them.[3]

[1] Guirá or Wirá is any bird, Tinga white, and Wasú for Guaçú, great. The latter is opposed to Mirim, Merim, Mini, or Mi, small.

[2] Vasconcellos (ii, 18) calls this sacrificial club Tangapema. Vieyra Tangapena (Fangapena being a clerical error), Ferd. Denis Yvera-pème, and others, Yvera-pèmi, Tangapé, and Tacapé. It is described in Part 2, chapter 28, and Varnhagen (1, 112) gives an illustration of what evidently corresponds with the Cuidarú of the Amazonian tribes. The common tomahawk, a paddle-shaped cutting club, corresponding with the North American weapon, was called Macaná, and on the Amazon as Tamarana.

[3] In scraping and shaving the prisoner about to be eaten, there was possibly some idea of ceremonial purification.

Caput XXIII.

How they danced with me before the huts, wherein they keep their idols
the Tamerka.

Then they led me from the place where they had shaved off
my eyebrows, to before the huts wherein the Tammerka their
idols were, and made round about me a circle in the middle
of which I stood. Two women were with me, and they tied
to one of my legs strings of objects, which rattled,[1] and
they also tied an ornament made of birds' tails, and of square
shape, behind my neck, so that it projected above my head;
it is called in their language Arasoya.[2] Thereupon the
womenkind all began together to sing, and to their time I
was obliged to stamp with the leg to which they had tied
the rattles, so that they rattled in harmony. But the leg
in which I was wounded pained me so badly that I could
hardly stand, for I had not yet been bandaged.

Caput XXIV.

How, after the dance, they took me home to Ipperu Wasu, who was to
kill me.

Now when the dance came to an end, I was handed over
to Ipperu Wasu, who kept me in careful custody. Then he

[1] These bunches of little bells (Cascaveis) were threaded nuts, whose
kernels had been replaced by pebbles: Nieuhoff describes them as made
from "the rind of the fruit Aguai". Making music when the victim
danced, they are compared by old writers with the bells used by the
morris-dancers in Europe.

[2] In the province of S. Paulo there is a mountain of old called Bira-
çoiava, and lately Araçoiáva, or Arassoiyába. The people derive it from
"Araçoyà" (properly Coaraçy), the sun, and "mba", a very general
term, meaning thing, shadow, and so forth: thus the title is "Escondrijo
do Sol" (hiding-place of the sun), and Arasoya may have some similar
signification. Guaiaciaba, "hair of the sun", was a term applied to
Europeans with fair locks.

told me that I still had some time to live. And they brought all their gods that were in the huts, and placed them round about me and said, that these had prophesied, that they would capture a Portuguese. Then said I, These things have no power, and also cannot speak, and they lie (in asserting) that I am a Portuguese, for I am one of the Frenchmen's allies and friends, and the country where I am at home (to which I belong), is called Allemanien. Then they said that I must lie, for if I was the Frenchmen's friend, what was I doing among the Portuguese ? They knew full well that the Frenchmen were just as much the enemies of the Portuguese as they. For the Frenchmen came every year with ships, and brought them knives, axes, looking-glasses, combs, and scissors, and for these they gave them Brazilwood, cotton and other goods, such as featherwork and (red) pepper. Therefore they were their good friends, which the Portuguese had not been. For these had in former years come into the country, and had, in the parts where they were still settled, contracted friendship with their enemies. After that time, they (*i.e.* the Portuguese) had also come to them, and they had in good faith gone to their ships and entered them, in the same manner in which they to the present day did with the French ships. They said moreover that when the Portuguese had collected enough of them in the ship, they had then attacked them and bound them, and delivered them up to their enemies who had killed and eaten them. Some of them also they had shot dead with their guns, and much more had the Portuguese in their haughty presumption done to them, having also often joined with their enemies for the purpose of capturing them in war.

F

Caput XXV.

How those who had captured me bewailed in angry mood, how the
Portuguese had shot their father ; this they would revenge on me.

And they further said that the Portuguese had shot the
father of the two brothers who had captured me, in such
manner that he died, and that they would now revenge their
father's death on me.   Thereupon I asked why they would
revenge this upon me ? I was not a Portuguese ; (adding
that) I had lately arrived there with the Castilians : I had
suffered shipwreck, and I had from this cause remained
among them.

It happened that there was a young fellow of their tribe,
who had been a slave of the Portuguese ; and the savages
among whom the Portuguese live had gone into the Tuppin
Imba's country to make war, and had taken a whole village,
and had eaten the elder inhabitants, and had sold those who
were young to the Portuguese for goods.   So that this young
fellow had also been bartered by the Portuguese, and had
lived in the neighbourhood of Brikioka with his master who
was called Anthonio Agudin,[1] a Gallician.

Those who had captured me had retaken the same slave
about three months before.

Now as he was of their tribe, they had not killed him.
The said slave knew me well and they asked him who I
was.   He said it was true, that a vessel had been lost on
the shore, and the people who had come therein were called
Castilians, and they were friends of the Portuguese.   With
these I had been, further he knew nothing of me.

Now when I heard, and having also understood that there
were Frenchmen among them, and that these were accustomed to arrive there in ships, I always persisted in the
same story, and said that I belonged to the allies of the

_____
[1] A correct Basque name, of which many end with -in.

French, that they were to let me remain unkilled, until such time as the Frenchmen came and recognized me. And they kept me in very careful confinement, as there were several Frenchmen among them who had been left by the ships to collect pepper.

Caput XXVI.

How one of the Frenchmen who had been left by the ships among the savages came thither to see me, and advised them to eat me, as I was a Portuguese.

There was a Frenchman living four miles distant from the huts where I was. Now when he heard the news he proceeded thither, and went into another hut opposite to that wherein I was. Then the savages came running towards me,[1] and said, " Now a Frenchman has arrived here, we shall soon see if you also are a Frenchman or not." I felt glad of this, and I thought, at all events he is a Christian, and he will say everything for the best.

Then they took me in to him naked as I was, and I saw that he was a young fellow, the savages called him Karwattu ware.[2] He addressed me in French, and I of course

[1] As we learn from Yves d'Evreux it was the custom for Europeans to travel with a guide-guard, whom they called Moussacat or Compère. Such is the Ghafir of Arabia and the Abbán of the Somali country, to mention no more.

[2] In chapter xxv, Karwattuware. European names being often unpronounceable to the Tupis, they gave nicknames to every one : in Yves d'Evreux for instance, we find a dragoman called Mingan or porridge. This word is probably Carauáta-g-uára, eater of the wild Bromelia Caraguatá, in Southey (i, 175) Craûta, in Niehoff (*loc. cit.*, 873), Karageata and vulgarly Gravatá ; there is a place of this name in the Bay of Rio de Janeiro. Vasconcellos notices a number of uses to which it is put : one of these is that the hollow leaves collect rain-water to relieve the traveller's thirst. The fruit is of an extreme acidity ; it destroyed the teeth of the unfortunate explorers of the Panama Isthmus, led by Lieut. Strain, U.S. Navy, as I was told by one of the survivors, Dr. Reinhardt, of Campinas, S. Paulo.

understood him not.   The savages stood round about us
and listened.   Now when I could not answer him, he said
to the savages in their language, "Kill and eat him, the
villain, he is a true Portuguese, my enemy and yours."
And this I understood well.   I begged him therefore for
God's sake, that he would tell them not to eat me.   Then he
said : "They want to eat you," upon which I remembered
the words of Jeremiah (cap. xvii.) who says : "Cursed is he
who putteth his trust in man."   And herewith I again went
away from them very sorrowful at heart ; and I had at the
time a piece of linen tied around my shoulders (where could
they have obtained it ?)   This I tore off and threw it before
the Frenchman's feet, and the sun had scorched me severely,
and I said to myself, "If I am to die, why should I preserve
my flesh for another ?"   Then they conducted me back to
the huts where they confined me.   I then went to lie down
in my hammock.   God knows the misery I endured, and
thus I tearfully began to sing the hymn,

> Now beg we of the Holy Ghost
> The true belief we wish for most.
> That He may save us at our end
> When from this vale of tears we wend.[1]

Then they said : "He is a true Portuguese, now he howls,[2]
he dreads death."

[1] Sanctum precemur Spiritum
Verâ beare nos fide,
Ut nos in hac reservet,
In fine nempe vitæ
Hinc quando commigramus
Doloribus soluti.
Kyrie eleison !

[2] The savage is ever
Trained from his tree-locked cradle to his bier,
The fierce extremes of good and ill to brook,
Impassive—fearing but the stain of fear—
A stoic of the woods—a man without a tear.
                    (*Gertrude of Wyoming.*)
Chapt. xli is not very complimentary to Tupi bravery, yet the southern

The above-mentioned Frenchman remained two days there in the huts : on the third day he went on his way. And they had agreed that they would prepare everything, and kill me on the first day after they had collected all things together, and they watched me very carefully, and both young and old mocked and derided me.

Caput XXVII.

How I suffered greatly from toothache.

It happened, when I was thus in distress, that to bear out the saying, " misfortunes never come singly," one of my teeth ached so grievously that I became emaciated from great pain. My master asked me how it was that I ate so little, and I told him that a tooth pained me. Then he came with an instrument made of wood, and wanted to pull it out. I then told him it ached no more : he wanted to pull it out violently.[1] But I resisted so much that he gave up his intention. "Yes," said he, "if I would not eat and

savages, like the northern, held nothing so dastardly and effeminate as outward signs of fearing death (Chapt. xxxvi) ; and no Christian martyr ever died with more constancy and fortitude than these human wild beasts. They held with Charlevoix (Histoire du Paraguay, i, 468) : "Après tout, il faut convenir que les barbares ont la vraie idée du courage, qui consiste plus et qui est moins équivoque dans la constance à souffrir les grands maux, que dans la hardiesse à s'exposer aux plus grands dangers." The defect of this view is that it makes courage a mere matter of nervous insensibility.

[1] Southey (i, 200) remarks, " It is said in the *Noticias* MSS. that the teeth of these people were not liable to decay. But the readiness with which teeth-drawing was recommended in this instance certainly implies a knowledge of tooth-ache." I have never yet seen a savage tribe that did not suffer from this "little misery of human life;" and yet, as a rule, wild men are more careful of their teeth than the civilised. Glas and other writers give interesting accounts of the precautions taken by the Guanches of Tenerife, who for fear of caries would not drink cold water after eating hot food.

become fatter again, they would kill me before the appointed time." God knows how often I have heartily desired that I might, if it were His Godly will, die without the savages perceiving it, that they might not work their will upon me.

Caput XXVIII.

How they took me to their chief king called Konyan Bebe, and how they treated me there.

Several days afterwards they took me to another village, which they call Arirab,[1] to a king named Konyan Bebe,[2]

[1] About ten miles to the east of Ubatúba Mirim is the village of Cairussú, probably that here alluded to. Half-way between the settlements runs the Pisinguara river, separating the provinces of Rio de Janeiro and São Paulo.

[2] Thevet, the cosmographer, writes Quoniambec, and Vasconcellos Cunhambeba, whilst Varnhagen translates it O voar de Mulher, the flying of a women. Cunha is a woman, and here we may note a curious trivial resemblance with γυνὴ, the teterrima causa belli, the Icelandic konu, and the English quean. Bebe means flying, hence the title of Abaré bébé (" flying father") given to a travelling missionary of the sixteenth century—P. Leonardo Nunes, who came to the Brazil in 1549 with Thomé de Souza, and who distinguished himself by his prodigious activity in charitable works. Cunha Bébé was Morubixabaçú (Mburu bicho in Southey), or Great Cacique, of the whole coast between Cabo Frio and the Bertioga, and from him the Ilha dos Porcos, or, as the people will have it, dos Portos, was anciently called Tapéra (ruin, abandoned settlement) de Cunha Bébé. Thevet has left a graphic description of his tall, broad frame, terrible countenance, and wrinkled brows; his legs adorned with rings, his lower lip protruded by a " bung", and his neck encircled with cowries, to which hung in front an enemy's tooth, like the king of Dahome's favourite decoration, or a large shell, also an African ornament. He boasted that he had caused five thousand of his enemies to be killed and eaten, a feat which even Marshal Narvaez might have envied. He carried in his canoe to S. Vincent the venerable F. José de Anchieta, after the latter had been to Iperoyg (Ipperoig, the Sharkwater) on a mission of peace between the Tapúyas of Ubatúba and Larangeiras. It is probable that this saintly personage reconciled him to the Portuguese, for we find him in 1564 assisting Estacio de Sá in expelling the French from Rio de Janeiro.

the principal king over all of them. Many others had assembled at his place and made great rejoicings in their
manner; they also wanted to see me, for he had ordered
that I also should be brought there that day.

Now when I came close upon the huts, I heard a great
noise of singing and blowing of horns, and in front of the
huts were fixed some fifteen heads on stakes. These belonged to a tribe who are also their enemies, and are
called the Markayas,[1] whom they had eaten. As they led
me past them, they told me that the heads were from the
Markayas, who were also their enemies. Then terror pos-
sessed me; I thought, thus they will also do with me.
Now as we were entering the huts, one of those who had
me in their keeping, went before me and spoke with loud
words, so that all the others heard it, "Here I bring the slave,
the Portuguese." And he appeared to think it was something worth seeing, when a man had his enemy in his power.
He said also many other things as is their custom, and then
he led me to where the king sat and drank together with the
others, and had made themselves drunk with the beverage
which they make, called kawawy. He looked savagely at
me, and said, "O our enemy! art thou come?" I said: "I
am come, but I am not your enemy." Then they gave me
also to drink. Now I had heard much of the king Konyan
Bebe, how great a man he was, also a great cannibal at
eating human flesh. And there was one among them who

---

[1] Called Marckayas (chap. xxxvii) and Karayas (? Part 2, chap. xi);
elsewhere Margajas (Margayas), Margaias, Maracás, and Maracuyás, an
insulting name, meaning wild cats (see Introduction). In chapter lii
we find that "Los Markayas" are neighbours and enemies of the Tupiniquins, occupied the coast between Espirito Santo and Rio de Janeiro,
spoke the Tupi tongue, and formed part of the great confederation. De
Lery records their bitter hostility to the Tupinambás of Rio de Janeiro.
In 1557 Villegaignon carried off ten lads of the tribe, aged from eight
to ten years, and presented them to Henri II, who bestowed them upon
M. de Passi and other courtiers. Hence the savages are often alluded to
by the French poets of the sixteenth century.

seemed to be he, and I went up to him and spake to him in the manner of their language, and said : "Art thou Konyan Bebe ? livest thou still ?"[1] " Yes," said he, "I still live." " Well then," said I, "I have heard much of thee, and that thou art so fine a man." Then he arose, and strutted before me with proud conceit, and he had a large round green stone, sticking through the lips of his mouth (as their custom is[2]). They also make white rosaries from

[1] Yves d'Evreux (pp. 31, 96, 221) gives the forms of address as follows :—
Ereiup Chetouasap—Art thou come, O my friend?
Pà—Yes !
Auge-y-po—That's well !—Marapé derere—What is thy name?—
Demoursousain Chetouasap—Art thou hungry, O my friend?
Pà, Chemoursosain—Yes, I am hungry !
Maé pereipotar—What will thou eat ? and so forth.
Alencar borrowing from de Lery (p. 286) says in Iracema (p. 166).
Ere ioubê—Hast thou come ?
Pa·aiotu—Yes, I have come !
Auge-be—Well said !
These specimens add another item to the absurdity of popular greetings all the world over, from the English " how do you do ?" to the Tupi style of asking the new comer " hast thou come ?"

[2] For a full description of this labret, lipstone or mouth-piece, see Part 2, (chap. xv), where four stones are also described. Some tribes wore them of an exaggerated size, hence the early travellers called the Aymoré savages, Botocudos from botoque a bung. The green stones alluded to may have been jade, of which I have seen a specimen in the Brazil, or possibly a crystal of olive-coloured tourmaline, the mineral which, being taken for emeralds, produced such an effect about A.D. 1562, and has named so many Brazilian mountains Serra das Esmeraldas. The labrets were of two kinds, one a round button (botoque), the other a cone varying from two to ten inches in length, with the small end worn downwards, and the upper worked into a crutch or cross-piece fitting the inner lip and preventing its falling out, (Ewbank sketches them. *Life in Brazil*, Appendix, p. 459). I sent home a specimen made of Jatahy gum much resembling a bit of barley sugar. Vancouver (iv, xxxvi) found on the west coast of North America oval labrets of polished fir-wood, from two and a half to three and four-tenths inches in diameter, the latter looking like platters or little dishes. The labret is also an East-African ornament worn in the upper lip by the Wahiáo and other tribes. Cook found it in California, Stedman in Surinam and Belcher amongst the Eskimos who had an upper labret, a lower and two cheek-pieces.

a kind of sea-shell;[1] such are their ornaments: of these the king had also some six fathoms length hanging round his neck. It was by his ornaments I perceived that he must be one of the noblest.

Thereupon he again sat down, and began to question me about what his enemies the Tuppin Ikins and the Portuguese were doing. And he asked further, why I had wanted to fire at them in the district of Brikioka, for he had been informed, that I had served there against them as a gunner. Then I said that the Portuguese had stationed me there and that I was obliged so to do. Upon which he said that I also was a Portuguese, and he spoke of the Frenchman who had seen me as his son, and said, that he who had seen me had stated, that I could not speak with him, and that I was a genuine Portuguese. Then I said, " Yes it is true, I have been so long out of my country that I have forgotten my language." Thereupon he observed, that he had already helped to capture and eat five Portuguese, who had all said that they were Frenchmen, and yet had lied. So that I gave up all hopes of life and resigned myself to God's will; for I heard nothing else from all of them, but that I should die. Then he again began to ask what the Portuguese said of him, they must surely be in terrible fear of him. I said: " Yes," they know much to tell of thee, how thou art wont to wage great war against them, but now they have fortified Brikioka more strongly. " Yes," he said, and therefore he

Nothing can exceed its ugliness except its uncleanliness : " the rume runneth out of the hole that they have in their lips," says Knivett with disgust.

[1] See Part 2, chap. xv, called Mattepin. This is the wampum of the New England " Redskins", also used by the Bube people of Fernando Po off the west coast of Africa. Every where it is made of chipped snail-shells, achatinæ and other species. The Tupins also wore teeth necklaces (Aiucará) taken from monkeys, ferocious beasts or human foes, the spoils of the latter could not be borne unless duly won, and for every new victim a tooth was added.

would catch them now and then in the wood as they had caught me.

I further said to him : "Yes, thy real enemies, the Tuppin Ikins, are equipping twenty-five canoes, and will soon appear and invade thy country ;" as also happened.

The while he so questioned, the others stood and listened. In short he asked me much and told me much ; boasting to me how he had already killed many a Portuguese, and savages besides who had been his enemies. During the time he was thus talking to me, the liquor in the huts was drunk up. Then they moved off to another hut to drink therein also, so that he ceased speaking.

After this those in the other hut began to carry on their jokes and to deride me. The said king's son having tied my legs together in three places, I was made to hop with joined feet through the huts ; at this they laughed and said, "there comes our meat hopping along." Upon this I asked my master (Ipperu Wasu) who had taken me there, whether he had led me thither to be killed. He said no, it was the custom, that foreign slaves were treated in this manner, and they again untied the ropes round my legs, thereupon they walked round about me and grabbed at my flesh, one said the skin of the head belonged to him and another that he claimed the fleshy part of the leg. Then I had to sing to them, and I sang spiritual songs. These I was asked to translate to them in their language, and I said, "I have sung of my God." They said my God was filth, that is in their language, "Teuire."[1] These words hurt me much and I thought, "O merciful God, how long-suffering Thou art !" Now on the next day when all in the village had seen me and had heaped every insult upon me, the king Konyan Bebe told those who had charge of me, that they were to watch me carefully.

Thereupon, when they again led me from out of the huts,

[1] In modern days written Tepoty or Typoty.

and were going to take me to Uwattibi, where they intended
killing me, they called mockingly after me that they would
not fail to appear at my master's hut, to drink over me and
to eat me. But my master always comforted me, saying
that I was not to be killed for the present.

Caput XXIX.

How the twenty-five canoes of the Tuppin Ikins, whereof I had told the
king, arrived, intending to attack the huts wherein I was.

Meanwhile it so happened, that the twenty-five canoes
belonging to the savage tribe of whom the Portuguese are
allies, and who as I also stated previous to my being captured, were desirous of proceeding thither to make war ;
it so happened (I say) that one morning they fell upon the
village.

Now when the Tuppin Ikins were about to attack the
huts, and together began shooting in upon them, those in
the huts became distressed, and the women prepared for
flight.

Then I said to them, "You take me for a Portuguese,
your enemy ; now give me a bow and arrows and let me go
loose, and I will help you to defend the huts." They handed
me a bow and arrows ; I shouted and shot and acted as like
them as I possibly could, and encouraged them to be of
good heart and valorous, and that no harm would come to
them. And my intention was to push through the stockade
which surrounds the huts, and to run towards the others, for
they knew me well, and also were aware that I was in the
village. But they watched me too well. Now when the
Tuppin Ikins saw that they could not succeed, they again
repaired to their canoes and sailed away. When they had
departed, I was imprisoned again.

Caput XXX.

How the chiefs assembled in the evening by moonlight.

About eventide on the day when the others had again gone off, and by moonlight they assembled together on the open space between the huts,[1] and debated among one another, and determined when they would kill me. Placing me also between them they derided and threatened me. I was sad, and looked at the moon, and thought to myself, "O my Lord and my God, assist me through this peril to a peaceful end!" Then they asked me why I so constantly looked at the moon: Then I said to them: "I see by her aspect that she is angry." For the face which is in the moon, appeared even to me to be so terrible (God forgive me this!) that I thought myself, that God and all creatures must be angry with me. Thereupon the king who was to have me killed, called Jeppipo Wasu, one of the kings of the huts, asked me, with whom is the moon angry? I said, "she looks towards thy huts." For these words he began to speak angrily to me. In order to recall the words, I said, "It will not be thy huts, she is angry with the Carios slaves," (which is also the name of a savage tribe). "Yes," said he, "upon them fall every misfortune, so be it." I thought no further about this.

Caput XXXI.

How the Tuppin Ikins had burnt another village called Mambukabe.

The following day news came from a village called Mambukabe, that the Tuppin Ikins, when they had departed from where I lay imprisoned, had attacked it, and that the inhabitants had fled, except a little boy, whom they had

---

[1] The Ocára described in note to chap. xxi.

captured, after which they had set fire to the huts. Then Jeppipo Wasu (who had power of life and death over me, and who treated me very cruelly), as they (the people of Mambukabe) were his friends and allies, repaired thither, to assist them in re-erecting their huts, and for this purpose took with him all his friends from his village. He also had the intention of thence bringing (potter's) clay and root-meal (mandioca) with which to prepare the feast and eat me. And when he left, he ordered him to whom he had presented me, called Ipperu Wasu, to look well after me. Thus they were absent perhaps more than a fortnight, and they prepared every thing there.

Caput XXXII.

How a ship arrived from Brickioka and inquired after me, and they gave a short account of me.

Meanwhile came a ship from the Portuguese of Brickioka, anchored not far from where I was imprisoned, and fired a gun, so that the savages might hear and come to parley.

Now when they became aware of their presence, they said to me, "There come thy friends the Portuguese, and perhaps they desire to know if thou still livest, and they may possibly wish to buy thee." Then I said, "It will probably be my brother," for I supposed that the Portuguese ships which sailed past that part of the country, would inquire after me. Therefore that the savages might not think I was a Portuguese, I told them that I had among the Portuguese another brother who was also a Frenchman. Now when the ship arrived and I said it must be my brother, they would not believe otherwise than that I was a Portuguese, and sailed close enough to the ship to be able to parley. When the Portuguese had asked, how it fared with me, they had answered them, that they were to inquire no further about

me. And the ship proceeded on her course, perhaps they
fancied I was dead. God knows what my feelings were
when I saw the ship sail away! They said among themselves: We have the right man, they already send ships
after him.

Caput XXXIII.

How the king's brother Jeppipo Wasu came from Mambukabe, told me
how his brother and his mother, together with all the rest had
fallen sick, and demanded of me, that I should intercede with my
God, so that they might recover again.

And I every day expected the others who, as stated above,
were away, and were preparing for me. Thereupon one day
I heard a howling in the huts of the king who was absent.
I became alarmed, and I thought they had come back, (for
it is the custom of the savages, that when one of them returns, after having been away no longer than four days, his
friends shout with joy). Shortly after the shouting, one of
them came to me and said, "thy part-owner has come and
says, that the others have fallen very sick." Then I rejoiced
and thought, "Here God desires to do something." A
little while thereafter my part-owner's brother, entering the
hut wherein I was, sat down by me and began to cry, and
said that his brother, his mother, and his brother's children
had all fallen sick together, and his brother had sent him
to me and he was to tell me: that I should intercede with
my God, so that they might become sound again. He also
said: "My brother imagines that thy God must be angry."
I replied, "Yes, my God in angry, because he wants to eat
me, and he has gone to Mambukabe and he is making
ready there." And quoth I to him, "You declare that I
am a Portuguese and yet I am none;" and I said to him:
"Go hence to thy brother, let him return to his huts,"
(adding) that I would then pray to my God for his recovery

Thereupon he told me that he was too ill to come, and that he knew well and had observed how if I but desired it, he would become well. And I told him, he was to wait until he was strong enough to come home to his huts, then he should be completely restored. He went back again with the answer to Mambukabe, which is four miles (leagues) from Uwattibi where I was.

Caput XXXIV.

How the sick king, Jeppipo Wasu, returned home again.

After several days, they all of them came home together sick. Then he (Jeppipo) ordered me to be led to his huts, and told me how they had been stricken with illness, and that I had well known it, for he still remembered that I had said the moon looked angrily towards the huts. When I heard these words from him, I thought to myself: "Surely it must have been through God's providence, that I last night, as aforesaid, spoke about the moon." I was in great joy at this and thought: "To-day God is with me."

Then I told him that it was true, because he wanted to eat me, though I was not his enemy, and therefore had misfortune come upon him. Upon which he said that nothing should happen to me if it turned out that he recovered. I knew not how best to pray to God, and thought, "if they regain health they will yet kill me, but if they die, the others will say, let us kill him, before more misfortune happens on his account," as they had already begun to say. I submitted the matter to God. He (Jeppipo) begged me hard that they might again recover. I walked round them, and laid my hands upon their heads as they desired me to do. God would not have it so, they began to die, first died one of their children, then his mother died, an old woman who intended baking the pots, wherein were to be made the beverages with which I was to be eaten.

After some days one of his brothers died, then another child, and another brother, who as beforesaid had brought me the news that they had fallen ill.

Now when he saw, that his children, his mother and his brothers were gone, he feared much, that he and his wives would also die. Then he said that I was to tell my God to withdraw his anger, so that he might live. I comforted him greatly, and told him there was no danger, but that when he recovered again he was not to think of killing me. Thereupon he answered " No," and also commanded those in the huts that nobody should injure me, or threaten to eat me. He nevertheless remained ill for a time, but he was (at last) restored to health, together with one of his wives, who was also ill. There died, however, about eight of his friends, besides others, who had treated me cruelly. Now there were yet two other kings from two other huts, the one named Vratinge Wasu, the other Kenrimakui. Vratinge Wasu had dreamt, that I had appeared before him, and had told him, that he was to die. And he came in the morning early to me and complained thereof to me, I said " No," he was not to be afraid, but that he also was not to think of killing me, or advise others to do it. Then he answered " no," as they, who had captured me would not kill me, so he also would do me no harm, and even if they killed me, he would not eat of me.

In like manner the other king Kenrimakui, had also dreamt of me, a dream which terrified him much, and he called me to his hut, and gave me to eat and then complained of it to me, and said, he had once been to war, and had captured a Portuguese, and had killed him with his own hands, and had eaten of him so plentifully, that his chest (stomach) had ever since been delicate. And (he declared that) he would eat of no other. So now he had dreamt of me such a terrible dream that he thought he was also to die. Him also I bade be of good cheer, but he was to take care never to eat human flesh again.

And the old women in the several huts who had also tormented me cruelly, tearing me, beating, and threatening to eat me, these same then called me " Scheraeire,"[1] that is, " my son—thou wilt surely not let us die. When we thus treated thee, we thought thou wert one of the Portuguese, whom we so much hate. We have also had several Portuguese and eaten them, but their God was not so angry as thine. By this we now see, that thou canst not be a Portuguese."

Thus they left me alone for a while, not knowing quite what to make of me, whether I was a Portuguese or a Frenchman. They said I had a red beard like a Frenchman, and though they had also seen Portuguese, yet these had all black beards.

After this panic, when one of my masters recovered again, they spoke no more to me about eating, but guarded me just as strictly, not allowing me to go about by myself.

Caput XXXV.

How the Frenchman who had commanded the savages to eat me, returned, and I begged him to take me with him. But my masters would not part with me.

Now the Frenchman Karwattu Ware (of whom I have before said, that he went away from me with the savages, who accompanied him, and who were friends of the Frenchmen) had remained there to collect the goods which the savages produce, namely (red) pepper, and a kind of feathers which they also have.

But when he was travelling back to that part of the country where the ships arrived, called Mungu Wappe and

[1] Shé (in Portuguese written Xé) is " I " or " my" and Táyra, Son, which in composition becomes She-r-áyra.

Iterroenne,[1] he had to pass through the place where I was. When he set out he expected nought but that they would eat me ; he had also commanded them so to do ; and, as he had been absent for some time, he little expected to find me otherwise than dead.

Now when he again came to me in the huts, he spoke to me in the savage tongue, and at that time I went about un-fettered. Then he asked me if I still lived, when I said " Yes, I thanked God, that he had preserved me so long." Perhaps he might have heard from the savages how this had happened, and I called him privately to a spot where the savages could not hear what I said, and told him that he saw plainly that God had preserved my life, also that I was no Portuguese, but a German, and had through ship-wreck with the Spaniards, come among the Portuguese, that he also might now tell the savages, how I had informed him that I belonged to his friends and allies, and that he desired to take me with him to where the ships arrived. For I feared that, if he did not do this, they would yet con-

[1] Mungu Wappe is probably Mamanguápe, not an uncommon name for villages and meaning a kind of wasp : there is a stream so called in the valley of the northern Parahyba. Iteroenne in chap. iv is called Iteronne and Iterone : it is the Nhiteroi of Jaboatam, the Nithero of Vasconcellos and the modern Niheroy, Nicteroy, Nictheroy or Nitherohy, usually translated " hidden water", but meaning according to Varnhagen (ii, 346) cold water, from Meteró (cold) and y or yg. At present it is applied to the town of Bragança popularly Praia Grande, which lies oppo-site the metropolis of the Brazil, and is the capital of " Rio Province." The authors use it for the Bay, now called Rio de Janeiro, which, how-ever, was more generally known as Genabara, Ganabara and especially Guanabara. The latter, says Varnhagen (i, 229) is probably an error of Guá-ná-pará for Paraná-guá, Sack of the sea, bay or bight, and is still preserved in Brazilian geography. Both Nictheroy and Guanabara are charmingly descriptive terms, supplanted by the unmeaning " Bay of Rio." The settlement afterwards called Bragança, dates from A.D. 1557 : in the days of Hans Stade it was held by the French Hugue-nots under Villegaignon, and they founded a colony which they called somewhat prematurely " La France Antarctique."

sider these statements as lies, and some time or other when in anger they might kill me.

And I made him an admonition in their savage language, and I asked if he had not a Christian heart in his bosom, or had thought that after this life there was no other, when he had so strongly advised that I should be killed ? Thereupon he began to repent and said, he had believed me to be no other than one of the Portuguese, who were such great villians, that if they were ever to catch any of them (the French) in that province of Brazil they would hang them at once—which is true ; also, said he, that they had to give way to the savages, and were obliged to be satisfied with the manner in which they proceeded with their enemies, for they were the hereditary enemies of the Portuguese.

According to my request, he told the savages that he had not well recognised me the first time, but that I was from Germany, and belonged to their friends, and that he wanted to take me with him to where the ships generally arrived. Then my masters said, " No ; " they would give me up to nobody unless my own father or brother came there, and brought them a ship-load of goods, namely, hatchets, mirrors, knives, combs, and scissors, and gave these to them ; for they had found me in the enemy's country, and I belonged to them.

When the Frenchman heard this, he told me that he well heard they would not part with me. Thereupon, I begged him, for God's sake, that he might send for me and take me to France in the first ship that might arrive. This he promised me, and he told the savages that they were to take care of, and not to kill me, for my friends would come soon to fetch me. With this he went away.

Now when the Frenchman departed, one of my masters, named Alkindar Miri (not he who was sick), asked me what Karwattuwara (which was the name of the Frenchman in the savage language) had given to me : if he was one of

my countrymen. I said " Yes." Quoth he, " why has he
not given thee a knife, which thou mightest have given to
me," and he became angry. Afterwards, when they all
became well again, they once more began to murmur about
me, and said among themselves that the Frenchmen were,
after all, not worth more than the Portuguese; so I began
to fear harm again.

Caput XXXVI.

How they ate a prisoner and led me thereto.

But it happened after several days that they wanted to
eat a prisoner, in a village called Tickquarippe¹ about six
miles [leagues] from where I lay imprisoned; so several out
of the hut where I was, also went, and led me with them,
and the slave whom they were going to eat belonged to a
tribe called Marckaya, and we sailed thither in a canoe.

Now when the time came for their wanting to drink over
him (for it is their custom, when they intend eating a man,
they make a drink from a root called kawi,² and when this
is drunk they afterwards kill him), on the eve of the day
when they intended drinking to his death, I went to him
and said to him, " Everything is prepared for thy death."
He laughed and said, " Yes." Now the cords wherewith
they bind the prisoners, called Mussurana, are made of cotton,

¹ Southey (i, 207) suggests " Iguarippe," but I found no village of that
name near Ubatúba. The distance would correspond with the Juqui-
riqueré River (see Preface), formerly known as the Curupaçe.

² See chapter xvii, Southey (i, 245) tells us that in the Curamuru
poem the liquor is called " Catimpoeira." The latter word, however,
means the dregs of Abati-yg, or maize-beer, and in the modern dialect,
" Cotimbao," a corruption, is applied to dirt in the tobacco-pipe, or dirt
generally. Cauïm is a word extended to many drinks, even civilised.
Thus Cauïm-pyranga (red) is wine from Europe; Cauïm-tata (fire),
spirits, the " fire-water " of the north. The latter was also called Tiquira,
meaning properly the distillation from Manioc.

and are more than a finger thick. "Yes," said he, he was
well prepared with everything, only the Mussurana was
not quite long enough (for it wanted about six fathoms in
length). "Yes," said he, "with us they are better ; " and
he spake in such manner as if he were going to a festival.

Now I had with me a book in the Portuguese language.
The savages had taken it from a ship which, with the
assistance of the French they had captured. This they gave
to me.

And I went away from the prisoner and read the book,
and I felt pity for him. Thereafter I again went to him
and spoke with him (for the Portuguese have also this same
tribe of Markaya for friends), and said, " I am also a
prisoner, as well as thou, and have not come hither that I
might eat of thee, but my masters have brought me with
them." Then, said he, he knew well that we eat not of
human flesh.

Further I told him he was to be of good cheer, for they
would only eat his flesh, but his soul would proceed to
another place, whither our countrymen's souls also proceeded, and where there was much happiness. He then
asked if this were really true. I said " Yes." But, quoth
he, he had never seen God. I said he would see Him in the
next life. Now when I had finished this discourse with
him, I went from him.

The night of the same day when I had spoken with him,
a great wind arose and blew so terribly that it carried off
pieces of the hut roofs. Then the savages began to be
angry with me, and said in their language, " Appo meiren
geuppawy wittu wasu Immon"—the bad man, the wizard
now makes the wind to come, for during the day he looked
into the thunder-skins (Donnerheude), meaning the book
which I had. And they said that I did it because the slave
was our (the Portuguese) friend, and that I, perhaps, intended thereby to hinder the feast through bad weather.

I prayed to the Lord God and said, "Lord, thou hast protected me thus far, protect me further," for they grumbled much at me.

Now when the day broke, the weather became fine, and they drank, and were well pleased. Then I went to the slave and said that the great wind was God, and that he wanted to take him away. Thereupon, the next day, he was eaten. How this is done you will see in the last chapters.

Caput XXXVII.

What happened on the home-voyage when they had eaten him.

When the feast had been held, we again sailed to our habitations, and my masters took some of the roast flesh with them, and we were three days on the home voyage, which may generally be done in about one day, but it blew and rained much. They therefore told me on the first day, when, in the evening, they were making huts[1] in the wood, wherein to rest, that I was to cause the rain to stop. There was a boy with us who had still a bone of the slave's leg, whereon there was left some flesh, which he ate. I bade the boy to throw the bone away. Then he and the others became angry with me, saying that it was their proper food. I let the matter rest there. We were three days on the journey.

When we arrived within a quarter of a mile (league) from the habitations, we could get no further, for the waves rose high. We drew the canoe on shore, and thought that the next day the weather would be fine, and that we could then take the canoe home; but it was equally stormy. Then they were of opinion to go by land, and afterwards, when the weather should become fine, to fetch the canoe. As we

---

[1] The modern Brazilians are remarkably skilful in setting up these travelling huts.

were about to leave, they ate, and the boy finished gnawing the flesh from off the bone. Thereupon he threw it away, and we started by land, and the weather became fine again. " Well," said I, " you would not believe me when I told you that my God was angry, and therefore the boy ate the flesh from the bone." "Yes," said the others, "had he but eaten it so that I had not seen it, the weather would have remained fine." Thus the matter ended.

When I again arrived there in the huts, Alkindar, who also had a share of me, asked me if I had now seen how they disposed of their enemies. Then I said "Yes, that you eat them appears terrible to me. The killing is not so terrible." " Yes," said he, " that is our custom, so we also do to Portuguese."

This same Alkindar was very spiteful to me, and would have been glad if he to whom he had given me had killed me ; for, as you have read before, Ipperu Wasu had presented a slave to him to kill, so that he should thereby obtain another name. Therefore Alkindar had promised him in return to present him with the first slave whom he might capture. Now as this did not appear to succeed in my case, he would gladly have killed me himself, but his brother prevented him in every way, for he feared that greater plagues might come upon him.

This same Alkindar, before the others led me to where they ate the prisoner, had once more threatened to eat me. When I came back again, he had, whilst I was absent, suffered from an eye-ache. He was obliged to lie still, and for a time he could not see. He told me constantly that I should speak with my God, so that his eyes might again become well. Then I said, " Yes, " but that he should afterwards meditate no evil against me. He replied " No." Then, after several days he was again restored to health.

Caput XXXVIII.

How a ship was again sent after me by the Portuguese.

Now during the fifth month of my stay with them, there
arrived another ship from the island of S. Vincent, for the
Portuguese are accustomed to sail well armed to their
enemy's country, and to barter with them, giving them
knives and reaping hooks (hepen) for mandioca meal, of
which the same savages there have much in various places,
and the Portuguese, who have many slaves for sugar cultivation, procure this meal, wherewith to feed these same.
And when the ships barter in such manner with these
savages, two or three of the latter arrive in a canoe, and
deliver the goods to them at the greatest possible distance. Then they declare what they want to have in return,
which is given to them by the Portuguese. But whilst the
two are near the ship, a number of full canoes keep in the
offing to look on, and when the trading is completed, the
savages oftentimes approach alongside, and skirmish with
the Portuguese and shoot arrows at them, after which they
again paddle away.

The before-mentioned ship's crew fired off a gun, so
the wild men might hear that a ship was there, and they
sailed thither. Then it appears that they had asked after
me, if I still lived. They, my captors, had answered " Yes."
The Portuguese had thereupon demanded to see me, for
they had a chest full of goods, brought by my brother, also
a Frenchman, who was with them in the ship.

Now there was with the Portuguese in the ship a Frenchman called Claudio Mirando, who had formerly been my
companion; this same I called my brother. He said, " I
will, perhaps, be in the vessel and inquire after you", for
he had already been on one voyage there.

And they returned again from the ship to shore, and told

me that my brother had once more come, and had brought
me a chest full of wares, and wished much to see me. Then
I said, "Lead me to within a certain distance of them; I
will speak with my brother—the Portuguese understand
us not—and I will tell him that he advise our father when
he returns home to come with a ship and bring plenty of
goods with him, and fetch me." This plan appeared satisfactory to them; but they feared that the Portuguese might
understand us, for they had in prospect a great war, which
they intended carrying out in the month of August, in the
country of Brikioka, where I was captured. I well knew
all their plans; therefore they feared lest I should tell something thereof. But I said, "No; the Portuguese do not
understand mine and my brother's language." Then they
carried me to within about a stone's throw of the ship,
naked, as I always went among them. I addressed those
in the ship, and said "God, the Lord, be with you, my dear
brothers. Let one alone speak to me, and let them hear
not otherwise than that I am a Frenchmen." Then began
one called Johann Senches,[1] a Boschkeyer whom I knew
well, and said to me, "My dear brother, for your sake have
we come hither in the ship, and we knew not if you were
living or dead, for the first ship brought no news of you.
Now the Captain Brascupas,[2] at Sanctus, has commanded us
to discover if you were still alive, and when we should hear
of your being alive, we must learn if they will sell you, and

[1] Juan Sanchez, a Vizcaino.

[2] See chapters viii and xiii. Braz Cubas, "Fidalgo da Caza d'El Rey"
was a noted man in his time, and travelled extensively over the new
Conquests. In 1543 he founded the Santa Caza de Misericordia, a hos-
pital for distressed seamen at (Todos os) Santos, here "Sanctus," which
thus acquired its name, and which, as the port of S. Vicente lost its
prestige, became the principal harbour of the Captaincy. In 1560 Braz
Cubas built a fort for the protection of the new town. In 1592 he died
at Santos, aged 85, and was buried in the Matriz, or mother church
of his own settlement. I have seen his tomb which is near the high
altar, and Varnhagen (i, 453) gives the epitaph.

if not, we must see whether we cannot capture several for whom to exchange you."

Then I said, " Now may God in eternity reward you, for I am here in great fear and danger, and I know not yet what they will do. They would probably have eaten me before this, if God had not wonderfully prevented it." Further I told them, " They will not sell me to you, therefore think not of it, and do not in any way shew otherwise than that I am a Frenchman, and for God's sake give me some wares, knives and fishing-hooks." This they did, and one went with a canoe to the ship and fetched them.

Now when I saw that the savages would not allow me to speak further with them, I said to the Portuguese, take heed, they have a war in view against Brikioka. Then they told me that their friendly savages were also preparing, and would attack the same village wherein they kept me ; and they bade me be of good heart, God would do everything for the best. As I well saw that they could not assist me, " Yes," said I, " inasmuch as my sins have merited this, it is better that God punish me here than in the next world, and pray ye to God that he may see me out of my misery."

Therewith, I commended them to God the Lord, and they wished to speak further with me ; but the savages would no longer permit me to parley with them, and again sailed back with me to the huts.

Then I took the knives and fishing hooks, which I gave to them saying, " All this my brother the Frenchman has given to me." Thereupon they asked me what it all was that my brother had spoken to me. I said that I had commanded my brother to try and escape from the Portuguese, and proceed to our native country and to bring a ship full of many goods, and to fetch me, for you are good men and treat me well, wherefore I would reward you when the ship shall come. And I had in such manner at all times to conciliate them as best I could, and this pleased them mightily.

Then they said to one another, " He must certainly be a Frenchman, let us henceforward treat him better." Thus I continued among them for a time, and told them, " A ship will soon come for me," and that they were to treat me well. After this they led me now and again into the forest, and when they had any work to do, I was obliged to help them.

Caput XXXIX.

How they had a slave among them who constantly lied about me, and would willingly have seen them kill me at once, and how the same was killed and eaten in my presence.

Now among them was a slave belonging to a tribe called the Carios, who are also enemies of the savages that are friends of the Portuguese. This same had been captured by the Portuguese and had then run away from them. Those who escape to them they do not kill, unless they commit some particular crime; but they hold them as their slaves, bound to serve them.

The said Cario (Carijó) had been three years among these Tuppin Imbas, and said that he had seen me among the Portuguese, and that I had shot several times at the Tuppin Imbas, when they had gone thither to make war.

Now the Portuguese had several years ago shot one of their kings, which king, the Cario said, I had shot, and he constantly urged them to kill me, for I was the real enemy, and he had seen it; yet he lied altogether, for he had been three years among them, and only a year had passed after my arrival at Sanct Vincente, whence he had escaped. And I constantly prayed to God that he might protect me from these lies.

So it happened about the year 1554, during the sixth month of my captivity, that the Cario fell sick, and his master who owned him begged me to help him, that he

might get well again and catch game, bringing something
for us to eat, especially as I knew well that when he brought
him anything, he also gave me thereof.   But that if I
thought that he would not recover again, he would give him
to a good friend, who might kill him and gain a name by
him.

And in such manner he had been about nine or ten days
sick.   Now they have the teeth of an animal which they call
Backe,[1] one of these (teeth) they sharpen, and then they cut
with it through the skin where the blood is sluggish, and it
runs out.   This, with them, is equivalent to our cupping.

Of these said teeth I took one and meant therewith to
open the middle vein.[2]   But I could not pierce it therewith
as the tooth was too blunt, and they stood round about me.
When I again went away from him and saw that it was useless, they asked me if he would recover.   I told them that
I had not succeeded, and that no blood had come, as they
had well seen.   " Yes," they said, " he will die, we will,
therefore, ere he dies, strike him dead."   I said, " No, do
not this, he may perhaps recover."   But it availed not, they
dragged him before King Uratinge's huts, and two of them
held him, for he was so sick, that he knew not what they
were going to do with him.   And so came the one to whom
he had been given to kill, and struck him on the head, so
that the brain sprang out, then they left him lying before
the huts and wished to eat him.   I told them not to do this,
as he had been sick, and they might also fall ill.   Therefore,
they knew not what to do.   But one came out of the hut
wherein I was, and called to the women to make a fire near
the dead man, and he cut his head off—for his eye and
appearance were loathsome from his disease, so he threw

---

[1] In p. 2, chap. ix, this rodent is more correctly written Pacca. The
Noticia do Brazil gives Paquá, but the name of the well-known cœ-
logenous animal is now generally pronounced Páca.

[2] O medici, mediam pertundite venam !—*Juvenal.*

the head away, and singed the skin off the body at the fire.[1]
Then he cut him up and divided him equally with the others,
as is their custom, and ate him all but the head and bowels,
of which they had a loathing, as he had been sick.

Thereafter I went now and again through the huts; in
one they broiled the feet, in another the hands,[2] and in a
third, pieces of the trunk. Then I told them, how that the
Cario whom they were there broiling, and were going to eat,
had at all times lied against me, and had said that I had shot
several of their friends when I was with the Portuguese,
and in this he had lied, for he had never seen me. You know
well, I continued, that he was several years among you, and
never was ill, but now on account of the lies which he told
about me, my God has become angry, and has stricken him
with sickness, and has put into your minds that you should
kill him and eat him. So will my God do unto all wicked
men who have worked me harm, and who would further injure me. At such words they were much terrified. I thank
Almighty God, that he, in everything shewed himself to me
so powerful and so gracious.

I THEREFORE BEG THE READER that he will take notice of
my writing. For I trouble myself not thus, in order that
I am desirous of composing something new, but solely to
bring to light the vouchsafed mercies of God.

And thus the time drew near when they wanted to go to
war, for which they had prepared themselves during the

---

[1] This disgusting scene reminds us of old Thevet, " Ceste canaille
mange ordinairement chair humaine comme nous ferions du mouton."

[2] The hands are everywhere considered an especial dainty. Every one
records from Vasconcellos (i, § 49), the story of the old woman, who
being asked by a Jesuit when she was at the point of death, if he
could bring her a little sugar, or something nice, replied, " O my
grandson, I have no stomach for anything. There is but one thing I
fancy. If I had the little hand of a tender little Tapuya boy, I think
I could just pick the little bones, but woe is me, there is nobody to go
out and shoot one for me ! "

three previous months. So I hoped constantly, that when
they went away, they would leave me at home with the
women, and that thus I might escape during their absence.

Caput XL.

How a French ship arrived, and traded with the savages for cotton and
Brazil-wood, to which ship I had lief gone, but it was not intended
by God.

About eight days before they purposed setting forth to
war, a French ship had arrived eight miles (leagues) off
at a harbour which the Portuguese call Rio de Jenero,[1]
and in the savage language Iteronne. There the French
are used to load Brazil-wood, so they now also came with
their boat near the village where I was, and took in exchange
from the natives pepper, monkeys, and parrots.[2] One
came out of the boat on shore, who understood the savage
tongue, he was named Jacob, and he traded with them. I
begged him to take me with him on board the ship, but my
masters said " No," they would not send me away in such
manner, but they wanted to have many goods for me. Then
I said to them that they were to carry me themselves to the
vessel, as my friends would give them enough goods. They
said " No, they are not thy real friends."

" For those who are here with the boat would have given
thee a shirt, as thou art naked, but they heed thee not"
(which was true). I replied, they will clothe me when I

---

[1] The Spanish form of Janeiro. The "River," or "Bay of January,"
which was known by this misnomer when Martim Affonso touched at it
on April 30, 1831, was so called from the day of its discovery by Gonçalo Coelho, and Amerigo Vespucci.

[2] When Boccacio represented this at the time of the Annunciation, the
people had not even heard of a parrot, he forgets that the African species
was well-known at Rome, and neglects his Persius.

" Quis expedivit psittaco suum χαῖρε ?"

get to the big ship. They said the ship would not sail away for the present, as they had first to go to war, but that when they came back they would bear me to it. And so now the boat was about to sail away again, for it had been anchored one night at the village.

Now when I saw that they were about to sail off again in the boat, I thought, " O Thou Gracious God, if the ship now also sail away, and take me not with it, I shall yet perish among them, for it is a people wherein no faith can be placed." With this thought I went out of the hut, towards the water, and they perceived it, and rushed after me. I ran before them, and they tried to catch me. The first who came up to me I struck away from me, and the whole village was after me ; yet I escaped them and swam to the boat. Now when I wished to get into it, the Frenchmen pushed me off, saying that if they took me away with them against the will of the savages, these might rise against them and become their enemies also. Then I sadly swam back to shore again, and thought, " Now I see it is God's will that I remain longer in misery." And if I had not tried to escape, I should afterwards have thought that it was my fault.

When I returned to the shore, they were joyful and said, " Now he comes back again." Then I reproached them and said, " Think you that I would so escape you. I have been to the boat and have told my countrymen that they are to prepare against the time when ye come back from the war and bring me (to them), and (they are to) collect a good many wares, and give them to you." This pleased them well, and they were once more satisfied.

Caput XLI.

How the savages set forth to war, and took me with them, and what happened on the expedition.

Four days thereafter, several canoes which were going to the war assembled by the village where I was. Then the chief, Konyan Bebe, also arrived there with his (boats), and my master said that he would take me with him. I proposed that he should leave me at home, and he would, perhaps, have done so, but Konyan Bebe declared that he must take me in their company. I allowed them to see that I went unwillingly, so that they might not suspect (as they would have done) if I had gone willingly with them, that I would try to escape them when they arrived in their enemies' country, and that they might keep watch over me less strictly. It was also my plan, if they had left me at home, to have escaped to the French ships.

But they took me with them, and they were thirty-eight canoes strong, each manned with eighteen, more or less, and some of them had prophesied about the war, with their idols, with dreams,[1] and with other foolery, according to their custom, so that they were well-disposed for the undertaking, and their intention was to proceed to the district of Brickioka, where they had captured me, and to hide themselves in the forest round about the place, and to take with them those who in such manner might fall into their hands.

And when we began this expedition it was in the year 1554, about the thirteenth day of August. Now in this month, as before-stated, a kind of fish, called in the Portuguese language Doynges, in Spanish, Liesses, and in the

---

[1] Perhaps it was with them as with the people concerning whom it was said " Sabini quod volunt somniant." This seems to have been effected after the practice of some years by the author of " Les Rêves et les moyens de les diriger." Paris, Amyot, 1867.

native language Bratti, pass from the sea to the fresh waters, therein to spawn ; and the savages call this season Pirakien. They then generally go to war on both sides, their enemies as well as themselves, in order to catch and to eat the fish on their journey; and on the voyage thither they proceed slowly, but on the return as quickly as they can.[1]

Now I always hoped that those who are friends of the Portuguese would also be on the war-path. For they also intended invading the other's country, as the Portuguese in the ship had before told me.

They constantly asked me during the voyage, whether they would capture anybody. I said, " Yes," that I might not anger them. I also told them that the enemies would meet us ; so we lay one night in a place which is also called Uwattibi.[2] Here we caught many of the fish Bratti, which are as large as a good-sized pike. And it blew strongly during the night, therefore they talked much with me, and asked me many questions, when I said that this wind blew over many dead men. And it so happened that another party of them had proceeded through the country up a river called the Paraibe.[3] " Yes," said they, " they have attacked the enemy's country close by, and several of them

---

[1] An invariable custom of savages, like asses returning to their stalls. The European traveller must therefore be very careful not to reserve for the home journey anything worth observing. I have learnt this by hard experience.

[2] The modern Ubatuba, for which see Preface.

[3] In Part II, chapter iv, Parabibe. This is probably the Parahybuna River, the north-eastern fork of the Parahyba, which rises in the western counterslope of the Serra do Mar, or eastern Ghauts, about twelve miles inland from Ubatuba. Varnhagen (i, 288) makes Paráhiba, Parnahiba, or Paranahiba, to mean Bad River, opposed to Pará Catú, Good River. Parahybuna would thus signify Bad Black River, from " Pará," the sea; "aib", bad ; and "una," black. As early as 1572, English settlers occupied the Parahyba for five years till expelled by the Governor of St. Sebastian, and Southey remarks (i, 318) that had not this contretemps occurred, " in another generation the Anglo-Tupi ' mamalucos'

H

have been killed, (which, as I afterwards learned, had really happened).

Now when we were within a day's journey (of the place) whence they intended carrying out their plan, they bivouacked in a wood on an island which is called San Sabastian[1] by the Portuguese; but the savages call it Meyenbipe.

As evening came on, the chief called Konyan Bebe went through the camp in the forest, harangued (his men), and said that they had now arrived close to the enemy's country, that everyone was to remember the dream which he would dream that night, and that they were to take care and have lucky dreams. When this speech was finished, they danced with their idols until night, then they slept. When my master lay down, he said that I was also to try and dream propitiously. I replied that I placed but little faith in dreams; as they were false. " So bring about, nevertheless, with thy God," said he, " that we capture some enemies."

Now when the day broke the chiefs assembled around a cauldron full of stewed fish, which they ate, and recounted their dreams, in so far as that they had well pleased them. Some danced with the idols, and they were willing to set forth early on the same day for their enemy's country, to a place called Boywassu Kange.[2] There they would then abide until evening came.

might have been found dangerous neighbours." I certainly cannot imagine a more terrible breed: the proverb says

Un' Inglese italianato
È un diavolo incarnato:

But what would be the Anglo-Tupi?

[1] So termed because discovered on that Saint's day, January 20. The native name Meyenbipe (in chapter xlii, Meyen) is quite forgotten. For an account of it see Preface.

[2] Properly Boy-assú cánga, the " big Boa's head," from Boya, boia, or boi, a cobra, a python, a snake generally, whence our "boa." Thus the large Brazilian python is called Gyboia, from " gy " an axe, and the scorpion (Anchieta, loc. cit. § xvii), is Bóiquíba for Kiýba (i.e., Coluber-pediculus, Jaguára Kiýba, or Jaguar-louse, being a flea). Canga

Now when we had set forth from the place where we had passed the night, named Meyenbipe, they asked me once more what my presentiments were. Then I said at haphazard, " by Boywassu Kange the enemy will meet us, be but brave." At this Boywassu Kange it was my intention to have escaped from them, when we had arrived there, for we were six miles (leagues) distant from the place where they had captured me.

Now as we in such manner sailed along the coast, we also saw canoes which approached from behind an island to meet us. Thereupon they cried, " Here also come our enemies, the Tuppin Ikins." But they tried to hide themselves, with their canoes, behind a rock, so that the others might pass them unawares. They soon saw us, and turned to escape homewards, and we rowed after them as fast as possible, for some four hours, when we caught them up, and there were five canoes full, all from Brickioka. I knew them all, one with another. There were six Mammelucks in one of the five canoes. These had been baptised, and two of them were brothers, one called Diego de Praga, the other Domingos de Praga. The two opposed great resistance, one with a blow-pipe, the other with a bow, and both defended themselves two whole hours against thirty odd

is the composite contraction for Acanga, a head. The name now generally written " Boisucanga" is preserved in a rocky point west of St. Sebastian, projecting southwards, and fronting the Alcatrazes group. It is about 30 miles (in the text 6 meilen), from the Barra di Bertioga, and has been mentioned in the Preface.

I said that we have taken the word "Boa" from the new world, where there are pythons, and not boas, and have applied it to a native of the old world. It may here also be noted that the North American rattlesnake story, in which a fang fixed in a boot killed several men successively, and highly interested our artless youth-tide, may be found in the Noticia do Brazil (chapter iii), about a " Gereraça" (Jararáca) snake duly recorded as having happened in the Capitania dos Ilheos. Of course it is a fable, as the poison gland would have been destroyed, or rendered harmless.

canoes of ours. Now when they had exhausted their arrows, the Tuppin Imba attacked them, captured them, and several were at once killed or shot. The two brothers were not hurt; but two of the six Mammelucks were severely wounded, and also several of the Tuppin Ikins, among whom was a woman.

Caput XLII.

How they disposed of the prisoners on the return voyage.

It was two good miles (leagues), out at sea, away from the land, where they (the enemies) were captured; and they (the victors) hastened, as fast as they could, back, in order to encamp upon the shore where we lay the night before. Now, when we arrived at the land of Meyen, it was evening, and the sun was about to set. Thereupon, they led their prisoners, each one his own, into his hut. Those who had been badly wounded they at once despatched and cut them in pieces according to their custom, and broiled[1] the flesh. Among those who were roasted that night were two Mammelucks who were Christians. The one was a Portuguese named George Ferrero,[2] the son of a Captain who had had him by a native woman. The other was named Hieronymus,[3] who was caught by a savage that belonged to the hut wherein I was, and his name was Parwaa. The same fried Hieronymus during the night at about a step's distance from where I lay. The said Hieronymus (may God have his soul) was a blood relation of Diego de Praga.

That same evening, when they had lain down, I went to the

---

[1] The frame-work for broiling flesh was called "Boucan"; whence our buccaneers. See chapter xlv, and Part II, chapter xi, where the process of boucaning meat is described.

[2] Jorge Ferreira.   [3] Jeronymo.

huts in which they kept the two brothers, purporting to speak
with them, for they had been my good friends at Brickioka,
where I had been captured. They asked me whether they
also would be eaten. I said that they must leave that to the
will of our Heavenly Father, and of his dear Son Jesus
Christ, who suffered on the cross for our sins, and in whose
name we were baptised with him unto death. " In him,"
said I, " I also believe, and he himself has also preserved
me so long among them, and whatever Almighty God does
unto us, therewith we must remain content."

Further the two brothers asked me how it fared with
their cousin Hieronymus. I told them that he lay before
the fire, and was roasting, and that I had also seen a piece
of Ferrero's son eaten. Then they wept. I comforted
them again, and told them that they knew well that I had
now been about eight months¹ among them (the savages),
and that God had yet preserved me. " This he will also do
by you, trust him." Further I said, " I ought to feel this
much more than you, for I am from a foreign land, and
not accustomed to the terrible deeds of these people ; but
you have been born and bred here in the country. " Yes,"
said they. I had become so callous, though, by misery that
I no longer felt it.

Now when I was thus conversing with them, the savages
ordered me to go from them into my hut, and asked what
matter I had to speak so long to them about. This made
me sorry that I had to go from them. I told them that
they must give themselves up entirely to God (as) they
saw well what misery we suffered in this vale of tears.
They replied that they had never experienced this so fully
as now, and said that they owed God at all events one
death, and they would die the more joyfully, as I also was

¹ In chapter xli, the author told us that the expedition took place
about the middle of August, 1554; consequently, he was captured either
in the beginning of that year or at the end of 1553.

with them.   Herewith I went out of their hut, and passed
through the whole camp, visiting the prisoners.   I wandered
about free, and nobody paid any attention to me.   I could
have escaped that time, for it was at an island called
Meyenbipe, which might be about ten miles (leagues) distant from Brickioka, but I refrained on account of the
Christian prisoners, of whom four were still alive.   For I
thought, " If I run away from them they will be angry,
and will immediately kill them.   Perhaps, meanwhile, God
will preserve us all together ;" and I determined, therefore,
to remain with them and to comfort them, as I also did.
But the savages were very well disposed towards me, for I
had before told them at hazard that the enemy would en-
counter us.   Now as this so happened, they said that I
was a better prophet than their Miraka.

Caput XLIII.

How they danced with their enemies when we encamped the next day.

The next day we arrived, not far from their country, at an
extensive chain of mountains called Occarasu.[1]   There they
encamped, in order to pass the night.   Then I went into the
hut of the chief king (called Konyan Bebe), and asked him
what he purposed doing with the Mammelucks.   He said
they were to be eaten, and he forbade me to speak with
them, for he was angry with them, as they should have
remained at home, and not have gone to war with his
enemies against him.   I told him he should let them live,
and sell them back to their friends.   He replied they should
be eaten.

And this Konyan Bebe had a large basket full of human
flesh before him, ate (a bit) off a leg, held it before my

---

[1] A corruption of Taquarussu or Tacuaruçu, the " Big Bamboo".

mouth, and asked if I also would eat it. I replied "Unreasoning animals hardly devour their kind; ought one man, therefore, to devour another?" He took a bite, saying, "Jauware sche;[1] I am a tiger-animal. It tastes well." With this I went from him.

That same evening he commanded that each should bring his captives before the wood to an open space, near the water. This was done. Then they assembled together, and made a large ring, wherein stood the captives. Then the latter had all to sing and to rattle with the Tammaraka idols. Now when the prisoners had danced, they began to speak, one after the other, boastfully saying, "Yes, we went forth, as it beseems valiant men, to capture and to eat you, our enemies. Now you have gained the upper hand, and have captured us, but we care not for this. Braves die in their enemy's country, and as our land is still large, the others will revenge us well upon you." "Yes," said the others, "you have already destroyed many of ours, and for this we will have our revenge of you." When these speeches were finished, each led his prisoner back to his quarters.

---

[1] Literally, "a Jaguar (am) I". The name of this feline in Tupi is "ja", us; and g-u-ara, great eater (the same etymology as the Guára wolf): the whole meaning great eater of us (men). This is the Felis Concolor, the Puma of Peru, the Painter (panther) of the United States; the American lion and colloquial Brazilian Onça Vermelha. According to P. Anchieta (*loc. cit.*, § xx), the Jaguar was dangerous to men; possibly, since the land has become populous, the wild beasts have lost heart. I never found any authentic account of an accident, except to dogs and monkeys, of which the puma is inordinately fond. Yet the backwoodsmen fear it at night. The same may be said of the tiger, or ounce (Part II, chapter xxx). The flesh of the young animal is said to be good eating. When Southey (iii, 898) discredits the tale about Nasil Lichma, the lion-pawed idol of S. Sebastian, because "there are no Lions in America", he forgets that foreigners have always called the puma "lion".

Except in the matter of cannibalism, Cunha-bebe's boast is not unlike those of Ali, the Asad Ullah el Ghalib and of Richard Cœur de Lion.

Thereupon, on the third day, we again reached their country, each leading his captive to his dwelling. Those in the village of Uwattibi, where I was, had taken eight savages alive, and three Mammelucks, who were Christians, namely, Diego and his brother, and yet another Christian, called Anthonio, whom my masters' sons had captured; and also they took home two other Mammelucks who were Christians, (ready) roasted, and to be eaten there. This was on the eleventh day of our journey out and back.

Caput XLIV.

How the French ship, to which they intended taking me, as they had promised me, when they returned from the war, etc., as recounted above, was still there.

Now, when we had again returned home, I demanded that they should take me to the French ship, for I had been to war with them, and had helped them to capture their enemies, from whom they had now heard it confessed that I was not a Portuguese.

They said "Yes," they would take me to it, but they must first rest and eat the Mokaen[1]—that is, the roasted flesh of the two Christians.

Caput XLV.

How they ate the first of the two roasted Christians, namely, Jorge Ferrero, the son of the Portuguese captain.

Now there was a king in some huts close to the huts where I was. The same was named Tatamiri.[2] He had

[1] See chapter xlii. In Part II, chapter xi, the word is spelt Mockaein; in both cases the terminal consonant being wrong. The modern Brazilians have adopted the form of "Moquem", from the Tupi Mocaem, *assar na labareda*, to broil in flame. "Barbacoa" was the Guaycuru word; whence our "barbecue."

[2] This would mean "the spark", from "tata", fire, and "Merim", small.

charge of the roasted bodies, and had caused much liquor to be prepared, according to their custom; and many of them had assembled, drunk, sung, and made great rejoicings. Thereupon, the next day after the drinking, they again cooked the roast flesh and ate it; but the flesh of Hieronymus, the other, was hung in the hut wherein I was, in a basket above the fire, exposed to the smoke during fully three weeks, until it became as dry as a piece of wood, from having remained so long over the fire uneaten.

This was owing to the savage, called Parwaa, who had charge of it. He had gone elsewhere to fetch roots for making the beverage which would be drunk (when feasting upon) the flesh of Hieronymus, so that the time passed, and they would not lead me to the ship before they had made their feast off (the remains of) Hieronymus, and had eaten the flesh. During this time the French ship had again sailed, for it lay about eight miles away from where I was.

When I heard this news I became sad, but the savages said they were in the habit of coming there every year, wherewith I must be content.

Caput XLVI.

How Almighty God worked a wonder.

I had made a cross of reed, and had raised it in front of the hut wherein I was. At this I oftentimes made my prayers to the Lord, and I had commanded the savages that they should not pull it up, for misfortune might ensue therefrom. But they heeded not my words. At a time when I was out with them fishing, a woman had torn up the cross, and had given it to her husband, who was to rub thereon a kind of Paternoster, which they make from snail shells,[1] because it was round. This grieved me sorely, and

---

[1] About this wampum, see chapter xxviii.

soon after it began to rain very hard, and to blow for several days. They came to my hut, and demanded that I should intercede with my God, that the rain might be stayed, for if it did not stop it would prevent their planting, and their time for planting had come. I said it was their fault, they had angered my God, by having torn up the piece of wood ; for by that piece of wood I was in the habit of holding discourse with my God. Now when they thought this the cause of the rain, my master's son helped me to erect another cross. It was, judging by the sun, about one hour after noon. When it was erected, the weather, which had been very stormy before mid-day, from that hour became fine. They marvelled all, and thought that my God did whatever I wished.

Caput XLVII.

How, one evening, I was out fishing with two savages, and God did a wonder through me, during a great rain and thunderstorm.

I stood with one who was also a chief. He was called Parwaa, and he had roasted Hieronymus. The same, with another and myself, stood and fished at close of day, when it began to rain hard, with thunder, and it rained not far from us, so that the wind brought the rain towards us. Then the two savages begged me to speak with my God, that the rain might not prevent us from the chance of catching more fish ; for I was well aware that we had nothing in the huts to eat. These words touched me, and I begged the Lord from the depth of my heart that he would, through me, show his might. The savages demanded it from me (I said), "Therefore (grant) that they may always see how thou, my God, art at all times with me." When I had ended the prayer, the wind and rain came rushing on, and rained within about six paces from us, and at the spot whereon we stood, we felt none. So the savage, Parwaa, said, " Now I see that thou hast spoken with thy God," and we caught several fishes.

When we came to the huts, the two told the other savages that I had spoken with my God, and that such and such things had come to pass, whereat the others wondered.

CAPUT XLVIII.

How they ate the other of the two roasted Christians, named Hieronymus.

Now when the savage Parwaa had ended all preparations, as before stated, he caused drinks to be made, wherewith to make merry over the flesh of Hieronymus. And whilst they were drinking, they brought the two brothers to me, and also another, by name Anthonio, whom my master's son had captured. They were four Christians together, and we were obliged to drink with them ; but before we would drink we made our prayers to God, that he would be merciful to the soul of Hieronymus, and also to us when our hour might come. And the savages gibbered with us, and were merry, but we felt great misery. The next morning early they recooked the flesh and ate it, and swallowed it in a very short time. The same day they took me off to be given away. Now when I parted from the two brothers, they begged that I would pray to God for them, and I gave them information, in case they could escape, as to which direction they were to take over the mountains, so as to be safe from being tracked, for I was acquainted with the mountains. This they also did, as I afterwards learned, for they got loose and escaped. If they were recaptured I know it not to this day.

Caput XLIX.

How they led me off to be given away.

They sailed with me to the place where they purposed giving me away, called Tackwara sutibi.[1] And when we were some distance from the shore, I looked round at the huts from which we had sailed, and there was a black cloud over them. I pointed it out, and said that my God was angry with the village, for having eaten of the Christian flesh, etc. Now when they had taken me there, they delivered me to a king called Abbati Bossange,[2] and they told him that he was to do me no harm, nor allow any to be done to me, for my God was terrible to those who did me evil. For this they had seen during the time I had been with them. And I also admonished·him, saying, that soon my brother and friends would come with a ship full of wares, that they were only to take good care of me, for then I would give them wares; and that I knew full well, how my God would soon conduct thither my brother's ships. This pleased them greatly. The king called me (his) son, and I went out hunting with his sons.

Caput L.

How the savages of the said place told me that the aforesaid ship from France had sailed away again.

They told me how the former ship, Maria Bellete by name, from Dieppe, and which I had so much wished to join, had

[1] Near S. Paulo is a village, Itaquaquecetuba or Itaquaqucetuba. This long but expressive word means, if I remember right, " the stone bearing much bamboo, that cuts like a knife": " Ita" signifying stone; "taquára", bamboo; "kyce", a knife; and "-tyba", túba or -uba, a desinent denoting abundance, like the Portuguese -al. For instance, "yby' Cui" is arêa, sand; yby' Cui tyba" is areal, a place with much sand.

[2] Abatybo Sanhé; *i.e*, to the Maize (go) quickly.

there taken in the rest of her cargo, namely, Brazil-wood, red pepper, cotton, featherwork, baboons, parrots, and such goods as were wanted at the former place, and that they had in the harbour of Rio de Jenero captured a Portuguese ship, and had given one of the Portuguese to a savage king, named Ita Wu,[1] who had eaten him. Also I learned that the Frenchman, who, when I was captured, had ordered the savages to eat me, was in the ship, and was returning home, and that it was the same ship which, when I ran away from the savages, and swam to their boat, would not receive me on board. That ship was lost on the return voyage, for when I arrived with the other vessel in France, nobody had heard what had become of her, as will be seen further on.

Caput LI.

How shortly after that I had been given away there, another ship arrived from France, called the Katharina de Vattavilla, which, through the providence of God, brought me away, and how this happened.

I had been about a fortnight in the village Tackwara sutibi with the king Abbati Bossange, when it happened one day that some savages came to me, and said that they had heard a firing, which must be at Iteronne, the harbour also called Rio de Jenero. Hearing with certainty that a ship was there, I told them that they were to take me to it, as, probably, my brothers would be there. They said "yes," and, nevertheless, detained me several days longer.

Meanwhile it happened that the Frenchmen who had arrived there, heard that I was still among the savages. The captain sent two men belonging to the ship, who, together with several savage kings, whom they had for friends in the place where I was, came to a hut, the king of which was called Sowarasu,[2] close to the hut wherein I was.

---

[1] Ita-u ; *i.e.*, Stone I eat.

[2] Sóo-ussu would mean the Big Animal.

The news was brought to me by the savages, that two men from the ship had arrived there. I was overjoyed, and went to them and bade them welcome in the savage tongue. When they saw me in such wretched plight, they had pity upon me, and divided their garments with me. I asked them why they had come, they answered, on my account, as they had been commanded to take me to the ship, and to effect this they were to use every means. Then my heart rejoiced at the mercy of God. And I said to the one of the two who was named Perot, and who knew the language of the savages, that he was to feign the following :—He was to be my brother, and he had brought me several cases full of merchandise, that they might take me with them to the ship to fetch the cases. And he was to make believe, that I would remain among them, and collect pepper and other produce, until the ships returned next year. Upon these pretexts they took me to the ship, my master going with me himself. All in the vessel had much pity on me, and treated me very kindly. Now when we had been about five days in the ship, the savage king Abbati Bossange, to whom I had been given, asked me where the cases were, that I was to demand them to be given to me, and that we might return home betimes. This demand I repeated to the ship captain, who instructed me to put him off until the vessel had its full cargo, in case they should become angry, and attempt to give us trouble, seeing that I was kept in the ship, or should work us some other treachery, since it is a people in whom none can confide. But as my master the king wanted positively to take me home with him, I detained him long with words, and told him not to hurry so much,[1] for he knew well that when good friends came together, they could not part again so quickly ; when, how-

---

[1] It is a characteristic of the savage, that he will keep you waiting six months; whilst, if you keep him waiting as many hours, he works himself up into a fever of " fussiness".

ever, they were about again to sail away in the ship, we would also return to our huts. In this manner I put him off.

At last, when the vessel was well laden, the Frenchmen in the ship all assembled together, and I stood near them, and my master the king, together with those whom he had with him, also stood there. And the captain caused the savages to be told through his interpreter, how he was much pleased that they had not killed me, after having caught me among their enemies. And he caused them further to be told (in order to take me away from them in a more gentle manner), that he had in this way ordered me to be brought from the land to the ship, so that he might give them something for having taken such good care of me, and that it was also his intention to give me some wares, and let me remain among them till his return, because I was known by them, and collect together pepper, and other goods that he wanted.

Now we had in such wise planned, that about ten sailors, who in some degree resembled me, should come together and state they were my brothers, and wanted to carry me home with them. This wish was taken into consideration; my said brothers would in no way consent that I should again go on shore with them, but they declared that I should return home, for our father wished to see me once more before he died. Then the captain caused them to be told that he was the captain of the ship, and was desirous that I should go back with them on shore, but that as he was only one man, and my brothers were many, he could not do anything against them. These pretexts were all made in order to part on good terms with the savages. And I also told my master the king that I should be glad to go home with them, but that he saw well my brothers would not consent. Then he went weeping about the ship, and said, if then they really wanted to take me with them, I was to return with the first ship, for he had considered me as his son, and was very angry with those of Uwattibi, for having wanted to eat me.

And one of his wives, who was with him on board the ship, had to cry over me after their custom, and I also cried according to their usage. After all this, the captain gave him sundry goods, which might amount to some five ducats in value, knives, hatchets, looking-glasses, and combs. Therewith they proceeded again on shore to their home.

In such manner did the Almighty Lord, the God of Abraham, Isaac and Jacob, help me out of the hands of these tyrants (barbarians); to Him be praise, honour, and glory, through Jesus Christ his dear Son, our Saviour. Amen.

Caput LII.

How the officers of the ship were named, and where the ship came from, and what yet happened before we sailed out of the harbour, and how long we were on our voyage to France.

The captain of the ship was called Wilhelm de Moner, and the mate, Françoy de Schantz. The ship was called the Catharina de Wattanilla, etc. They rigged the ship again to sail to France, when it happened that one morning, while we were still in the harbour called (Rio de Jenero), a small Portuguese ship came by, sailing out of the harbour. It had been trading with a tribe of savages, whom they have for friends, called Los Markayas, whose country is bounded by the country of the Tuppin Ikins, whom the French have as friends. These two nations are great enemies.

And this was the ship, which (as before stated), was sent after me, to purchase me from the savages, and it belonged to a factor called Peter Rösen. The Frenchmen armed their boat with firearms, and sailed up to them, intending to take them; they also took me with them, that I might tell them to surrender. But when we attacked the ship, they beat

us back again ; some Frenchmen were shot, others were
wounded, and I also was wounded by a shot to near death,
and much more severely than any of those wounded who
still lived again. I called in my anguish to my Lord, for I
felt nothing else than the agony of death, and implored the
merciful Father, that as He had saved me from the hands
of the heathen, He might grant me my life, and restore me
to Christian countries, where I might proclaim to mankind
His mercies vouchsafed unto me. And I regained complete
health. Praised be the merciful God from eternity to
eternity.

On the last day of October, Anno Domini 1554, we sailed
out of the harbour of Rio de Jenero, and again made for
France. We had fair winds at sea, so that the sailors wondered,
and thought it must be a special gift of God (as it also was).
Even so, the Lord did a visible wonder by us on the sea.

On Christmas eve, there came about the ship many fish,
which are called porpoises ; of these, we caught such a
number, that we had enough victual for some days. In the
same manner, on the eve of the day of the Three Holy Kings
(Epiphany), God also bestowed an abundance of fish upon
us ; for there remained, at that time, but little else for us to
eat, save what God gave us from the sea. Thereupon, about
the 20th day of February, of the year 1555, we arrived in
the kingdom of France, at a small city called Honflor,[1]
situated in Normandy. During the whole return-voyage
we saw no land for nearly four months. I assisted them in
discharging the vessel, and when that was done, I thanked
them all for the kindness shown me. Thereupon, I requested a passport from the captain ; but he would much
rather that I made another voyage with him. When, however, he saw that I would not stay, he obtained a passport
from Moensoral Miranth,[2] the Governor of Normandy.
The same, when he had heard of me, ordered me before him,
and handed me the passport, whilst my captain gave me

---

[1] Honfleur.   [2] M. l'Admiral (?).

my viaticum (travelling means). I took my leave, and proceeded from Henfloer to Hebelnoeff, and from Hebelnoeff to
Depen.[1]

Caput LIII.

How, at Depen, I was taken to the house of the captain of the "Bellete"
(the house-owner being absent on his command), which had sailed
before us from Brazil, and had not yet arrived.

It was from Depen that came the former ship, "Maria
Bellete", in which was the interpreter who had commanded
the savages to eat me, and in which he intended returning
to France. In it also were those who would not take me
into the boat when I escaped from the savages, also the
same ship-captain, who, as the savages told me, had given
them a Portuguese to be eaten. For they had taken a ship
from the Portuguese, as before stated.

The said crew of the "Bellete" had not yet arrived with
the vessel when I came there; although, according to the
reckoning of the ship "Wattuuilla", which arrived out
there after them, and which brought me back, they should
have returned home three months before us. The wives
and relations of the said crews came to me, and asked me
if I had not seen them. I said, " Indeed, I have seen them;
there are, in the ship, some godless men, be they who they
may". Then I recounted to them, how one who was in the
vessel had commanded the savages to eat me; but Almighty
God had protected me; and I told them further, how they
had been with their boat near the huts wherein I was, and
had bartered pepper and monkeys from the savages; but
that when I had run away, and had swum off to those in the
boat, they would not take me in, and I was therefore obliged
to swim back to shore among the wild men, which at that
time was a terrible sorrow to me. Also, that they had given
to the savages a Portuguese, whom they had eaten; and I
told them how they would show no mercy unto me. By all

[1] Dieppe.

this I now well see my beloved God meant so well by me, that I, praise be to God, am here before you, to bring you the newest tidings. Let them come when they like. But I will be a prophet to you, that God will not suffer such unmerciful cruelty and want of pity, as they showed me in that country (may God forgive it them !), to remain unpunished, whether sooner or later; for it was evident that my sighs had moved God in Heaven to pity. I told them further, how well it had gone, during the voyage, with those who had bought me from the savages, which was also the truth. God sent us fine weather and wind, and gave us fish from the depths of the sea.

They lamented greatly, and asked what I thought about it, and whether it was not possible that they might still be living. In order not to make them too disconsolate, I said that they may possibly still return; although most people, and I also, could not suppose otherwise, but that they must have perished with the ship.

After all these discourses I parted from them, and said that they were to inform the others, if they arrived, how God had helped me, as I had been there.

From Depen I sailed with a ship to London, in England, where I remained several days. Thereafter, I voyaged from London to Seeland, from Seeland to Antdorff. In such wise has Almighty God, to whom all things are possible, helped me back again to my fatherland. To Him be praise for ever! Amen.

My prayer to God, the Lord, whilst I was in the power of the savages, who purposed to eat me :

" O Thou omnipotent one, Thou who hast created heaven and earth, Thou God of our forefathers, Abraham, Isaac, and Jacob, Thou who hast so mightily led Thy people Israel out of the hands of their enemies, through the Red Sea, Thou who hast preserved Daniel among the lions; to Thee I pray, Thou eternal power, that Thou mayest deliver me out of the hands of these tyrants, who know Thee not, for

Jesus Christ, Thy dear Son's sake, who delivered us prisoners from eternal captivity. But, Lord, if it be Thy will that I should suffer so cruel a death at the hands of these people who know Thee not, and say, when I speak to them of Thee, that Thou hast no might to deliver me out of their hands, then strengthen me in the last hour, when they fulfil their intentions on me, that I may not doubt of Thy mercy.

"And as I shall in this misery suffer so much, so grant me hereafter peace, and preserve me ever from the future torments, of which all our forefathers have been fearful. But, blessed God, Thou canst well deliver me out of their power, help me, I know full well Thou canst help me, and when Thou hast delivered me, I will attribute it to no mere fortune, but to Thy helping mighty hand only, for now no human power can save me. And when Thou hast helped me out of their power, I will praise Thy mercy, and proclaim it among all nations to whom I may go. Amen."

I cannot well believe, that from his heart a man can pray,
Unless that risk and crosses and great trials haunt his way;
For when the body liveth as it wills to live, and thrives,
The wretched creature all its days against its Maker strives.
Therefore, to him whom God vouchsafed to tempt with tribulation,
He alltimes means that it shall end by bringing true salvation.
Thereof let no man ever doubt,
Thus gifts by God are brought about.

No comfort, weapon, shield, is found to man at any time,
But who alone is armed with faith and God's own word divine.
Therefore, O each and every man of true God-fearing heart,
Unto thy sons no better gift than this thou canst impart;
Than willingly the Word of God to read and comprehend;
For thus in time of sorest need thereon they may depend.

Therefore, dear reader, think not fit on me to cast the blame,
That I have done this work of mine for aught of earthly fame,
'Tis done in God Almighty's love, in honour and in praise,
Who knows the hearts of mortal men, their thoughts and all their ways.
To Him, dear reader, I commend thee;
May He protect, and so defend me.

END OF THE FIRST PART.

PART THE SECOND.

A VERITABLE AND SHORT ACCOUNT

Of all the by me experienced manners and customs of the
Tuppin Imbas, whose prisoner I was.

They live in America; their country is situated in 24 degrees on
the south side of the equinoctial line, and their country
is bounded by a river called Rio de Jenero.

PART THE SECOND.

Caput I.

How the voyage is made from Portugal to Rio de Jenero, situated in America, in about 24 degrees of the Tropic of Capricorn.

Lissebona is a city in Portugal, situated in 39 degrees to the north of the equinoctial line. In order to sail from Lisbona to the province of Rio de Jenero, in the country of Brazil, which is also called America, the islands called the Canaries, belonging to the King of Spain, have first to be reached. Six[1] of them are here named. The first—Grand Canaria; the next, Lanserutta; the third, Forte Ventura; the fourth, Il Ferro; the fifth, La Palma; the sixth, Tineriffe. Thence to the islands, called Los Insules de Cape Virde;[2] that is to say, the Islands of the Green Headland, which green headland lies in the country of the black Moors, also called the land of Gene. The said islands lie under the Tropic of Cancer, and belong to the King of Portugal. From the islands, the direction sailed is south-south-west, to the country of Brazil, and it is a great wide ocean; often three months long and more are sailed, before the country is reached. First, the Tropic of Cancer is passed, so that it remains behind. Then, through the *linea Æquinoctialis;* and, upon leaving the north side behind, the north star,

[1] The seven are—1. Lanzarote or Lanserote, nearest the coast; 2. Next to it, Fuerteventura; 3. Grand Canary; 4. Tenerife; 5. Gomera; 6. Hierro, in Portuguese, Ferro; and, 7. La Palma. The author omits Gomera, which lies west of Tenerife. See Part I, chapter vi.

[2] Part I, chapter vi.

which they also call *Polum articum,* is no longer seen. After this, the height of the Tropic of Capricorn is reached, and one sails along under the sun. And when the height of the Tropic of Capricorn is passed, after midday the sun is seen down in a northerly direction. There is always great heat between the two tropics, and the above-mentioned country, Brazil, lies partly within the tropics.

Caput II.

How the country, America, such as I have partly seen, is situated.

America is a great country, inhabited by many tribes of savage people, who show much difference in language, and there are in it many strange animals. The land is joyful to behold, the trees are at all times green; it has no wood that resembles the wood of this country, and the people go naked. It is in the part of the world which lies between the Tropics, and at no time of the year is the cold so great as it is here at Michaelmas. But that part of the country which lies south of the Tropic of Capricorn is rather colder. In it live the tribe of savages called Carios, who use skins of animals, which they delicately prepare, to clothe themselves with ; the women of the said savages make things of cotton-wool yarn, like a sack underneath and open above ; these they draw on, and call in their language Typpoy.[1] There are in this country many fruits of the earth and of the trees, on which man and beast live. The people are

[1] See Part I, chapter xx, where the hammock is called Inni. According to Varnhagen (i, 458), "Tipoia", like Tanga and Moxinga (a whipping), is an African word, and it is still used throughout Angola. Hans Stade, however, knew nothing of Africa, and records what he heard. In Brazil, "Tipoya" was applied to the sleeveless shirts of "Indian" converts, sewn by the women with a thorn of the Murumuru palm. The hammock, in Portuguese, is named Redesinha, when made of network. The Sedan-chair of Bahia was known as a "Serpentina".

coloured reddish-brown,[1] on account of the sun, which burns their bodies. They are a well-shaped race, cunning in all malice, much inclined to pursue their enemies, and to eat them, etc. Their country, America, is several hundred miles (leagues) long from north to south, of which I have sailed along the coast about five hundred, and I have been at many places in the interior.

CAPUT III.

Of a great chain of mountains which is in the country.[2]

There is a chain of mountains, which may reach to within about three miles of the sea, in some places it is further off, also it lies sometimes nearer, and it begins in about the latitude of the Boiga de Todolos Sanctus,[3] a place so called where the Portuguese have built a city, and live. And the said chain extends along the sea fully 204 miles ; and in 29 degs. latitude, on the south side of the equinoctial line, the mountains at places end, where the distance from the sea

[1] A correct description of the " Red Skins", who are red only where the skin is sunburnt. The older travellers did not much insist upon the colour, which is now considered characteristic of the race. Gil Barbosa, the scribe who accompanied Cabral, makes them pardos, manheira de vermelhados. P. Lopes de Souza, who visited Bahia in A.D. 1531, declares that the Tupinambás, men and women, were white and well made, and that the latter would not envy their sisterhood of the " Rua Nova de Lisbôa". De Lery describes them to be swarthy like Spaniards ; Cazal says, " Côr baça tirando a vermelhada."

[2] A fair description of the Eastern Ghauts of the Brazil, whose presence forms the wonderful charm of " Rio Bay".

[3] Bahia de Todos os Santos, so called because discovered by Gonçalo Coelho on All Saints' Day (Nov. 1st), in A.D. 1501. Varnhagen's first date (Dec. 25th) was an error, afterwards owned by himself. Thomé de Souza, the first governor-general, who arrived at his head-quarters on May 29th, 1549, changed it to "Cidade de São Salvador", the " Festival of Plenary Indulgence", commemorating the " Precious Blood of our Lord Jesus Christ". It is now called Bahia, the Bay *par excellence.*

is eight miles. Behind the highlands lies similar land. Many fine rivers flow from amongst the mountains, and in them there is much game. Among these highlands is a savage tribe called the Wayganna,[1] who have no fixed dwelling-places like the others, and who live before and behind (*i.e.*, on both sides of) the mountains. These same Wayganna make war against all the other tribes, and when they can capture them they eat them. In like manner they are also done to by the others. They follow the game into the highlands; they are clever at shooting it with the bow, and they show much ingenuity in other things, such as slings[2] and traps, wherein they catch game.

There is also in the mountains much wild honey, which they eat. They invariably learn the cries of animals and the songs of birds, in order the more easily to creep up to and shoot them.

---

[1] These were probably the Goáinazes (*Noticia*, Part I, chap. lxiii), Goyanás or Guayanás (see Introduction); the name is popularly derived from "Guaya", people, and "na", esteemed—the esteemed people. They occupied, says Jaboatam, fifty leagues of coast, from Angra dos Reis to Cananéa, where they met the Carijós. They lived in caves or underground dwellings (Part II, chapter iv), wore the skins of beasts, fought in the open field, enslaved but did not slay their prisoners—Hans Stade asserts the contrary—and were easily civilised. They practised vivisepulture of men as well as women, and when a Royalet died some of his vassals were buried with him. When disease or old age made a brave weary of his life, he was tarred with resin and feathered with the plumes of many-coloured birds; "the people then with festivity and dancing, placed him in an earthen pot under a heavy cover of baked clay, and he went to his doom more joyful and gladsome than to his first nuptials". The coffin was presently lowered into a hole, earth was heaped upon it, "and thus," says the astonished old chronicler, "the man was buried twice". Potted skeletons are often dug up in the valley of the Southern Parahyba river.

[2] The sling was a favourite weapon amongst the Tupis. Caramuru (iv, 46) mentions this Funda. They do not seem to have used the "bolas", whose simplest form was a stone attached to a string. Presently it would be doubled, and thus Ovalle (iii, 7) tells us that a stone bullet at one end, and at the other a ball of leather or other light sub-

They kindle their fire with two pieces of wood, as also do the other savages. Usually they roast the flesh, which they eat. They travel, taking with them wife and children. When they encamp anywhere near their enemies' country, they make hedges[1] close around their huts, so that they cannot be suddenly surprised; also partly on account of wild animals. Moreover, they place sharp thorns (called Maragaeibe Ju[2]) round about the huts, even as we here plant foothooks; this they do from fear of their enemies. The whole night they keep up a fire near them,[3] and when day breaks they put it out, so that no one may see the smoke and track them.

The head-hair they wear long; they also allow their fingernails to grow. They have rattles, called Maracka, like the other savages; these they consider as gods; they have their drinks and their dances, and teeth of wild animals wherewith they cut. They chop with stone wedges,[4] as did the other tribes before they had traded with the ships.

stance was used by the Pampas Indians. South America also, according to Charlevoix (ii, 67), had the two-stringed pellet-bow, the "Stone bow" of Shakespeare, still commonly used in India.

[1] This is the Kraal (Portuguese Corral) of Somali-land and Zanzibar, Angola and Kafir-land, to mention no other part of Africa.

[2] Maraja-aybe-jú would mean the thorn (jú) of the bad (ayú, aib, or aybe), Maraja tree. I found the Mpangwe (Fans) of the Gaboon using the caltraps of mediæval Europe; the usual article was a bamboo splint. The Tupis probably perferred the Bombax thorn (Part II, chap. xxvii).

[3] The same was the practice of the North American Indians and many African tribes; the Somal, for instance, do so.

[4] These Ituque, or Stone-knives, are mentioned by Nieuhoff. The remnants of the Tupi race have not yet ended with the "Stone Age". They have every variety of fashion, palæolithic and neolithic, from the coarsest axes of dark blue sandstone (See Part II, chapter ix), for opening shell-fish, to fine lava and arrow-heads of rock-crystal (alluded to in Part II, chapter xv), and admirably finished hatchets of apple-coloured jade, the latter probably brought or washed down from the Andes. I deposited with the Anthropological Society (No. 1) of London sundry of these "stone wedges" found in the "kitchen-middens", near Santos. See Part II, chapter ix.

They also often fall upon their enemies when they want to capture them, and they sit down behind dry wood, which stands near the hostile huts. This they do, so that if any come from out of the huts to fetch wood they may capture them.

They also behave more cruelly to their enemies than their enemies do to them; for example, they often cut their arms and legs off when alive, to show their great hatred. The others, however, first strike their dead before they cut them up to be eaten.

CAPUT IV

What the dwellings of the Tuppin Imba savages, whose prisoner I was, are like.

They have their dwelling-places in front of the above-mentioned great chain of mountains, close to the sea ; they also extend for some sixty miles (leagues) behind the range; and out of the mountains a river flows into the sea, whose banks in one place they inhabit, and which they called the Paraeibe. Along the sea-coast they have about twenty-eight miles (leagues) of ground, which they occupy, and they are on all sides surrounded by enemies. Northwards they are bounded by a savage tribe called Weittaka,[1] who

[1] These are the Guaitacá (Plur., Guaitacazes) of Fr. Gaspar, and the Ouctacuzes of Abreu e Lima's "Compendium". They held sixty miles of country from the Reritygb to the Southern Parahyba River, and it is still called the " Campos dos Goaytacazes"—those fertile prairies, of which " Campos" is now the capital, between Rio de Janeiro and Espirito Santo. They were good swimmers ; they fought in the open country, and they did not devour their prisoners. Others represent them as " human tigers"; and, at any rate, they were able to expel Pedro de Goes from his Captaincy of S. Thomé or Parahyba do Sul. Southey (i, 46) is right in saying that the " Goaytacazes" did not burrow like the " Gonynazes". See Part II, chapter iii.

are their foes; on the south, their enemies are called the Tuppin Ikin; landwards, their enemies are the Karaya;[1] then the Wayganna, in the mountains close to them; and yet another tribe called Markaya, who live between them. By these they are much persecuted. The before-mentioned tribes also make war upon one another, and when any of them take a prisoner, they eat him.

They prefer erecting their dwellings in spots where they are not far from wood and water, nor from game and fish. After they have destroyed all in one district, they migrate to other places; and when they want to build their huts, a chief among them assembles a party of men and women (some forty couples), or as many as he can get, and these live together as friends and relations.

They build a kind of hut, which is about fourteen feet wide, and perhaps a hundred and fifty feet long, according to their number. The tenements are about two fathoms high, and round at the top like a vaulted cellar; they thatch them thickly with palm leaves, so that it may not rain therein, and the hut is all open inside. No one has his specially-prepared chamber; each couple, man and woman, has a space of twelve feet on one side; whilst on the other, in the same manner, lives another pair. Thus their huts are full, and each couple has its own fire. The chief of the huts has also his lodging within the dwelling. They all have commonly three entrances, one on each side, and one in the middle; these are low, so that they must stoop when they go in and out.[2] Few of their villages have more than seven huts. They leave between their abodes a space wherein they kill their prisoners. They are also in the habit of

---

[1] See Part II, chapter xi.

[2] The low door is universal amongst savages and the semi-civilised, from the Hindu hut to that of the Chiquito, who, though equal to his neighbours in stature, was so called by the Spaniards on account of the dwarfish entrances to his abode. The objects secured are, coolness in hot weather, heat in cold seasons, and freedom from flies and other such pests.

making, round about their villages, forts which are as follows: they plant a palisade, made of split palm trees; this stockade may be about a fathom and a half high, and is so thick that no arrow can penetrate it; small holes are pierced therein, from out of which they shoot arrows. And outside of the stockade they make yet another of great high rails; but they plant them not close together, only so that a man cannot creep through. And some of them are wont to place the heads of those whom they have eaten on the rail, before the entrance to the huts.

Caput V.

How they make fire.

They have a kind of wood, called Urakueiba,[1] which they dry, and then they take two sticks of it, a finger thick, and rub one upon the other, till it produces dust, and the heat resulting from the rubbing lights the dust. Therewith they make fire.

Caput VI.

The places wherein they sleep.

They sleep in things called in their language Inni, and made of cotton-wool; these they tie to two posts above the ground, and constantly have fire near them at night. They also do not willingly, for any purpose, leave their huts during the dark hours without fire, so much are they afraid of the devil, whom they call Ingange,[2] and often see.

[1] The wood is called Biribá, by Alencar (*O Guarany*, i, 356). Like stone weapons, the fire-drill was universal amongst savages from Europe to Australia. All the civilised peoples of antiquity had vestal virgins, probably to commemorate the difficulty of obtaining fire, and the artificial light is still the highest test of civilisation.

[2] In the *Noticia*, Part II, chap. lxxv, "Anganga". De Lery calls him

CAPUT VII.

How skilful they are in shooting wild animals and fish with arrows.

Wherever they go, be it to the wood or near the water, they always have with them their bows and arrows. When they pass through the forest, they look straight up at the trees, now and again. Whenever they hear any noise of large birds, monkeys, or other animals that inhabit trees, they go thither, and try to shoot them, and they follow

Ayguan, and others Angai, Agnen, Aignen, Uracan, Hyorocan (hence our hurricane, through ouragan?), and Anhanga, the popular modern form. Barrère (1743) terms an idol "Anaantanha" (from Anhanga, and tanha, a figure). Alencar (*Iracema*, 171) derives it from "Anho", alone, and an, ang, or anga, a ghost or larva, vulgarly translated soul and spirit. Che-an, however, seems to mean the vital principal; Angata, mental agitation; Angûera, the soul of the body; Angai, a bad spirit; and Pitanga, a child (from pitár, to suck, and anga, life or soul). In modern usage, Anhanga is a lemur, a larva, a phantom, an evil ghost opposed to the beneficent lares. In the city of S. Paulo there is a streamlet called Anhangabahu-hy, which Varnhagen translates (i, 218) agua de diabrura: the tradition is, that the Red-skins there saw for the first time a negro, and therefore named it "Water of the black devil"; hence, also, in 1772, the celebrated Bartolomew Bueno was known as "O Anhanguera or Amigo do Diablo"; in fact, the Devil's Brother of the Brazil. This also explains Southey (ii, 162), *Anhaguiara, or Mistress of the Devil*.

The Tupis suffered severely from these creatures of their own imagination. Besides the Anhanga, Nieuhoff and others give the Taguai and Taquaiba; the Timoti and Tauvimama; the Macachera, or evil spirit, that haunts roads and paths (espirito dos Cuminhos); the Chinay, that sucks human blood (vampire); the Curupira, from Curumim or (Konnouny, Yves d'Evreux) pappoose and pira, a bad spirit, the ghost of a child; the Caa-poru or forest-dweller, meaning an evil being that haunts woods, and hence the popular abuse Caipira; the Upiara (Oiára) or Merman; the Curipira, Will-o'-the-Wisp, which some translate hill and dale devil, others devil of mind and heart; the Marangigogna or Marangiguana, marsh devil; the Amignao, manes or remainders of the soul after death, and the Giropary (Yves d'Evreux), Garupary, Jerupary, or Jurupari or Yurupari, from Juru or Yuru (a mouth), and Apara (twisted or crooked). No wonder that the old missionaries declared the country to be "farcy de diables".

until they get something. It is seldom, when one of them
is out in the chase, that he returns empty-handed.

In like manner they pursue fishing close to the shores of
the sea. They have keen sight; and, whenever a fish
jumps, they shoot at it; few of their shots miss. As soon
as one is hit, they jump into the water, and swim after it.
Some large fish, when they feel the arrow within them, go
down to the bottom; after these they dive well nigh six
fathoms deep, and bring them up.

Besides this, they also have small nets; the thread wherewith they knit them is drawn from long leaves, which they
call Tokauns.[1] And when they wish to fish with nets, several of them assemble, each taking his own station in a place
where the water is not deep. Then some of them form a
ring, and beat the water; the fishes dive deep, and come
in such manner to their nets. He who catches the most
divides it with the others.

Often, also, come down those who live far from the sea,
catch many fish, bake them hard, pound them, and make
thereof powder,[2] which they dry well, that it may last a
long time. This they take home with them, and eat with
root-meal; for, otherwise should they carry the fish home
with them baked, it would not last long, as they do not
salt it; also does this powder occupy less space than fishes
could whole.

[1] Yves d'Evreux gives Toucon; Southey (i, 214), Tocon; and others,
Ticum, Tocum, and generally Tucum. It is the "Black palm" of Pigafetta (lib. I), of which he says Brazilian bows are made, and the astrocaryum Tucum of Martius. I have described it in the *Highlands of the
Brazil* (ii, 349).

[2] See also Part II, chapter x. This "fish-powder" (Pirá-kuí) was universally used by the Tupis, and it may fairly be recommended to civilised
travellers in wild regions: the same may be said of fish-soup, about
which everyone speaks, but which hardly anyone knows how to cook.

Caput VIII.

What appearance the people have.

They are a race of well-made body and figure, both women and men, like the people of this country, only that they
are brown from the sun; for they all, young and old, go
naked; also they wear nothing over their sexual organs,
and they disguise themselves with painting. They have no
beards; for they pull the hair out by the roots whenever it
grows, and they pierce holes in the mouth and ears, wherein
they hang stones, that are their jewels, and they deck themselves with feathers.

Caput IX.

Wherewith they hew and cut, as they can obtain no Christian tools, such as axes, knives, and scissors.

They had formerly, and before ships came to the country,
and they have still in many parts of the country, where no
vessels arrive, a kind of blackish-blue stone, fashioned like
a wedge. The widest part they make tolerably sharp; it
may be about a span long, two fingers thick, and of a hand's
breadth. Some are large, others small. Then they take a
thin reed, and bend it about the head of it, tying it firmly
with bast.[1]

The iron wedges which the Christians give them in several places, have the same shape. But now they make the

---

[1] This is a contemporary description of how the stone axe was
mounted. So all the weapons of the kind collected and inspected by
me in Brazil had a clean " waist" or groove either worn or chipped, so
that no sharp edge might cut the " bust-rope" or " tie-tie", here called a
reed (ein schmal Reydelin). The author does not mention axes with
eyes, into which the haft was inserted: these were made of iron by the
traders. See **Part II**, chapter iv.

handle in another way : a hole therein, through which they insert the wedge. This is the axe with which they hew.

They also take the teeth of wild hogs, and grind them to make them sharp, and then tie them between two small sticks. Therewith they scrape their bows and arrows, so that they become round as if they were turned.

They also use the tooth of an animal called Pacca ;[1] this they grind sharp at the point, and when they have bodily ailments produced by the blood, they scratch themselves in the place which hurts them. It then bleeds, and such is their cupping.

Caput X.

What their bread is, how their fruits are called, how they plant them, and prepare them to be eaten.

In those places where they intend to plant they cut down trees, and leave them for about three months to dry, then they light fire among them and burn them.[2] After this they plant their roots between the trunks, from which the former derive support ; they are called Mandioka, which is a tree about a fathom in height, giving out three roots. When they want to eat of the roots, they pull up the tree, and break off the roots ; then they break off twigs from the

[1] " Agoutis et Pacs", says Yves d'Evreux, chapter xvii. See Part I, chapter xxxix. The tooth of the Cutía was also used for scarifying purposes ; also flakes of rock-crystal, lancets of fish teeth (the Kakaon of Nieuhoff, p. 875), and thorns of the Carnahúba palm. The women were the operators. Wounds were treated by exposing them to a hot fire, so as to " draw out the humours" (of Hippocrates) and cicatrisation was induced by anointing them with copaiba-oil.

[2] This is the modern Brazilian style of cultivation, and it remarkably resembles that of Unyamwezi. The traveller in both countries cannot fail to remember the curious contrast of " black jacks" and white ashes, with the marvellous green outside the clearing, and the sky of blue and gold above.

stem, and stick them again into the earth. These put forth roots, and in three months become so large as to be eatable. They prepare these roots in three different ways.

Firstly, they rub them upon a stone, into small crumbs, and then they press off the juice with a thing made of hollow palm trees, called Tippiti,[1] in such manner, that it becomes dry; afterwards they rub it through a sieve; and, lastly, they bake, with the meal, thin cakes. The utensil in which they dry and bake the meal is of burnt clay, shaped like a large dish.

They also take the roots fresh, and put them in water,[2] leaving them to rot therein; then they remove them and place them above the fire in the smoke, allowing them to dry. The root thus dried they call Keinrima,[3] and it keeps

---

[1] Tapeti in the *Noticia do Brazil*, and usually typpyti. In Nieuhoff (p. 859), tapití is the grater used, instead of the wheel, to powder the root, and he calls the wooden mortar in which it is pounded Tipiratí. It is generally applied to a sleeve-like bag of matting, in which the manioc-meal is placed for drawing out and pressing, until the noxious juice has oozed away.

Cassava or Cassada is the Antillean word for manioc (Manioch in Yves d'Evreux), the root and the flour (farinha de Páo). The wild plant was called Maniba, Cuaçu-Mandiiba, or Cuguaçuremia (*Noticia* and Nieuhoff). The leaf-bunch, eaten as spinach, was Manikoba (-oba, a leaf.) There were many kinds of manioc, as Manipipocamerim, Mambaru, Tatu, Manaibuna, Paratí, Manetinga, etc. In fact, the nomenclature, as usual with savages, was profuse; and the subject would fill a volume.

[2] This is the second way of preparing the poisonous manioc root; called by the Tupis " Uî Púba", and by the Brazilians Farinha d'agua.

[3] Nieuhoff writes Kaarima, and explains it by " toasted Puba" (vulgarly Fuba), or Mandiopuba, manioc sliced and softened in water for four or five days. This Kaarima was made into porridge (Mingaopomonga), into cakes, and into a dish, termed Minguipitanga, which also contained meat or fish, " reddened" (pitanga) with peppers. The poisonous juice, called Manipoera, was boiled down to make Cassireep, as in the well-known West Indian dish " pepper-pot", and Tapucu was the worm bred by the decomposed juice. The dried sediment of the exposed water was Tipiaka, our " Tapioca", and this was also made into cakes.

a long time. When they want to use it, they pound it in a mortar made of wood, when it becomes white like corn-flour, therefrom they make cakes called Byyw.[1]

They also take rotten mandioka before they dry it, and mix it with the dry and the green. From this they prepare and dry out a meal, which lasts fully a year, and which can be eaten as it is. They call this meal Vy-than.

They also make meal from fish and flesh, and do it in this way: they roast the flesh or fish above the fire in the smoke, and they allow it to become quite dry; then they pull it to pieces, dry it once again on the fire in pots called Yueppaun.[2] Thereupon they pound it small in a wooden mortar, and they pass it through a sieve, reducing it in such manner to powder. This lasts a long time; for they have not the custom of salting fish and meal.[3] Such meal they eat with the root-meal, and it tastes pretty well.

---

[1] Uî or Uy, contracted from Kuí, was generically farinha de páo, wood-meal, manioc-flour, which the British sailor compared with sawdust. Vy-than, in De Lery "Ouy-entan"; and in Nieuhoff "Viata", is Uî-atá, the thoroughly dried and toasted manioc-flour, called by the Portuguese Farinha de Guerra, and still used on their man-hunts by the armies of the King of Dahome. It is opposed to Uî-púba or water-flour (Ouy por, De Lery, and Viapua, Nieuhoff, p. 860), which, of course, was softer. Nieuhoff gives five different kinds of farinha.

[2] Uî-panera, corrupted from the Portuguese "panella", would mean flour-pot; the native term was Cambocý.

[3] Instead of salting it, they sun-dried or boucan'd it, and then reduced it to powder. As a rule, the Brazilian savages ate no salt, except those on the coast, who extracted a brown, bad substance from sea-water. They were Agriophagi, eaters of flesh and fish, whose diet contained enough saline matter to supply the blood; and, as in Abyssinia, the place of salt was taken by Kyinhn or pepper. (See Note to Part II, chapter xxvii.) The more civilised used Jekitaia (Inquitai in the *Noticia*, chapter xlviii; and Jequitaya in Marcgraf), pepper and salt in a small gourd which, wetted with water, formed the favourite sauce.

CAPUT XI.

How they cook their food.

There are many tribes of savages who eat no salt. Some of those amongst whom I was a captive ate salt, of which they had learnt the use from the Frenchmen, who trade with them. But they informed me how the people of an inland tribe called the Karaya,[1] whose country is bounded by theirs, made salt from palm trees, and ate the same, but that those who eat much thereof did not live long. And they prepare it in this manner; for I saw it, and helped to do it. Having felled a thick palm tree, they split it into small splinters; then they make a stand of dry wood, lay the splinters thereon, and burn them to ashes, from which they make lye, and this they boil till the salt separates from it. I thought it would have been saltpetre, and tried it in the fire, but it was not; it tasted like salt, and it was of gray colour. But the majority of the tribes eat no salt. When they boil anything, be it fish or flesh, they generally add green pepper thereto, and when it is pretty well done they lift it out of the broth, and make with it a thin pap, which they call Mingau.[2] They drink it out of calabashes, which they have for vessels. Also, when they want to cook any food, flesh or fish, which is to last some time, they put it four spans high above the fire-place, upon rafters, and make a moderate fire underneath, leaving it in such manner to roast and smoke, until it becomes quite dry. When they afterwards would eat thereof, they boil it up again and eat it, and such meat they call Mockaein.

[1] See Part I, chapter xxviii.
[2] De Lery writes Myngam, and Yves d'Evreux describes " Migan" as " potage", or épaisse bouillie of farinha. In Part II, chapter xxviii, it is applied to broth made of man's flesh. Modern Brazilians still preserve the name (Mingáo), and the use of the article. There were many other kinds of pap and porridge, Mindipiro, etc.

Caput XII.

What kind of regimen and order they have in government and laws.

They have no particular government or laws ; each hut has a head-man, who is their king. For all their chiefs are of one tribe, one command and authority; thus they can do whatever they will. One may perhaps be more experienced than the other in war, so that in this way, when they go to war, more deference is shown to him than to the others. Such was the before-mentioned Konyan Bebe. Otherwise, I have observed no particular authority among them, than that the youngest observe obedience to the eldest, as their custom is.

Whenever one slays or shoots the other, the friends are ready in return to kill him,[1] although this seldom happens. They also obey the chiefs of the huts, in what they order : this is done without any compulsion or fear, but from good-will only.

Caput XIII.

How they bake the pots and vessels that they use.

Their women make in this way the vessels which they use. They take clay and reduce it to mud, wherefrom they make whatever utensils they want. They leave it some time to dry, and they know how to paint it ornamentally. And when they want to burn these pots they tilt them up upon stones, and then they put over them a quantity of dry tree-rind ; they light this, and herewith the pots become so baked that they glow like hot iron.[2]

---

[1] And, it may be observed, savages are apt to make scant distinction between accidental homicide and murder with malice prepense.

[2] Of course the potter's wheel was unknown. Yet, some of their vessels show rudiments of art, and the fact that they could make jars

Caput XIV.

How they make their beverages wherewith they drink themselves drunk,
and how they order their drinking.

The womankind make the drinks; they take the mandioca
root, and they boil great jars full. When it is boiled they
take it out of the jars, pour it into other pots or vessels, and
allow it to get cool. Then the young girls[1] sit down to it,
and chew it in their mouths, and the chewed stuff they put
into a separate vessel.

When the boiled roots are all chewed, they put the stuff
again into the pots, and once more fill them with water.
This they stir up with the chewed roots, and then again
they heat it.

They have especial vessels, which are half buried in the
ground, and they use them like we here do as casks for
wine or beer. Into these they pour the chewed stuff, and
close it up well; it then ferments by itself, and becomes
strong. They allow it in such manner to stand for two
days, then they drink it and become drunk therewith. It
is thick, but of agreeable flavour.

Each hut makes its own drink. And when a village
wants to make merry with it,[2] which generally happens once

large enough to hold corpses, proves that they had attained a certain
amount of skill. I may suggest that this style of burying the human
body was to return it, as it were, to the womb whence it sprang. According to the *Noticia* (chapter lxxvi), they staked the body round, so
that earth might not fall upon it—a Moslem practice.

[1] In Bolivia and other parts of South America old women are preferred
for chewing the manioc and maize. I heard of a sharp Yankee, who
invented a machine in order to imitate the " chaw", which much resembles a dentist's cast of the palate. Unfortunately, he could not
produce human saliva by machinery, and thus all his " chaws" were
" bogies".

[2] This is the style of drinking which I found in African Unyamwezi.
Hans Stade makes his Tupis rather a " jolly" and Bacchanalian race, very
different from the appreciation of Pero Lopes, "Nunca faziam modo
senam de tristeza, nem me parece que folgaram com outra cousa".

a month, the men first go all together to one hut, and drink out there. This is so carried on in succession, until they have drunk out the drink in all the huts.

They sit around the vessels from which they drink. The women help them to the liquor in due order; some stand, sing, and dance around the vessels; and, on the spot where they drink, they also void off their wine.[1]

The drinking lasts through the whole night; they also dance between the fires, shout, and blow trumpets; they make a terrible noise when they wax drunk. They are rarely seen to become quarrelsome.[2] They also behave generously to one another; whatever food one of them has more than his neighbour, that he divides with him.[3]

<hr>

Caput XV.

What are the ornaments of the men, and how they paint themselves, and what their names are.

They make a tonsure upon their heads, allowing a small cross (crown) of hair about it, like a monk. I have often

[1] In Unyamwezi the standing bedstead has a slope from the pillow to the feet, in order to obviate the consequences of over-indulgence in Pombe.

[2] This absence of quarrelling in their cups and of "losing temper", generally, is remarked both by De Lery and by Yves d'Evreux. Thus the Tupis contrasted favourably with the North American savages, who are easily maddened by drink, and then become capable of the most abominable cruelties.

[3] Like the modern Krumen or Krooboys, the Tupis had most things, except their wives and children, their ornaments and weapons, in common—with them *la propriété c'est le vol* would be self-evident as regards food. Thus they had little to quarrel about, and theft was unknown. In the wild parts of the Brazil, upon the Ribeira d'Iguape, for instance, when I first travelled (1865), boxes might be left open without the least danger. But a little leavening of colonists from the Southern States of the North American Union so changed the social state, that next year locks and padlocks could not keep out pilfering fingers.

asked them whence they took this form of cultivating the hair. They said that their forefathers had seen it on a man, who was called Meire Humane,[1] and who had done

[1] This is a subject to be treated rather in a volume than in a foot note. For Meire (Maïr and other forms), see Part I, chap. ii. Here it would simply signify "master".

It is satisfactory to find in Hans Stade a version of this much-vexed story before it was taken in hand by the Portuguese. All along the eastern coast of America, from Florida to the Plata, there were traditions of a mysterious white emigrant, who everywhere had the same name. Columbus found the "Indians" worshipping painted devils called Zemes. Enciso (1519) records that "Sumi" was adored by the Caribs or Guaranís of Cuba, and in Hayti he became Zemi ; in Paraguay he was Pay (father) Zome ; and elsewhere he was Pyzome, Zome, Zoe, Summay, Zamna (Central America), and especially Sumé. Possibly, the word was "Tamoï"; literally, a grandfather ; mythologically (pp. 85-88, Une Fête Brésilienne, etc.), a regenerator of peoples, son of Maire Monan, Monam, Monang, or Monhang (as in Monhang-pora or generation). The latter term is derived by some from Mona, to build ; whilst others render it old, ancient ; a deity who, like Prometheus, brought down fire from heaven and placed it between the shoulders of the Aig or Sloth (Bradypes Tridactylus, Linn.) Sumé, whom we will assume to be the type of many shipwrecked Europeans that were cast upon the Brazilian coast long before the official discovery of the country, appeared coming from the sea or eastward, at Maranham, at Pernambuco, at Bahia, at Cabo Frio, at S. Vicente, and other parts, where his *pegadas* or footprints in the rock were and are still shown. He was either alone or accompanied by a boy, who also left traces. A white man, with long beard and flowing raiment, he became a kind of Triptolemus, Prometheus, and Esculapius, in one, teaching the savages the preparation of manioc, the use of fire, the removal of the body-hair, and the knowledge of simples and poisons, especially of Maté, herb of Saint Thomas, which was deadly till the Apostle miraculously changed its properties. At last, when some bad Indians attempted to destroy him, he walked towards the sea, and went as mysteriously as he came.

This "légère croyance des Sauvages Austraux", manipulated by Yves d'Evreux (pp. 438-449), by Padre Vieira, by Vasconcellos (who treats it at great length) ; and by a host of ecclesiastical writers, speedily became doctrine. Sumé was evidently Tuma, S. Thomas, whose incredulity sent him to this unpromising mission-field, and the boy was his guardian angel. The myth spread even into the interior, and vestiges of S. Thomas were found not only upon the coast, but also at São Thomé das Letras, near Campanha of Minas Geraes, in Paraguay, and even near

many wonderful things among them ; for he is supposed to have been a prophet or an apostle.[1]

Further, I asked them wherewith they had been able to cut off the hair before the ships had brought them scissors. They said that they had taken a stone implement, had held another implement underneath, and upon this they struck off the hair ; then they made the tonsure in the middle with a scraper, a transparent stone, which they used much for shearing purposes.[2] Further, they have a thing made of red feathers, called " kannitare";[3] this they bind around the head.

They also have in the nether lip a large hole,[4] which they make from early youth. When they are still young a little hole is pricked through with a pointed deer-horn ; in this they stick a small stone or a piece of wood, and they then

the Rio Diamante, South of Andine Mendoza. The legend is treated of by Varnhagen (*History*, i, 136, and in " Sumé". Lenda mytho-religiosa Americana do Madrid, 1855). See also the *Noticia do Brazil* (pp. 47, 48), and *Anthropologia*, vol. i, No. 1, pp. 52, 57.

The tonsure prevailed amongst many Tupi tribes, who therefore had the generic name of " Coroados", the crowned. In some cases, according to Nieuhoff, only the chief was shaved in the shape of a crown ; whilst others removed the hair, as many Indians still do, from the fore-part of the head, and allowed the rest to grow long. The fact is, that the " tonsure"-form gave a taste of mystery to a practice common throughout the savage world.

[1] In this sentence we suspect Portuguese influence ; but, as Hans Stade was an ardent Catholic, he might easily have detected " a prophet or an apostle" for himself.

[2] Evidently rock-crystal, of which beautiful specimens, in the shape of lance-heads, may be seen in the curious museums of the Atlantic cities in the Brazil.

[3] The correct word is Acangátara, from Acánga, a head ; and tára, to take, the infinitive of the verb a-jar. This diadem of feathers, alluded to by every old traveller in the Brazil, was an effective and picturesque ornament.

[4] See Part I, chapter xxviii. Africans usually pierce the upper lip, which gives a beak-like aspect to the mouth, but the effect is not so un-clean as boring the lower lip.

grease it with their salves.[1] The hole thus remains open. Now, when they are big enough to bear arms it is made larger for them; for then they insert therein a large green stone.[2] This is so shaped, that the narrow end above comes to hang inside the lips, and the thick one outside. And their lips at all times hang down from the weight of the stone. They also have on both sides of the mouth,[3] on either cheek, another small stone.

Some have them of crystal, which are small but long. And also they wear an ornament, which they make out of large snail-shells; these they call Mattepue.[4] It is made like a crescent, to hang round the neck, and it is snow-white; they call it Bogessy.[5]

They also make from shells white necklaces, which they hang round their necks; these are about the thickness of a straw; they have much trouble in fashioning them.

They also tie feather plumes to their arms, and paint themselves black, also with red and white plumes, gaily mixed, and the feathers they stick on to the body with gum taken from trees.[6] This they spread on the places where they want to feather themselves. They also daub (with

[1] This is precisely the African system of boring the ears and lips, which I have described in the "Lake Regions of Central Africa".

[2] Nieuhoff (877) mentions "crystal, smaragd or jasper, of the bigness of a hazel-nut: this stone they call 'Metara', and if it be green or blue, 'Metarobi'; but they are most fond of the green ones."

[3] Amerigo Vespucci relates that he saw one man with seven holes in his face.

[4] See Part I, chap. xxviii. De Lery calls this wampum Bou-re. "Mattipue" is Matapú, the ornament worn by the chief "Uapixanas".

[5] Evidently Uru-assú, the big Urua, a shell found in Brazilian rivers. The South African Balonda wear a round ornament of the same kind, two of which are the price of a slave, and Dr. Livingstone (*First Journey*, chap. xvi) describes and sketches it. I found the same in the Lake Regions; and, of course, the inland people value it the more according to their distance from the sea.

[6] Thus, as it has been remarked, "tarring and feathering" came from the New World.

gum) the feathers, which then stick on. And they paint one arm black and the other red; the legs and the body are treated in like manner.

They also have an ornament made of ostrich plumes, which is a large round thing of feathers; this they tie to their posteriors, when they set forth to war against their enemies, or otherwise when they make a feast. It is called Enduap.[1]

They call themselves after wild animals, and they give themselves many names, but yet with this difference. At first, when they are born, a name is given, which they keep only until they become capable of bearing arms and of killing enemies. As many foes as a man has killed, so many names does he take.

Caput XVI.

What the women's ornaments are.

The women paint themselves under the eyes, and over the whole body, also in the before-mentioned manner, as the men paint themselves. But they allow the hair to grow

[1] Nhundu-apuam would be a ball or globe of the American ostrich, the Nhundu (Tupi, not to be confounded with the Nhandú) or Ema: the latter is a Portuguese corruption of the Arabic Ne'ámah (نعامة), the Abestruz, Struthio Rhea Linn., and not to be mistaken, as Southey does (ii, 341) for the "Emu". Father Merolla, in 1682 (Part I, Voyage to Cuzco), calls the bird Hiema. Pigafetta and all old travellers, mention this tail-piece, whose appearance is very whimsical. Thevot and De Léry call it Araroye; Yves d'Evreux (p. 23) speaks of "une rondache faite de plumes de la queue d'austruche". The Noticia (chap. clv) describes it as "huma roda de pennas de Ema". I found something of the kind amongst the Mpange (Fans) of the African Gabon, who wore a quaint kind of tail-piece, like that which adorns a hen's posterior. Ostrich feathers were used as ornaments in triumph by the Greeks and Romans. The universal choice points to some symbolic meaning; possibly, it was to teach warriors the Parthian practice attributed to the ostrich.

long, like other women. They have no particular ornaments, except in the ears where they drill holes, in which they hang objects about a span long, round, and about the thickness of a thumb, called in their language Mambibeya.[1] These are also made of shells, called Mattepue.

Their names are called after those of birds, fishes, and tree-fruits. They have from youth but one name ; but as many prisoners as the husbands kill, so many names the women give themselves. When one picks lice from the others, she eats the lice. I have often asked them why they did this. They said, that they were their enemies, who eat their heads, and that they would be revenged on them.[2]

There are also no regular midwives. When a woman is in child-birth, whoever is nearest, man or woman, runs up to her. I have seen them go about on the fourth day after they had brought forth.[3]

They carry their children on the back, in slings made of cotton-wool, and do their work with them. The children sleep, and are well satisfied, however much they (the mothers) stoop and move about with them.

---

[1] The Dictionaries give Namby and Namby-porá as the names of ring and ear-ring.

[2] So, says the *Noticia* (chap. clix), " O que não fazem pelos (piolhos) comer, mas em vingança de a morderem". This may result from, or may have given rise to, their practice of cannibalism. It is hard to believe that man-eating was necessary in a country so full of game, and where the waters abounded in fish (Part II, chap. xxv). The *Noticia do Brazil* (p. 47) expressly tells us of the Aimores, "Comem estes selvagens carne humana por mantimento, o que não tem o outro gentio, senão por vingança de suas brigas, e antiquidade de seus odios." Revenge, and perhaps superstition, would supply sufficient motives.

[3] Easy parturition and rare miscarriage are the prerogatives of savage and barbarous peoples, chiefly because the women, after conception, separate from their husbands. They rarely bring forth in sorrow, and after the short labour the mother bathes herself and her new-born in the nearest water ; whilst the husband is put to bed in his hammock for a longer or a shorter period, seldom less than twenty-four hours, and in some cases till the navel-string fall off. At the end of his work, Nieuhoff (p. 878) adds some unpleasant details. See Part II, chap. xxix.

Caput XVII.

How they give the child its first name.

One of the savages who helped me at work had a son born to him by his wife. Some days afterwards he called together his nearest neighbours in the huts, and consulted with them what name that was valiant and terrible he should give the child. They proposed to him many names, which did not quite please him. He thought that he would give it the name of one of four forefathers, and said that the children who bore those names throve well, and became cunning at catching slaves. He then named the four forefathers : the first was called Krunen, the other Hermittan, the third Koem, the fourth I have not retained. I thought, when he spoke of Koem, that it must be Cham (Ham). But Koem means, in their language, the morning.[1] I told him that he was to give him this name, for the same had no doubt been that of one of his forefathers. One of these names the child kept. In such manner they give their children names, without baptism or circumcision.

Caput XVIII.

How many wives each of them has, and how he manages them.

The greater part among them have one wife, but some of them more. Several of their kings have thirteen or fourteen wives. The king, called Abbati Bossange, to whom I was the last time presented, and from whom the Frenchmen

---

[1] Coéma is the morning; Coéma piranga (literally, Morgen-roth) is Aurora, the blushing. It is to be observed that Hans Stade generally makes harsh the liquid and musical sounds of the Tupi tongue by changing or eliding terminal vowels; by contractions; by permuting initials into consonants; and, in fine, by his system of barbarous spelling.

bought me, had many wives, and she who had been his first was the principal among them.[1] Each had her own lodging in the huts, her own fire, and her own root-plantations. That one with whom he cohabited, and in whose lodging he stayed, gave him food. This went round in such manner :[2] the children which they have, when they are boys, and are growing up, are taught the chase, and what they bring in each gives to his mother, who cooks it, and then divides it among the others. The women agree well together.[3] They also have the custom of one presenting the other with a wife if he be tired of her. They also sometimes present one another with their daughters and sisters.

Caput XIX.

How they are betrothed.

They betroth their daughters when they are still young, and when they grow up and arrive at puberty[4] they cut the

---

[1] The rule of all polygamous peoples, from the Tupis to the Mormons, is, that the first wife is *the* wife. According to Gabriel Soares, the senior had her hammock slung nearest the husband's, and at night a fire was kept burning between each two wives. Some tribes also distinguished number one by a peculiar name.

[2] This is somewhat according to Moslem law, which, following the Talmud, allows four wives, but compels the husband to keep a separate establishment, mounted on an equal footing, for each one, if she demand it.

[3] Another instance that the plurality system or patriarchal marriage does not make a " bleak house". In semi-civilisation, as in " the•East", disorders may result from it ; but, amongst savages and barbarians, it produces a division of labour which tends to the comfort and happiness of the woman. The same is the case in communities on the border lands of old and settled societies. It is curious to see the women of the " Saints" persisting against being subjected to monogamy ; but, though it is an anachronism, it is not an anachorism. The petitions for permissive polygamy in Massachusetts must be explained on different motives.

[4] When arrived at the age of puberty, girls, according to Gabriel

hair from their heads, scratch peculiar marks into their backs, and tie several teeth of wild animals round their necks. Thereupon, when the hair has grown again, and the incisions are healed, one nevertheless still sees the scars of the cuts; for they put something therein that may remain black when they are healed. This is held as a great honour.[1]

When such ceremonies are ended, they deliver the maiden up to him who is to have her, without any further ceremony. Men and women also conduct themselves decently, and sleep with one another privately.[2]

Further, I have also seen that one of their chiefs went in the early morning through all the huts, and scratched the children's legs with a sharp fish-tooth, in order to intimidate them : so that, should they become unmanageable, the parents might threaten them, that the said chief would come, the better to keep them quiet.

Soares loosened the tight ligatures which, bound under the knees, caused the legs and feet to swell. They also wore cotton strings round the waist and wrists, to show that they were marriageable; and if they were not virgins they broke the cords.

[1] In Tupi the tattooing (tattuir in Portuguese) was called Coátiar or Cuatiar—to stripe like a Coati (?), opossum. See Part II, chap. xxx. Hence a secretary was called "Quatiaapobara", he who paints (Southey, ii, 337). The colouring matter was of any burnt gum (according to Yves d'Evreux), especially the " copal" of the Jatoba tree (known as Jatoba-ycíca), or the brown-coloured juice of the Jenipapo tree, the Genipat of De Lery (Genipa Americana).

[2] These tribes appear not to have been so grossly vicious as those of whom Gabriel Soares says, " Não ha lingua honesta que refira, nem onvidos Catholicos que ouçam os factos, que obram estos Gentios para satisfação de sua sensualidade". (See *Noticia do Brazil*, chapter xcvi, " Que trata da luxuria d'estos barbaros".)

Caput XX.

What are their chief valuables.

There is no community of goods among them : also they know nothing of money. Their treasures are birds' feathers, of which he who has many is rich ; and he who wears his stones in the lips of his mouth, is also one of the richest.

Each couple, consisting of man and woman, have their own plantation of roots, whereof they eat.

Caput XXI.

What their greatest honours are.

They hold in honour him who has captured and slain many enemies. For this is customary among them, so many enemies as one of them slays, so many names does he give himself. And those are the noblest among them who have many such names.

Caput XXII.

What they believe in.

They believe in a thing which grows, like a pumpkin, about the size of a half-quart pot. It is hollow inside ; they pass through it a stick, cut a hole in it like a mouth, and put therein small stones, so that it may rattle. Herewith they rattle when they sing and dance, and call it Tammaraka.

Of these, each of the men has one of his own. Now, there are among them some who are called Paygi ;[1] these

[1] This subject again, like " Tupa" and " Sumé", is extensive. In the Lingua Geral, the priest was called Pay' (pronounced Paeu) and Paya ; he was Pawa in the United States; Beyé or Boyé in the Western Islands;

are esteemed among them as fortune-tellers are here. The
same travel through the country once a year to all the huts,
and assert that a spirit had been with them, who came from
foreign places far off, and had given them the power to
cause all the Tammaraka (rattles), which they selected, to
speak and to become so powerful as to grant whatever was
supplicated from them. Everyone then desires that this
power might come to his own rattle. Upon this they make
a great feast, with drinking, singing, and soothsaying, and
they perform many curious ceremonies.[1]   The soothsayers

Payé in Guiana; Peeaio (Harcourt) in the Wiapoc; Piaché in the Orinoco; in Hans Stade, Paygi and Pagy (Part II, chap. xxvi); and elsewhere, Pey, Pagi, Piayé, and Pagé: evidently variations of one word.
It was adopted by Christianity: Pay abaré oçu etê (the Real Great Big
Father) was the Pope; Pay abaré Guaçú was a prelate or a Jesuit (also
Pay' abúna, "black father"); Pay' Missa Monhangára (who does Mass)
was the common priest; and Pay' tucúra (grass-hopper priest) was the
monk from his hood.

The order evidently corresponds with the Medicine Man or the Rain
Doctor of the South African tribes; and it combined the offices of priest
and physician, augur and magician, ordeal-man and poisoner, juggler
and ventriloquist. The Pay' Ayba (Padre Bravo) would represent the
bad Sorcerer; the "Tempestaire", who claimed to govern the sun, moon,
wild beasts, and so forth. The College of Pagés would represent a
council of Druids or any other medicine men. Southey (ii, 162) believes
female Pagés to be rare: they appear, however, both in history and
fiction, witness the Tanajúra of the Uraguay poem by José Basilio da
Gama. See also Hans Stade, Part II, chap. xxiii.

The good missioners, who saw the Devil in every faith except their
own, of course made their barbarous rival a priest of the foul Fiend.
They could not discern the soul of good in things evil, such as slavery
and cannibalism. But the institution had its uses: it was, and it is,
the first step towards emerging from the purely savage state. It gave
method and direction to the vague fears which primæval man shared
with the gorilla; it created a comparatively learned class, whose business in life was to study and to think; and it taught the art of govern-
ing as well as of being governed. Of course the time came when it
had done its work, and then, as is the course of things human, it was
succeeded by something better, and was looked back upon, not with respect and gratitude, but with a childish and unreasonable horror.

[1] We find the Tupis progressing beyond the rattle. Barrière, who

thereupon appoint a day in a hut, which they cause to be vacated, no women or children being allowed to remain therein. Then the soothsayers command that each shall paint his Tammaraka red, ornament it with feathers, and proceed thither, and that the power of speech shall be conferred upon them. Hereupon they go to the hut, and the soothsayers place themselves at the head, and have their Tammaraka sticking close to them in the ground. The others then stick theirs also hard by : each one gives these jugglers presents, which are arrows, feathers, and ornaments, to hang to the ears ; so that his Tammaraka may on no account be forgotten. Then, when they are all together, the soothsayer takes each man's Tammaraka singly, and fumigates it with a herb, which they call Bittin.[1] Then he places the rattle close to his mouth, and rattles therewith, saying to it: "Nee Kora,[2] now speak, and make thyself heard, art thou therein ?" Presently he speaks in a soft voice, and just a word or two, so that one cannot well perceive whether it is the rattle or he who speaks. And the other people believe that the rattle speaks ; but the soothsayer does it himself. In such manner he proceeds with all the rattles, one

wrote about a century after Yves d'Evreux (*Nouvelle Rélation de la France Equinoxiale*, etc., etc., Paris, 1743), speaks of a " Piayerie", a figure (of course of the Devil) of soft and sounding wood, three to four feet high, with long tail and claws, which the Pagé, after blowing upon the sick, carried out of the wigwam and beat, until it ceased to haunt his patient. Certain images of Saints have been subjected to the same process.

[1] German for P'ty' (see Introduction) or Pytýma, the common form (in chap. clxiv of the *Noticia* misprinted Patem), the Betum of Damião Goes and Balthazar Telles, and the Betume of Piso. The Bretons have preserved the original word, which was brought over from Brazil ; and we read in Scarron—

    S'il avait l'haleine importune
    Comme d'un homme qui petune.

Nicotianum Tabacum, or Herva Santa, was, in fact, the incense of the Tupi ritual.

[2] " Anheeng" (Enheeng or Nheeng) ; *i.e.*, speak and " Coyr", now.

after the other: each one then believes that his rattle contains great power. Thereupon, the soothsayers command
them to go to war, and to capture enemies, for that the
spirits in the Tammaraka desire to eat the flesh of slaves.
Then they go forth to make war.

Now, when the soothsaying Paygi has made gods out of
all the rattles, each one takes his rattle, calling it his dear
son, builds for it a separate hut, wherein he places it, puts
food before it, and demands from it everything that he
wants, just as we pray to the true God. These are now
their gods. Of that very God who created heaven and
earth, they know nothing, they consider the heavens and
the earth to have existed from eternity; and they know
nothing particular about the creation of the world.

For they say, once there had been a great water, which
had drowned their forefathers, some of whom had escaped
in a canoe, and others on high trees. Which, I opine, must
have been the Deluge.[1]

---

[1] Like all races, the Tupis preserved traditions of *a* Deluge, but not
of the Babylonian Deluge, as the missionaries would naturally suppose.
Their legends, as might be expected from an analphabetic people, are
wild and incoherent.

One tradition declares that the first populators of the Brazilian coast,
two brothers, Tamoyo and Tabayara, landed at Cabo Frio, north of Rio
de Janeiro, the Promontory of Cannibals, whose population claimed to
be of Carib (Caraïb) race. The senior settled there, and his descendants
spread to north of Bahia. The junior, when disputes had arisen touching a certain talking parrot, coasted down to the Rio de la Plata,
ascended it, and settled on the southern bank : thus his family peopled
the Pampas, Chili, Peru, and other parts. Presently, the sons of
Tamoyo were visited by a flood, which drowned all flesh, save a man,
his wife, and his children. This was Tamandaré (Vasconcellos calls him
Temenduaré or Temendoaré), which appears to signify Timandonar,
" he remembers" (Figueira, *sub voce*). Deucalion and Pyrrha climbed
with their young up a Pindó palm, which touched the sky ; and when
the flood abated, they descended at Cabo Frio, the cradle of the race. I
wonder that it has not been called Mount Ararat, especially when a
certain theologian proved that Noah landed near Pernambuco, and

Now, when I first came among them, and they told me thereof, I thought there was such a thing as a devil-spectre (evil spirit); for they had often told me how the rattles spoke. But when I went into the huts wherein were the soothsayers, who were to make them speak, they were all obliged to sit down; and, seeing the imposture, I went from out of the huts, thinking what an unfortunate beguiled people it was.

Caput XXIII.

How they make soothsayers of the women.

They first go into a hut and take all the women, one after the other, and fumigate them. After this, the women are made to yell and jump, and run about until they become so exhausted, that they fall on the ground, as if they were dead. Thereupon, the soothsayer says, " See, now she is dead; soon I will bring her to life again"! When she comes to herself, he says that she is now able to foretell future things; and when they go to war, the women must prophesy about the war.

One night the wife of my master (to whom I was presented to be killed) began to prophesy, and told her husband that a spirit had come to her from foreign lands, who demanded

when Belem of Pará has been so often confounded with Bethlehem of Judæa.

Another tradition represents Sumé to have had two sons—Tamandaré, or Abel, while Cain was represented by Aricoute, or Agitated Day. After a quarrel the former struck the earth, when water issued, extending to the tree-tops, but both escaped by climbing the highest. This was supposed to have taken place only five or six generations before A.D. 1555. Of course it was "universal", as it extended seven or eight hundred leagues from Cabo Frio to the Rio de la Plata ; and, by the very nature of all deluge-stories, there must be a family likeness ; either one person is saved, or two, generally, but not always, man and wife, or a whole family.

to know from her how soon I was to be killed, and asked
after the club wherewith I was to be slain, and where it
was. He answered her, it was not far off; all the preparations were ready; only, he inclined to think, that I was no
Portuguese, but a Frenchman.

When the woman had finished her prediction, I asked her
why she sought after my life, inasmuch as that I was no
enemy; and whether she did not fear that my God would
send her some plague. She said I was not to mind this, for
they were foreign spirits, who wanted to have information
about me. Of such ceremonies they have many.

Caput XXIV.

Wherein they sail on the water.

In the country is a species of tree called Yga Ywara:[1]
they separate its bark entire from the trunk, from top to
bottom, making a stage for the purpose round about the
tree, in order to take it off completely.

Thereupon, they take the bark and carry it from the
mountains to the sea; they heat it with fire, bend it high
up in front and behind,[2] lash two pieces of wood above it in
the middle, so that it may not stretch: and thus they make
canoes wherein thirty of them can sail forth to war. The
bark is of the thickness of a thumb, about four feet wide
and forty feet long: some are longer and others are shorter.

[1] Yga-ywero, a big canoe, capable of holding forty men, so corpu-
lent, we are told, were the trees. Ubá was the bark Coracle, the "birch"
of the Northern Continent. Yga (Iga) and Ygara (Igara) was any
canoe, and Igaripe (in Ferd. Denis, "Ygarité) was of bark. The Mara-
catim was a large war canoe, with the Maraca rattle at the prow (tim=
nose or snout). European ships were called Igarassú, big canoes.

[2] It may be added that nothing can be more graceful than the shapes
borrowed by the Brazilians from the savages who preceded them: the
local craft vies in beauty with that of Venice.

These they paddle very quickly,[1] and sail therein as far as they wish. When the sea becomes stormy, they draw up the canoes on the shore, until the weather becomes fine. They do not venture more thon two miles out to sea, but sail far along the coast.

Caput XXV.

Why one enemy eats the other.

They do this, not from hunger, but from great hatred and enmity, and when they are fighting, during war, one, impelled by great hatred, calls out to the other, " Dete Immeraya, Schermiuramme, heiwoe"; or, "·May every misfortune come upon thee, my meat !" "De Kanga Yuca eypota kurine"; or, "This day I will yet break your head !" " Sche Innamme pepicke Reseagu"; or, " To revenge my friend's death on thee, am I here!" "Yande soo, sche mocken Sera, Quora Ossorime Rire, etc."; or, " Thy flesh shall this day, before the sun sets, be my roast !" All this they do from great enmity.

Caput XXVI.

How they make their plans, when they purpose carrying war into their enemies' country.

When they desire to carry war into their enemies' country, their chiefs assemble, and deliberate how they will do it. This they then make known through all the huts, that they may arm themselves. And they name the fruit of some kind of tree, when it becomes ripe, (as the time) when they

---

[1] So the African surf-boat, worked by many paddles, which can "put on steam", or "stop her", at a moment's notice, is the only safe craft for crossing dangerous river-bars.

will set forth; for they have no denominations for year[1] and day. They often determine a time for setting forth, when a kind of fish spawn, which are called Pratti in their language, and the spawning time they call Pirakaen. At such time they equip themselves with canoes and arrows, and with provisions of dry root-meal, which they call Vythan. Thereupon, they consult with the Pagy, the soothsayers, whether the victory will be on their side. These, then, probably say "Yes"; but they also command them to pay attention to the dreams which they dream of their enemies. If the greater number dream that they see the flesh of their enemies roasting, this means victory. But when they see their own flesh roasting, it bodes no good; they must remain at home. Now, when the dreams please them well, they make ready, brew much drink in all huts, and drink and dance with the Tammaraka idols, each one begging of his, that he may help him to capture an enemy. Then they sail away. When they come close upon their enemies' country, their chiefs command them, on the eve of the day

---

[1] The year is mentioned by the earliest travellers. Vespucci (Lettere) found the reckoning kept by pebbles. Pigafetta (Book 1) says that age was proved by showing son, grandson, great-grandson, and great-great-grandson still living. The term used for year was Acajú or Cajú, the Cashew nut, which Nieuhoff calls Acaguakeya, Akajuti, or Itamabara; it flowers in August and September, and fruits in December and January. The savages kept every year a stone of this fruit, which was their grape, and thus could remember their age. They observed the stars, and called them Jacy-tata, fire of moon. Amongst some tribes, says Nieuhoff, the year began with the rise of Taku or the Rain-star; amongst others, with the heliacal rising of the Pleiades; and they knew Polaris, which, from its apparent want of motion, they called the Dead Star. They divided the year into two seasons with great correctness. The first was Coaraçy-ara, sun-season or heat, and the second was Almana-ara or rain-season. According to De Lery, they reckoned their years by moons. Weeks were obtained by observing the changes of Ja-cy, "our Mother", the Moon. New moon was Ja-cy peçaçu; the first quarter was Ja-cy jemorotuçu; full moon was Ja-cy Cabroçú, and the last quarter was Ja-cy Jearoca.

upon which they intend invading the enemies' country, to recollect the dreams which they may dream during the night.

On one expedition, when I was with them, as we came close to their enemies' country in the evening, when it was their intention to attack the foe during the next night, the chief went through the camp, and told them that they were to remember well the dreams which they would dream that night. He commanded further, that the young men should, when the day broke, shoot game and catch cattle. This was done; the chief had it cooked, and he then called together the other chiefs, who came before his hut. He made all sit down upon the ground, in a circle; food was given to them, and when they had eaten they recounted the dreams, so far as they pleased them, and then they danced for joy with the Tammaraka. They reconnoitre their enemies' huts during the night, and attack in the morning, as the day breaks. When they capture one who is severely wounded, they at once kill him, and take the roasted flesh home with them. Those who are still sound they carry back alive, and afterwards they kill them in their huts. They attack with loud yells, trample hard upon the ground, and blow trumpets made of pumpkins. All have cords bound round them, wherewith to tie the enemies, and they adorn themselves with red feathers, so that they may know themselves from the others. They shoot rapidly, and they also cast on their enemies' huts fiery arrows, wherewith to burn them. When one is wounded they have their specific herbs wherewith they heal the hurts.

Caput XXVII.

What their weapons are.

They have bows, and their arrow-heads are of bone, which they sharpen, and bind thereon. They also make them of the teeth of a fish, which is called Tibeset Tiberaun,[1] which are caught in the sea. They also take cotton-wool, mix it with wax, tie it to the piles of the shafts, and set fire thereto; these are their burning arrows. They also make shields of the bark of trees, and others of wild beasts' skins, and they bury sharp thorns like our foot-hooks (caltraps).

I have also heard from them, but did not see it, that, when they wish to do so, they can, in this manner, drive their enemies from the forts with pepper, which grows there. They make great fires when the wind blows, and then they throw thereon a quantity of pepper:[2] if the fumes were to strike into their huts, they would have to evacuate them. And I readily believe it, for I was once with the Portuguese, in a province of the country called Braunen-bucke, as hereinbefore mentioned. There we remained, lying dry, with a ship in a river, for the flood had left us; and many savages came, thinking to take us, but they could not. Upon this they threw heaps of dry underwood between the ship and the shore, also intending to drive us away with pepper fumes, but they could not light the wood.

---

[1] Here we should probably read Yperu (the Tupi name for the Portuguese) Tubarão, a squalus, a shark. See Part I, chap. xxii.

[2] This reminds us of the Chinese "stink-pots" and pepper-pots". For descriptions of the many pimentos or peppers growing wild in Brazil, see Part II, chaps. x and xxxvi; the *Noticia do Brazil* (chap. xlviii) and *Highlands of the Brazil* (i, 103). The generic name is Kyg'nha, by corruption Quiya and Cuihem; the most common varieties are the Cuihem-oçú, Cujepia, Sabaa, Pesihe-jurimu, and Comari or Comarim.

Caput XXVIII.

With what ceremonies they kill their enemies and eat them, and how they proceed with them.

When they first bring their enemies home, the women and children beat them. Thereupon, they paint the captive with grey feathers, shaving his eyebrows from above his eyes; they dance about him, tie him securely that he may not escape them, and give him a woman, who takes care of him, and who also has intercourse with him.[1] And when she becomes pregnant they bring up the child until it is full grown; after which, whenever they take it into their heads, they slay it and eat it.[2] They give him plenty of food, keeping him in this manner for a time; they prepare everything; they make many pots, wherein they keep the drinks; they bake peculiar vessels, wherein they put the compounds wherewith they paint him; they get ready feather-tassels, which they tie to the club with which they will kill him, and then twist a long cord called Mussurana, wherewith

---

[1] Cases are known of the women running away with the captive and saving the child thus born, despite the theories of the savages in which they were brought up. Usually the concubine was expected to attend the death of her man, to weep a little, and to eat a bit of his flesh.

[2] Tupi physiology, on this point at least, resembled that of the Hebrews, who doubtless borrowed from the older Egyptians. The child was in the loins of its father (Heb. vii, 10) : the male parent was the sole progenitor, and the mother was only the nidus or nest, the depository of the fœtus. Curious consequences resulted from this theory. In the first place, the son of a male captive was a slave for ever—as in Africa, there was no freedom for the born servile. Secondly, the parents had different names for "son" and "daughter": the father, for instance, said "Tayra", or being from my blood ; the mother, " Membira", my born ; and the captive's child, was " Cunha Membira", or son of a woman, *i.e.*, without a father ; also all fruit-bearing trees were called males, the barren being females. Vespucci tells us that the Caribs ate their own children by captive women and caponized them for easier fattening : the tribe in question must have been exceptionally ferocious.

they bind him before he is to die. When they have all the requisites together, they fix upon a time for his death, and they invite the savages from other villages to proceed thither at that time. They then fill all the vessels with liquor, and a day or two before the women make the drinks they lead the prisoner once or twice to the area, and they dance around him.[1]

Now, when those who come from afar are all gathered together, the chief of the huts bids them welcome, saying, " Now come, help to eat your enemy !" The day before they begin to drink they tie the Mussuruna cord round the prisoner's neck. The same day they paint the club, called Iwera Pemme, wherewith they intend to dispatch him, and which is shaped in the form here described. It is more than a fathom in length, and over it they spread a sticky substance : they then take egg-shells, which are of a grey colour, and are laid by a bird called Mackukawa ;[2] these

[1] With all their ferocity and outrageous cannibalism, the Tupis, I may observe, did not invariably practise upon their prisoners the hideous tortures which disgraced their wild brethren in North America. One of their practices, however, has hitherto been supposed peculiar to Abyssinia. " Ha alguns d'estes barbaros, que são tão carniceiros, que cortão aos vencidos depois de mortos suas naturas, assim aos machos, como ás femeas, os quaes levão para darem a suas mulheres, que os guardão depois di mirradas no fogo, para nas suas festas as darem a comer aos maridos por reliquias, o que lhes dura muito tempo."—*Noticia do Brazil*, chap. clxviii.

[2] Generally Maculo ; in *Prince Max. of Wied Neuwied* (iii, 3), Macucára (Tetrao Major, Linn. ; or Tinamus Brasiliensis Lath.) According to Lacondamine, the eggs saved the life of Madame Godin. This gallinaceous bird, which can be caught by dogs, lays upon the ground greenish-blue eggs, about the size of a goose's. It has been successfully domesticated in the Brazil, and there is no reason why this should not be done in Europe. The gallinaceæ seem to be easily acclimatised in all save the Polar zones, and much still remains to be done in that way by civilised man. For instance, the whole of thé Penelope family, especially the Jacú and the Jacú-pema (P. Superciliaris Linn.), would be valuable imports, superior in flight, as in flesh, to the pheasants. I have seen these also tame in Brazil. Again, the Curassow family, the

they crush to powder, which they spread over the club.
Then a woman sits down, and traces lines in the adhering
egg-shell-dust. Whilst she paints, a lot of women, who are
standing about her, sing. When the Iwera Pemme is decked
out as it should be, with feather-tassels and other objects,
they hang it in an empty hut to a pole, above the ground,
and then they sing around it during the whole night.

In like manner, they paint the prisoner's face; also,
whilst the woman is painting him, the others sing. And
when they begin to drink, they take with them the prisoner,
who drinks with them, and they chat with him.

Now, as the drinking comes to an end, they rest the day
after, and they make for the prisoner a hut on the place
where he is to die. Here he lies during the night, well
guarded.[1] Towards morning, some time before daylight,
they begin to dance and to sing round about the club, wherewith they intend killing him, and they continue until day
breaks. Then they take the prisoner out of the hut, which
they pull down; they clear a space; they take the Mussurana from off his neck; and they tie it round his body,
drawing it tight at both ends. He stands bound in the
middle, many of them holding the cords at both ends. They
let him stand thus for a while, and they place small stones
close to him, that he may throw them at the women,[2] who
run around him and threaten to eat him. These same are

Hocco or Mutum (Crax Alector) is a more showy bird, and better eating
than the turkey. As yet, we have borrowed two birds from America,
the turkey and the Manilla duck; one from Central Asia, the pheasant;
two from India, the peacock and the domestic fowl; and one from Africa,
the Guinea fowl.

[1] I can hardly imagine a man not being able to escape from so futile a
race of savages, and many must have done so. Probably the "brave"
would have disdained thus to save his life.

[2] Other authors relate that the victim is allowed some length of rope,
in order that he may the better injure his slayers; in fact, he was
allowed to die fighting.

now painted and ready, when he is cut to pieces, to run with his four quarters round the huts. In this the others find pastime.

Now, when this has been done, they make a fire about two feet from the prisoner : this fire he must see. Then a woman comes running about with the club Iwera Pemme ; turns the feather-tassels in the air, and shouts with joy, running before the prisoner that he may see it.

When this is done, a man takes the club, goes with it and stands before the prisoner, and holds it before him, so that he may look at it. Meanwhile, he who is going to kill him, together with fourteen or fifteen others, go and paint their bodies grey with ashes. Then the slayer proceeds with his companions to the place where the prisoner is, and the other, who stands before the captive, delivers up the club to him. The king of the huts now interposes, takes the club, and places it once between his legs who was to slay the prisoner.

This is considered a great distinction among them. He who has to kill the captive again takes the club, and then says, " Yes, here I. am ! I will kill thee, for thine have also killed and eaten many of my friends." Answers he, " When I am dead, I shall yet have many friends, who will revenge me well." Hereupon, the other strikes him on the head from behind, so that his brains are dashed out. At once he is seized by the women, who drag him to the fire, scrape all his skin off, making him quite white, and stop up his posterior with a piece of wood, so that nothing of him may be lost.

When the skin is scraped off, a man takes the body and cuts the legs off above the knee, and the arms. Then four women come and carry away the four pieces, and run with them round the huts, raising great cries of joy. Thereupon they cut off his back with the posterior from the fore-part : this they then divide among themselves ; but the entrails are kept by the women, who boil them, and with the broth they make a mess called Mingau. This they and the children drink, the bowels they devour, and they also eat the flesh from off the head: the brains in the head, the tongue, and whatever else is eatable, the young ones eat. When this is done, all go home again, and take their share with them. He who has killed the prisoner gives himself one more name, and the king of the huts scratches his upper arm with a wild beast's tooth. When it is properly healed, the scars are seen; that is the distinction he gains thereby. He must lie that same day quietly in a hammock,[1] his people giving him a small bow, with an arrow, wherewith to pass the time shooting into wax. This is done in order that his aims may not become uncertain from the shock of the death-blow. All this I have seen and have been present at.

They also cannot count any certain number beyond five; when they would count more, they point to their fingers and toes. If they desire to speak of any greater number, they point to four or five persons, as many fingers and toes as they want to express.

[1] This is the Gésine and the Couvade of the Bearn and Basque peoples. Vasconcellos quotes Fr. João de Peneda, Strabo (Lib. III) and others, to show that it has existed amongst many ancient peoples: the Iberians, the Corsicans, and the Tibareni (Apoll. Rhodius, ii, 1012). Marco Polo (ii, 41) found it amongst the Tartars, and all travellers of the sixteenth century remark it amongst the South American tribes, the Caribs, the Jivaros, and others. The father took to his hammock, and lay there (*dans ses couches*) for a time lest any accident happen to the newly-born; if the progenitor died, the offspring being part of him, also perished. A similar reverence for life, eccentrically displayed, forbade the lying-in husband to kill anything or even to eat eggs during the wife's pregnancy. It is curious that Southey, who fairly explains the practice (i, 248; iii, 165), should rank this practice with observances wholly unaccountable. See Part II, chap. xvii.

Caput XXIX.

Account of sundry beasts of the country.

There are in the country deer like ours; wild pigs of two
kinds, of which one resembled those in this country; the
other is called Teygasu[1] Dattu, small like a young pig.
The same is very difficult to catch in the traps, which the
savages use for the purpose of catching game.

There are also baboons of three species. The kind called
Key, is that which is brought to this country. There is
another species named Ackakey,[2] which is seen jumping
about in great numbers on the trees, making a great noise
in the forest.

And there is yet another kind called Pricki;[3] these are

[1] Tayasu, or Tagaçu (Tajasu of the *Noticia*, chap. c), in Tupi was a
wild pig, generically the Aper of Anchieta, the Sus Tajassu of Linn.
The word is derived from Caa-etê, virgin forest, and Çuu (suu) game,
the C being changed for euphony into T, and the word meaning " game
of the virgin forest". That alluded to in the text is the Peccari, the
Tayatatú, Tattetú, Cattete, and commonly Caïtete; in Espirito Santo it
is known as Bakarin, and in Luso-brasilian, Porco do Matto. This
"wart-hog" or " hog with navel on the back", as old travellers call it, is
the small porcupine-quilled Dicotyles Torquatus, of white colour, turning to grey and silver, on a black base, without tail, very fierce and fond
of biting, and hard to tame : the flesh is good, and the chiefs of certain
tribes used the teeth by way of necklace. The other is a much larger
species, known in Tupi as " Tayu tinga", and to the colonists as Porco
de Queixo Branco (white-cheeked hog) or Queixada from the clashing
of its teeth. The *Noticia* gives two species, the Tajasutiraqua and the
Tajasuetu. It haunts in droves the wilder parts of the Brazil, and cuts
off the paths. The traveller, unless he can climb a tree or a rock, would
be instantly devoured even to the nails : I have thus been detained
several days.

[2] Caya is the generic term for monkey, also written Cayarára.
" Ackakey" (Áca-Caya) is the horned-monkey (also name of a fish), and
Cayanhanga (*Noticia*, chap. civ, " Caieunhanga), the " bogio diabo", or
devil monkey.

[3] See Buriqui, before noticed.

red; they have beards like goats, and they are as large as an average sized dog.

There is also a kind of animal called Dattu,[1] which is about a span in height, and a span and a half long; it is everywhere about the body covered with armour, on the belly only it has none. The armour is like horn, closing together with links resembling mail; it has a small but long-pointed snout, and a long tail; it frequents rocky places; its food is ants, and the flesh is rich. I have often eaten of it.

CAPUT XXX.

There is also a kind of game, called Serwoy,[2] which is as large as, and which has a tail like, a cat; its hair is whitish-grey, and also blackish-grey. And when it breeds it bears about six young, and it has a slit in the belly, about half a span in length. Within the slit there is yet another skin; for its belly is not open, and within this slit are the teats. Wherever it goes, it carries its young in the slit between the two skins. I have often helped to catch them, and have pulled the young ones from out of the slit.

[1] The Tatú, Tato or Dasypus, is the well-known Armadillo (a Spanish word), called by the Dutch "Schilt-Verken", or shield-hog. There are many species: D. Gigas, Minutus, Sexdecim-cinctus, Tricinctus, Villosus, Niger, Hybridus, Orbicularis, and Chlamydophorus Truncatus (Harlan), the latter very rare.

[2] This is the Cuati, Quatý, or Coatim (the opossum, Viverra Nasua Linn. Ureus Nasua Cuv.), from Cuá, the waist, and tim, the nose; because, living in the woods, it sleeps on trees doubled up, like a dog, with the snout at its side. The plantigrade extends to the basin of La Plata; it is carnivorous, but eats vegetables, and is easily tamed, although troublesome and destructive. Pietro Martire and other old travellers describe it as having the forehand of a fox, the hind parts of a monkey, the feet of a man, and the ears of a bat. The Cuati must not be confounded with the Cotía (Cavia Aguti Linn.; Dasyprocta Aguti Ilig., or Dasyprocta Azaræ Lich.)

M

In the country are also many tigers,[1] which devour the people, and which commit great ravages. There is also a kind of lion, which is called Leoparda; that is to say, grey lion.[2] And many other singular animals are found.

The beasts called Catiuare[3] exist on land and in water. They eat the reeds which stand on the fresh water shores; and when they are alarmed by anything, they dive to the bottom. They are larger than a sheep, and they have heads something like that of the hare, but larger, and short-eared; their tails are stumpy, and their legs somewhat long. They also run swiftly on land, from one river to the other; the hair is greyish-black. They have three balls on each foot, and they taste like hogs' flesh.

There is also a kind of large water-lizard, and others on shore, which are good to eat.[4]

[1] In the original, Thiegerthûr, which must bet he ounce, opposed to the jaguar or puma, here called lion and leopard. The ounce (Felis discolor) is popularly called Onça Pintada; the old animal (Tigre Sovado) is said to attack men : it is a great eater, and the skin, which is some-times five feet three inches long, is valued for shabracks The Jaguar-ete-hun ("true black ounce"), the Onça Preta or Parda, is found prin-cipally in and about Paraguay ; the very rare and beautiful pelts may be compared with those of the black leopard on the Niger and in Western Africa.

[2] See Part I, chap. xliii.

[3] The well-known Cavia Capybara Linn. (Anchieta, " de Glire Ca-pyûára, hoc est, herbas pascentia"), a water-hog, whose name is derived from Capim, grass, and G-uara, an eater. I have described it in the *Highlands of the Brazil* (i, 3). "Larger than a sheep" must be taken *cum grano ;* but probably in those days German mutton did not reach the size of the modern Saxony breed, otherwise the account is very cor-rect.   Like mackaws and parrots, dogs and monkeys, it was made a pet of and domesticated in the days of Anchieta, "ut catuli aluntur domi".

[4] The water-lizard is the Cayman or Jacaré (in the *Noticia do Brazil,* Jaguaré) mentioned by Anchieta, chap. § ix, de Crocodilo, "Sunt et Lacerti itidem fluviatiles qui Jacaré dicuntur". The annotator's note (18) also describes the Caymans of the Amazonas, which " Maculam cioceam sub collo habent".

Caput XXXI.

Of a species of insect like small fleas, which the savages call Attun.[1]

There are small insects, which are like fleas, but smaller, called in the savage tongue Attun, and bred in the huts by the uncleanliness of the people. These same creep into the foot, and only cause a tickling sensation when they enter, eating themselves into the flesh, so that one scarcely feels it. If it is not perceived and pulled out at once, it lays a bag of eggs, round as a pea. Then, when one feels it and pulls it out, a small hole of the size of a pea remains in the flesh. I have known them, when I first arrived in the country with the Spaniards, badly to injure the feet of some of our companions, who heeded them not.

Caput XXXII.

Of a kind of bat[2] of the country, and how at night, during sleep, it bites into the toes and foreheads of the natives.

There is also a kind of bat, which is larger than those here in Germany. These beasts fly during the night into the huts and about the hammocks, wherein the people sleep.

[1] Father Michael Angelo describes these pests (Pulex Penetrans or Subentrans), and opines that the "Guattini" were one of the plagues of Egypt. F. Merolla (*Voyage to Congo*) calls them Nigua, and describes them well. The common Tupi name is Tunga (misprinted in the *Noticia*, chap. cxxiv, Jumga) and Tumbýra; hence De Lery, Claude d'Abbeville, and Yves d'Evreux term them Ton or Thon. The common flea was Tungasu. They are the "Pharoah's lice" of Angelo and Carli. The Portuguese name is Bicho do pé, ill-judged, because the insect also burrows under the hand-nails, as St. Hilaire found out. Azara reckons thirteen species. Hans Stade's description, as far as it goes, is very correct. Compare with F. Denis (Notes to Yves d'Evreux, p. 416), Koster (ii, 19), Southey (iii, 861), and *Highlands of the Brazil* (ii, 187).

[2] This Vampire, Phyllostoma Spectrum, in Tupi Andyra (Andura of

And when they perceive that anyone sleeps, and lets them, they fly to the feet, and bite a mouthful, or they bite into the forehead, and then fly away again.

Whilst I was among the savages, they often bit my toes; and when I awoke, I saw the toes bleeding. But they generally bite the savages in the forehead.[1]

Caput XXXIII.

Of the bees of the country.

There are three kinds of bees[2] in the country. The first is quite similar to those of this country.

The others are black, and as large as flies. The third are small like gnats. These bees all lay their honey in hollow trees, and I have often cut out honey with the savages.

the *Noticia*), and Morcego of the Portuguese, is familiar to every Brazilian traveller. These rhinophylls bite and suck any projecting part : I have heard of a man's nose suffering (*Highlands of the Brazil*, i, 10).

[1] There can hardly be any reason for this difference of treatment.

[2] The *Noticia* (chap. xci) enumerates the Uehú, Tapiuca, Taturama, Cabece, Caapoam, Cabatan, Saracoma, Cabaobajuba, and Copueroçú. Nieuhoff gives twelve kinds. Our principal authorities upon the subject of Brazilian bees are Spix and Martius, St. Hilaire (*Voyage dans les Provinces de Rio de Janeiro et de Minas Geraes*, ii, 371), and Dr. Gardner, the botanist, who travelled in 1836 to 1841. Most of the insects are stingless, and the honey (called by the Tupis Ira) is very liquid, whilst the wax is too dark to be valuable. The kind called Tatuira emits, as the name expresses, a burning fluid, and is generally plundered at night. Other species, as the Sanharó, Burá, Uruçu-boi, Chupé, Arapua, and Tubi, defend themselves, when attacked, by biting, not by stinging. The Jata, Mondura, and Nandacaya give the best honey, the Uruçu and the Mumbuçu give the most. The Irapuan (usually called Arapuá), from Ira, honey, and puam, round, because the comb is so shaped ; is fierce and stings painfully. Padre Anchieta (*loc. cit.*, § xxxii, de Apibus) mentions Eíraaquâyetá, a poison-honey : like that of Sardinia, according to the classics, *contrahit nervos, dolorem et tremorem immittit*, etc.

Caput XXXIV.

Of the birds of the country.

There are also many singular birds there, a kind called Uwara Pirange,[1] which have their feeding-grounds on the sea-coast, and make their nests on the rocks, which lie close to the shore. They are nearly as large as hens; they have long beaks, and legs like a heron, but not so long. Their peculiarity is, that the first feathers which grow on the young are whitish-grey; when they become fledged, the plume is blackish-grey. With these it is known that they fly one year, then they change these feathers and the whole bird becomes as red as any red paint can be, and so it remains. Its feathers are much prized by the savages.

Caput XXXV.

Account of several trees of the country.

There are trees there which the savages call Inni Papoeeywa,[2] and on these grow fruits not unlike apples. This fruit the savages chew and squeeze the juice into a vessel. Herewith they paint themselves; when they first spread it over the skin it looks like water; then, after a while, the skin becomes as black as ink. This dye lasts till the ninth day; then it disappears, and not before, however much they may wash themselves in water.

[1] The Tantalus Ruber before described. See Part I, chap. xix.
[2] The papaw tree (Carica Papaya), generally called Mammoeira, from the fruit Mammão being shaped like mammæ. The Dutch term it the melon tree. Southey (iii, 317) explains it in a foot-note, "a sort of bread-fruit, probably the Mammea Americana".

Caput XXXVI.

How cotton-wool[1] grows, and the Brazilian pepper, also sundry other roots, which the savages plant for food.

The cotton-wool grows on shrubs, about a fathom high, with many branches; when it flowers, it produces balls, which, when about to ripen, open, and the wool in these balls surrounds black kernels, which are the seed from which it is planted. Of these balls the shrubs are full.

The pepper of the country is of two kinds: the one yellow, the other red;[2] both, however, grow in like manner. When green it is as large as the haws that grow on hawthorns. It is a small shrub, about half a fathom high, and has small leaves; it is full of peppers, which burn the mouth. They pluck it when it becomes ripe, and they dry it in the sun.

There are also roots, which they call Jettiki,[3] of pleasant taste. When they plant them they cut small pieces, which are placed in the earth: these then grow, and spread over the ground, like hop trees, throwing off many roots.

Conclusion.

Hans Stade wishes the reader God's mercy and peace.

Kind reader! This, my navigation and travel, I have purposely described with brevity, only to recount how I first fell into the hands of the barbarous people. Therewith to shew how mightily against all hope, the Helper in need, our

[1] The cotton-plant was called by the Tupis "Maniú"; in the *Noticia*, chap. lii, "Manym".

[2] The black (and white) being, as is well known, Asiatic species.

[3] The Tupi word is Jetyca, also applied to the batata or sweet potato. Southey (i, 20) opines that the word Iuhame or Anhame, whence our "yam", is not Haytian nor Tupi, but probably South African.

Lord and God, has delivered me from out of their power. Also that everyone may hear, that Almighty God, now, as much as ever, wonderfully protects and accompanies His believers in Christ among the godless, heathen people; also that for this you all may be thankful with me to God, and trust to Him in the time of need. For He Himself says : " Call to me in the time of need, and I will save thee, and thou shalt glorify me."

Now, many might say : " Yes; were I to print all that during my life I have attempted and seen, it would make a big book." It is true ; in such manner, I should also be able to describe much more. But the case here is different. I have sufficiently, here and there, pointed out the object which induced me to write this little book, and thus we all owe to God praise and thanksgivings, that He has preserved us from the hours of our births to the present hours of our lives.

Further, I can well conceive that the contents of this little book will seem strange to many. Who can help this ? Nevertheless, I am not the first, nor shall I be the last, to whom such voyages, lands, countries, and people are well known. These same will certainly not scoff at such things, of which they have become convinced ; rather they will henceforward become the more convinced of them.

But can it be expected that he who is to be sent from life unto death, should be in the same frame of mind as those who stand afar and look on, or who hear the tale thereof? Anyone may answer this question for himself.

Also, if all those who sail to America should fall into the hands of their barbarous enemies, who would wish to proceed thither ?

But this I know verily, that many an honest man in Civilien (Seville), Portugal, and France, also some in Antdorff in Braband, who have been in America, must bear me testimony that what I write is true.

But for those to whom such things are unknown, I first of all call God to witness.

The first voyage which I made to America was in a Portuguese ship, whose captain was called Pintyado.[1] We were three Germans on board : one, called Heinrich Brant, was from Bremen ; the other was called Hans von Bruckhausen, and myself.

The other voyage I made from Seville in Spain to the Rio de Platta, a province in America so called. The admiral of the ships was named Don Diego de Senabrie; there was no German with me on that voyage. But at last, after much adversity, peril, and danger at sea and on land suffered during this one voyage, which, as before stated, lasted two years, we were shipwrecked at an island called S. Vincente, situated close to the mainland of Brazil, and inhabited by Portuguese. There I found a countryman, one of the sons of the late Eoban, of Hesse, who received me kindly. Besides this one, the Schetzen, merchants of Antdorff, had a factor called Peter Rösel : these two must bear me witness, as to how I arrived, and how I ultimately was captured by the cruel barbarians.

Further, the seafarers who bought me from the savages came from Normandy in France. The captain of the vessel, Wilhelm de Moner, was from Wattauilla. The mate, whose name was Françoy de Schantz, came from Harflor ; the interpreter from Harflor was called Perott. These honest people (may God reward them for it in eternal happiness) have, after God, helped me to reach France ; they have helped me to obtain a passport ; they have clad me ; and they have given me food. These must bear witness for me where they found me.

Thereupon, I embarked at Dieppe in France, for London in England, where the merchants, connected with the Dutchmen, learned from the ship captain, with whom I

[1] Penteado.

went thither, all about my circumstances. They made me their guest, giving me the viaticum ; thereupon, I sailed to Germany.

In Antdorff I went to the house of Von Oka, to a merchant called Jaspar Schetzen, to whom the before-mentioned Peter Rösel in Sanct Vincente is factor, as above related. To him I brought the news, of how the French had attacked his factor's ship at Rio de Jenero, but had been repulsed. The said merchant presented me with two imperial ducats, wherewith to pay my way. May God reward him for it !

Now, should there be any young man who is not satisfied with this writing and testimony, let him, so that he may not remain in doubt, with God's assistance, begin this voyage. I have herein given him information enough, let him follow the spoor ; to him whom God helps, the world is not closed !

To Almighty God, who is all in all, be Glory, Honour, and Praise, from Eternity to Eternity ! Amen.

Printed at Franckfurdt on the Mayn, by Weygandt Han, in the Schnurgassen at the sign of the Pitcher.

THE END.

For EU product safety concerns, contact us at Calle de José Abascal, 56–1°,
28003 Madrid, Spain or eugpsr@cambridge.org.

www.ingramcontent.com/pod-product-compliance
Ingram Content Group UK Ltd.
Pitfield, Milton Keynes, MK11 3LW, UK
UKHW010344140625
459647UK00010B/821